Learning In College

I CAN RELATE

Mary K. Bixby, Ed.D.
University of Missouri–Columbia

Prentice Hall
Upper Saddle River, NJ 07458

Library of Congress Cataloging-in-Publication Data

Bixby, Mary K.
    Learning in college : I can relate / Mary K. Bixby.
      p.   cm.
    Includes bibliographical references and index.
    ISBN 0-13-011465-0
    1. Study skills—United States. 2. College student orientation—
United States. I. Title.
LB2395.B54 2000
378.1'70281—dc21   99-15638
                                                CIP

Credit lines are included beginning on page 211, constituting a continuation of the copyight page.

Publisher: *Carol Carter*
Acquisitions Editor: *Sande Johnson*
Managing Editor: *Mary Carnis*
In-House Liaison: *Glenn Johnston*
Production: *Holcomb Hathaway, Inc.*
Director of Manufacturing and Production: *Bruce Johnson*
Manufacturing Buyer: *Marc Bove*
Editorial Assistant: *Michelle M. Williams*
Marketing Manager: *Jeff McIlroy*
Marketing Assistant: *Barbara Rosenberg*

Printed in the United States of America

10 9 8 7 6 5 4 3 2

ISBN 0-13-011465-0

Prentice-Hall International (UK) Limited, *London*
Prentice-Hall of Australia Pty. Limited, *Sydney*
Prentice-Hall Canada Inc., *Toronto*
Prentice-Hall Hispanoamericana, S.A., *Mexico*
Prentice-Hall of India Private Limited, *New Delhi*
Prentice-Hall of Japan, Inc., *Tokyo*
Prentice-Hall Pte. Ltd., *Singapore*
Editora Prentice-Hall do Brasil, Ltda., *Rio de Janeiro*

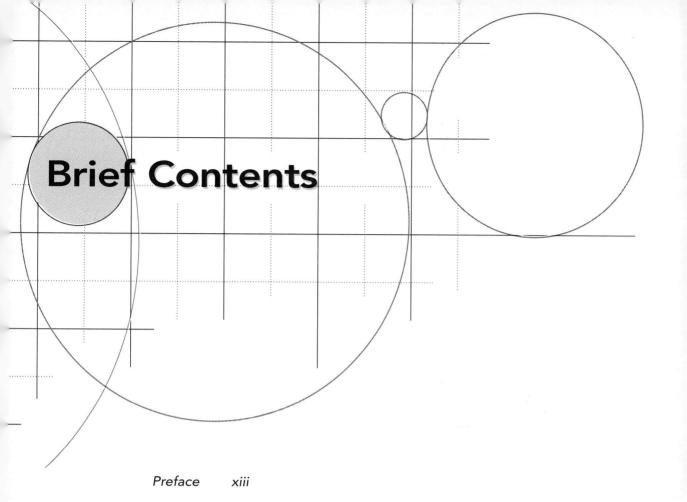

Brief Contents

Preface   xiii

PART I   RELATING INFORMATION   1
Learning and Understanding

CHAPTER 1   Information Management Systems   3
Getting It and Getting It Together

CHAPTER 2   Language and Thinking   27
It's Reading and Writing

CHAPTER 3   Language and Thinking   57
It's Listening and Speaking

CHAPTER 4   Questioning and Conquering the Exams   71
Testing, Testing

PART II   RELATING WITH PEERS AND INSTRUCTORS   93
Learning and Understanding

CHAPTER 5   Socializing Your Learning with Peers   95
"Within the Zone"

CHAPTER 6   **Relating With Your Instructors**   **107**
Meeting of the Minds

CHAPTER 7   **Catching on to Learning Styles and Teaching Styles**   **121**
The Essential Classroom Connection

PART III   RELATING WITH YOUR INSTITUTION   133
Learning and Decision Making

CHAPTER 8   **Negotiating the System**   **135**
Finding Your Place

CHAPTER 9   **Exploring Majors and Careers**   **155**
Why, When and How

CHAPTER 10   **Managing Time, Jobs, Money, and Stress**   **169**
Keeping It All Together

PART IV   RELATING TO THE TWENTY-FIRST CENTURY   185

CHAPTER 11   **Making Meaning in the Twenty-First Century**   **187**
The Future Is Yours

Endnotes   201
Bibliography   207
Credits   211
Index   213

Contents

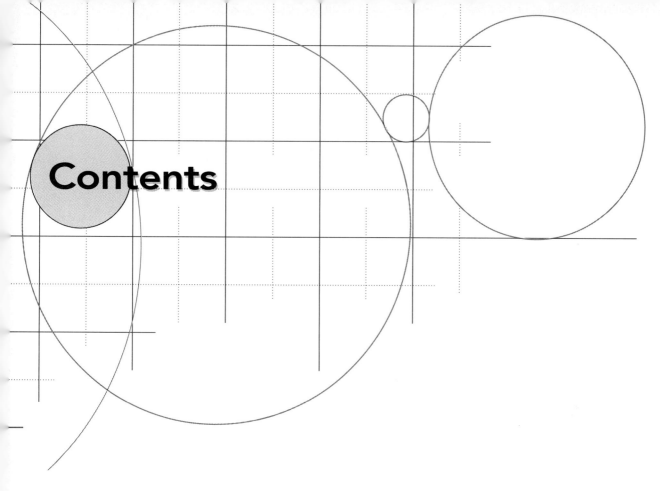

Preface   *xiii*

PART I   RELATING INFORMATION   1
Learning and Understanding

CHAPTER 1   Information Management Systems   3
Getting It and Getting It Together

Changing Social and Learning Behavior: Natural and Necessary   4

Becoming Successful, Satisfied Students   4

Decoding Your Syllabus   5

Starting College by Capturing the Lectures: Note Taking and Note Learning   7

General Characteristics of Good Note Taking   7

Expanding Your Learning with Different Notes/Book Systems   12

Learning Through Writing to Learn, Drawing to Learn, and Transmediation   16

Writing to Learn   16

Drawing to Learn   19

Charting   21

Transmediation, or Symbol Switching   21

Invitation: Invent Your Own Systems for Learning   22

Journal Reflections   22

Experiences   23

Can You Relate?   26

CHAPTER 2 Language and Thinking   27

It's Reading and Writing

Literacy: Reading, Writing, Understanding, Remembering   27

Reading: Motivation and Concentration vs. Boredom   28

     Effective vs. Ineffective Reading   28

     Skimming vs. Scanning   29

     We Are All Better Readers Than We Think   30

     Vocabulary Development   31

     A Simple Reading Format (Not SQ3R!)   31

     To Mark, or Not to Mark, the Text   32

Getting to be a Better Reader—A Pricele$$ System   33

     Procedure: Reading Improvement   33

A World of Reading Materials, A World of Relationships   34

     "Efferent vs. Aesthetic" Reading   35

     Humanities/Literature Texts   37

     Social/Behavioral Science Texts   38

     Foreign Language Texts   39

     Mathematics Texts   41

     Science Texts   44

     Collected Essay Readings   45

     Paperback Novels   45

     Journal Articles   45

     Newspapers and Weekly Magazines   45

     Electronically-Retrieved Print Sources   46

Memory Systems   46

     Sensory Memory   47

     Short-Term Memory   47

     Long-Term Memory   48

     Forgetting   49

     Memory and Comprehension Improvement   50

     Be Selective in Your Approaches to Learning   53

Journal Reflections   53

Experiences   53

Can You Relate?   56

CHAPTER 3 Language and Thinking   57

It's Listening and Speaking

The Listening–Speaking Connection   57

The Functions of Oral Communication   58

Impediments to Oral Communication: Communication Apprehension   59

Purposes of Listening   59
  The Listening–Reading Connection   59
  Getting to Be a Better Listener   60
  Other Tips for Listening   61
  To Tape or Not to Tape   61
Purposes of Speaking   62
  The Speaking–Writing Connection   62
  "Interactional Scaffolding": A Classroom Strategy for Dialogue   63
  Getting to Be a Better Speaker   64
Final Observations About Listening and Speaking   65
Journal Reflections   66
Experiences   67
Can You Relate?   69

CHAPTER 4 Questioning and Conquering the Exams   71

Testing, Testing

Getting the Cues: What to Study   71
Format-Specific Preparation Strategies and Tactics   72
  Objective Tests   72
  Subjective Tests: Are They More Difficult Than Objective Tests?   76
  Conquering Test Anxiety   81
Living Through Final Exams   83
  Debunking the Myths About Final Exams   84
  Truths About Strategies for Final Exam Preparation   84
Standardized Tests   85
  Myths About Standardized Tests   85
  Defining the Common Standardized Tests   86
  Standardized Tests Strategies   88
Journal Reflections   88
Experiences   89
Can You Relate?   90

PART II RELATING WITH PEERS AND INSTRUCTORS   93

Learning and Understanding

CHAPTER 5 Socializing Your Learning with Peers   95

"Within the Zone"

Bringing Together the Academic and Social   95
The "Zone of Proximal Development" (The What?)   96

Forming Study Groups   96

Interacting in Study Groups/Group Projects   97

Learning With and From Peers: A Summary   102

Journal Reflections   102

Experiences   103

Can You Relate?   104

CHAPTER 6 Relating With Your Instructors   107

Meeting of the Minds

Instructors, Teaching Assistants, and Tutors   108

Instructors   108

Teaching Assistants   110

Tutors   111

Research Assistants   111

Office Hours and Appointments   111

Strategies for Working with Instructors in Their Offices   114

Before the First Exam   114

After the First Exam   115

Throughout the Semester or Term   116

After the Course Has Ended   116

Distinguishing Between the Course Content and an Instructor's Personality   116

Other Out-of-Classroom Learning Opportunities   117

Shopping Around for Instructors   117

Selecting a Mentor (An Act of Serendipity)   117

Journal Reflections   118

Experiences   118

Can You Relate?   120

CHAPTER 7 Catching on to Learning Styles and Teaching Styles   121

The Essential Classroom Connection

Personal Learning Styles and Personality Types   122

Ancient Measures   122

Contemporary Measures of Learning and Personality Styles   122

Applications of Learning Styles Information   126

Looking at Teaching Styles   127

Relating Learning Styles to Teaching Styles   128

Journal Reflections   129

Experiences   130

Can You Relate?   131

PART III RELATING WITH YOUR INSTITUTION   133
Learning and Decision Making

CHAPTER 8 Negotiating the System   135
Finding Your Place

Your Institution   135
The System: People and Policies   137
  In Loco Parentis and Matters of Conduct   138
  Plagiarism and Academic Dishonesty   140
  All Students Have Basic Rights   141
Getting to Know Campus Resources and Student Services   141
  Support Services and Facilities: The Places for Assistance   142
Staying in College Means Getting a Life   142
  Multiple Senses of Belonging   144
Inclusion and Diversity on Campus   145
  Who Are Currently Attending Colleges and Universities?   146
  Whom Do the Educational Statistics Overlook?   148
Relating to the Community through Volunteerism and "Service Learning"   150
Journal Reflections   151
Experiences   152
Can You Relate?   153

CHAPTER 9 Exploring Majors and Careers   155
Why, When, and How

Majors and Careers: Two Sides of the Coin?   155
General Education Requirements: How Do These Relate?   156
  "Core" Courses: Why?   156
  "Enriched Majors"   156
  Study Abroad Opportunities Enrich Your Major and Your Life   157
Undecided, Major-Changing, and Decided Students   158
  "Undecideds"   158
  "Major-Changers"   158
  "Decideds"   160
How, With Whom, and When to Choose a Major   160
  Who Can Help? Working with Academic and Faculty Advisors   160
  Interest Inventories Can Help   161
  Electronic Information Sources   161
  Undecided? Interview Some Instructors   164
Will Employment Projections Affect Changes in Major-Seeking Trends?   164

Journal Reflections   165
Experiences   165
Can You Relate?   166

CHAPTER 10 Managing Time, Jobs, Money, and Stress   169

Keeping It All Together

Myths and Truths About Time/Task Management   170
Managing Your Time   170
College Responsibilities: Different Approaches to Unique Situations   174
   Enforced Study Halls   174
   Employed While Taking Classes? A Job: To Have or Have Not   174
   Commuters and Time Management: Sing Your Homework?   175
   Children, Family, and College Responsibilities   176
Managing Money   177
   Identify Your $ Habits   177
   Beware of Credit Cards and Your School's "EZ" Charge Systems   177
Low-Risk Ways to Pay for College   178
   Federal Aid, State Loans, and Other Grants   178
   Scholarships, Etc.   179
   Employment   179
   Other   179
   Taxpayers Relief Act of 1997   180
Managing Stress   180
   Physical Self-Care   181
   Emotional Self-Care   181
   Social Self-Care   182
Journal Reflections   182
Experiences   182
Writing Experiences   184
Can You Relate?   184

PART IV RELATING TO THE TWENTY-FIRST CENTURY   185

CHAPTER 11 Making Meaning in the Twenty-First Century   187

The Future Is Yours

On to a Four-Year School, Graduate School, or What?   187
   What Do Master's Degrees Provide?   188
It's a New Millennium   189
Reading, Writing, Speaking, and Listening After College: Always a Learner   189
   Literacy and Competencies in the Workplace   191

Diversity in the Workplace   192

Teamwork: From College into the Workplace   192

Joy and Serenity: Working and Learning with Children and Elderly People   193

Supportive Experiences: Sharing How Print Works   193

Points to Keep in Mind when Working with Children   194

Ideas for Working with Junior High and High School Students   194

Working and Learning with Senior Citizens   196

A Word about Technologies and Technology Education   196

Journal Reflections   197

Experiences   198

Can You Relate?   199

ENDNOTES   201

BIBLIOGRAPHY   207

CREDITS   211

INDEX   213

I dedicate my book to my parents, Bob and Mary, who read and wrote with me when I was just a "wee tot" and gave me a typewriter to play with at a very early age.

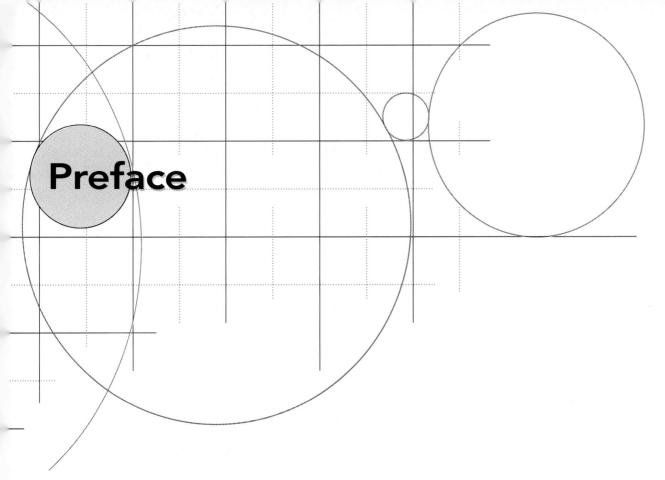

Preface

After twenty years of working and learning with college undergraduates, I have come to the conclusion that the world of college preparation courses, freshmen seminars and "study skills" classes has been offering a limited range of materials for students. I have several shelves of books in my office that I could not in good conscience ask students to purchase for the course that I coordinate, "Learning Strategies for College Students."

Learning to learn is indeed serious business, but we shouldn't be eternally gloomy or dogmatic. I have fun with my students. Therefore, I wanted to write a book on learning that was fun and even occasionally funny. (I sometimes poke fun at some situations you will no doubt encounter along the way. Some of what life deals us deserves humor. . . . Can you relate?)

Learners and Instructors! Give this book a chance . . . it's a little different.
Many how-to-do-better-in-college books discuss ways to get off to a good start, and then they end. However, this book challenges you to think and speculate about your present, your future, and *The Future*. Another related theme of this book is the importance of valuing diversity and inclusion. The material challenges you to think about those who differ from you in matters of age, race, ethnicity, religion, ability/disability, sexual orientation, country of origin, and socioeconomic standing. By virtue of your choosing to attend college, you are now a citizen of the world; you've moved out and away from your old, accustomed neighborhood.

This book emphasizes learning through reading, writing, speaking, and listening strategies and emphasizes the important relationships between and among the language systems.

The main theme of this book—and thus its title—emphasizes the importance of understanding relationships between written and spoken language; the importance of relationships with your peers, instructors, and your school, your relationship with various kinds of information; and the interconnectedness of all aspects of the college experience. Many students leave college because they did not form worthwhile academic and social relationships; they go home and wonder what they missed that other students seemed to "catch on to." What they may have missed is the power of understanding and maintaining relationships.

This book offers insights into theories about language and learning. Part I is "Relating Information: Learning and Understanding." In suggesting and giving examples of a variety of ways to learn, it explains why certain approaches are more powerful than others in certain kinds of learning situations. Learners and instructors deserve to know the reasons for approaches to learning and college success, not just what to do that seems to work. Therefore, bear with me as I continue to share learning theory along with practical information.

Part II concerns "Relating with Peers and Instructors: Learning and Understanding." The focus is your working and learning with others.

Part III is "Relating with Your Institution: Learning and Decision Making." Part IV, "Relating to the Twenty-First Century," invites you to think about work, parenting, and the meanings of technologies.

This book is not a "workbook." Flip through the pages—give it a once over—you'll notice an absence of fill-in-the-blank activities that are designed to, but usually do not, make you think deeply about yourself and the world of college. My philosophy about learning is, if you can explain a concept in conversation or write about it in an informed, intelligent way, the concept is truly yours. I have an incredible bias for reading, writing, speaking, and listening as means of understanding and learning. I also believe that if you want to know about a person's life and experiences or what it is like to be that person, ask her or him. Interviewing those players involved in the workings of your school is a powerful way to find out the "inside story" of the world of college. (See "Eight Good Reasons to Use Writing as a Learning Strategy" in Chapter 1 for my rationale for writing, writing, and more writing!)

This book recognizes and respects all students. *Learning in College: I Can Relate* is intended for and dedicated to all learners: traditional and non-traditional, parents and potential parents, students in two-year, four- or five-year programs, first-time and returning students from all over the country, international students, and all the many, many instructors.

No one is left out of this conversation about going to college. The examples of note taking styles, approaches to learning and learning styles, assignments, syllabuses, methods of preparing for and conquering test material, and other information are authentic content about people's lives. I've made every attempt to include information relevant to and representative of all college learners. Even if you were born in the 1950s or before, there are references to situations and events that have had lasting meaning for you.

Recurring Features of the Text Help You To Learn in a Variety of Ways

Each chapter has certain recurring features. They offer invitations for critical reflecting, writing, working with others, and applying ideas and strategies found in each chapter. Sometimes they are reasonably straightforward; other times, they are intended to be a bit of a challenge to think and write or draw in inventive, non-traditional ways and forms. Your instructors may use any of these thinking–writing tasks as part of their course evaluation procedures. The recurring end-of-chapter challenges include:

- The "Journal Reflections" are prompts or challenges to do some reflecting and writing about issues that make a difference in your college work and life. They are meant to invite you into the casual, "anything goes," private, first draft writing and doodling that the journal format allows. Let your mind go and your pen loose in writing your journal reflections.

- The "Experiences" activities are often collaborative activities that invite you to work with a partner or in a small group. These are meant to be interactive, and often they require using information from the chapter in combination with information that you obtain from outside sources such as instructors, staff, and other students. Some of the experiences ask you to consider "What if?" situations you may encounter in college.

- The "You Can Relate" end-of-chapter essay questions are of two varieties: one type invites you to integrate text, class discussion, and your own experiences to synthesize the main theme of the chapter. Writing this type of essay helps you bring together and assess what you have learned about the topics in the chapter.

  The second type of essay is less focused on your retelling the chapter and more focused on critical thinking and writing. These essay questions give you quotations to discuss, hypothetical situations to explore, and ideas to challenge. These writing assignments require longer essays than do the other recurring chapter activities, yet they are not all meant to be graded work.

An Invitation to Learners

My invitation and hope for you as you read and use this book as student or as an instructor is that you begin to understand, appreciate, and use the concept of relationships. Begin to experiment with and explore among all the learning strategies, courses, majors, instructors, helping professionals, and fellow students available to you. May you achieve all the goals that you have for school, for work, and for all your life's adventures. There are so many adventures waiting for you; have some fun along the way!

Mary K. Bixby, Ed.D.
Columbia, Missouri

ACKNOWLEDGMENTS

These people are very responsible for making this book "come true":

My fantastic assistant and partner Christine Wilson, for believing in me and for all the days and weeks she spent turning my idle ramblings into a beautiful book.

My reviewers, for their insights and excellent guidance: Karen R. Olson, University of New Mexico; Carmen Springer-Davis, Casper College; Nancy LaChance, DeVry Institute of Technology, Phoenix; Rober Spier, Hartnell College; Humberto Segura, Amherst College; Christy Cheny, Valencia Community College, University of Georgia, Athens.

My "informal" reviewers who have been with me since graduate school: Peter Hasselriis, Professor Emeritus of Education, University of Missouri–Columbia; Dorothy Watson, also Professor Emeritus, University of Missouri–Columbia, who has always loved responding to my deathless prose; and Dr. Patricia Jenkins, University of Missouri–Columbia, friend since "gradual school."

Dr. Dorothy King, Westminster College, Fulton Missouri, read every word, laughed at my jokes, and provided wonderful suggestions all through my writing process; Doug Clark of the University of Missouri Learning Center, for his help with math and Internet topics; my associates at MU who contributed their expertise—Brenda Noblitt, Student Financial Aid, and Patrick Kane, MSW, LCSW, assistant professor of social work, and an expert on stress reduction; Sabrina Friedman, MU journalism major, for her piece on Web access; and Lamara Warren, former student and friend, for her technical assistance.

My editor, Sue Bierman, for all her help, understanding, and empathy. It's a gift when an editor can be a caring friend. Michelle Williams, my assistant editor, for taking such good care of me and finding the answers to my many questions. My production team at Prentice Hall, including Mary Carnis. The members of the Center for the Expansion of Language and Thinking (CELT) for helping me remember why I believe what I do about language and thinking. The students at the University of Missouri–Columbia, who have been my teachers for twenty years. Jeff McIlroy, now in Prentice Hall marketing, for finding "the learning doctor." The student reviewers from Learning Strategies section 2B during the fall of 1998 for their wonderful comments and queries.

My long-time colleagues at the University of Missouri Learning Center, and in particular my director, Bonnie Zelenak, for appreciating the author in me and for supporting my work at MU for twenty years.

My family, especially my son Michael, and my good friends for their support, encouragement, and understanding.

Finally, the teaching team of faculty, staff, and students who have kept *Learning Strategies for College Students* an important, high-energy program for first-years for 10 years. These people teach outside their regular, full-time appointments, and have helped me learn so much about learners.

ABOUT THE AUTHOR

Mary K. Bixby, Ed.D., is an Assistant Professor of Education at the University of Missouri–Columbia. For over ten years, she has been the director of MU's First-Year Experience Program. An expert on reading, writing, and learning, she has been a Resource Learning Specialist with the MU Learning Center for twenty years. Much of her work involves Hispanic and African-American students and has helped to raise retention levels among underrepresented groups at MU. She has worked with Native American teachers, students, and aides in Arizona and New Mexico; in 1991 she was a member of the teaching exchange program with the University of Western Cape, Capetown, South Africa. Dr. Bixby has presented at numerous national conferences, including the National Council of Teachers of English; written articles about whole language teaching; and co-authored *Whole Language Strategies for Secondary Students,* a text for secondary language-arts methods classes. Bixby is also a member of CELT (Center for the Expansion of Language and Thinking) and is a recipient of the 1999 Excellence in Education Award.

Learning In College

I CAN RELATE

PART **I**

Relating Information

LEARNING AND UNDERSTANDING

CHAPTER 1   Information Management Systems:
Getting It and Getting It Together

CHAPTER 2   Language and Thinking:
It's Reading and Writing

CHAPTER 3   Language and Thinking:
It's Listening and Speaking

CHAPTER 4   Questioning and Conquering the Exams:
Testing, Testing

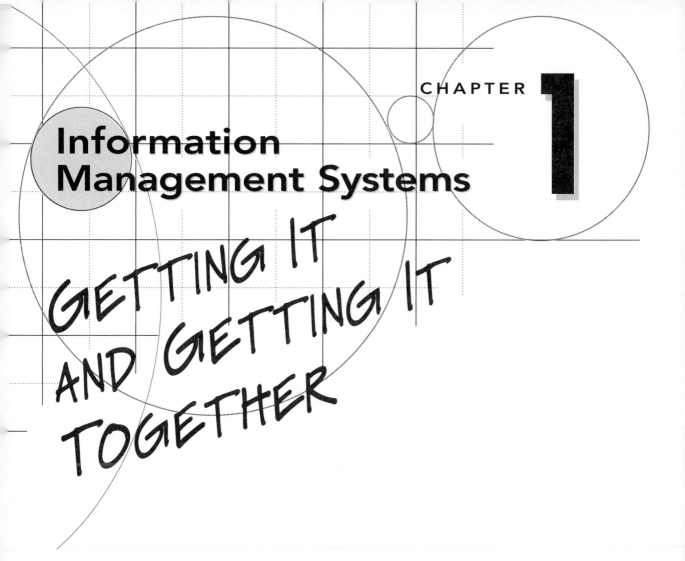

CHAPTER **1**

Information Management Systems

GETTING IT AND GETTING IT TOGETHER

Are you ready? Getting started in college can be quite an adventure. College students, with you among them, start their college careers by using and doing what they already know about learning. Based on observations of thousands of first-year students' study behaviors, some trends are evident. When first approaching college-level work, before the necessary process of experimentation and trial and error to improve their performance begins, many first-year college students, even you, may tend to do some of the following.

- Take incomplete, somewhat disorganized notes
- Study class notes and textbooks separately, making learning more difficult
- Study in long, infrequent sessions, usually late into the night
- Wait until a test is only a few days away to begin to prepare
- Study all the information without prioritizing the most important areas
- Memorize details, often to the exclusion of main concepts
- Read the text assignments inefficiently, rarely, or never, ignoring the information in class notes as a potential study guide
- Reread, highlight material and assume they've mastered it, yet have no means of **self-assessment** of their learning apart from their test scores
- Study alone
- Visit instructors rarely, only to inquire about specific contents or grades
- Procrastinate and mismanage their time

self-assessment a means of evaluating what you know and how well you know it as an ongoing part of day-to-day study

- Suffer from frustration, have more stress, and receive lower grades than they received in high school or a two-year college
- Do not understand why they aren't achieving the same level of success they did in their prior schooling

CHANGING SOCIAL AND LEARNING BEHAVIOR: NATURAL AND NECESSARY

Do any of the above sound familiar? That's all right! You have a place to start to change your study strategies into powerful learning tools. Change can be so scary that you don't want to risk it, and you may wonder: "What if I approach schoolwork differently and I don't succeed? Will it be because I shouldn't have taken the risk to change? Should I stick with what I've always done?"

Look, you are well aware of how you've handled schooling up to this point in your life and how much success you've achieved, so why not find out what you *really* can do with a few systematic changes? It will require a process of experimentation over time to develop new academic and social behaviors and relationships. This book offers you a multitude of ways to strengthen and *shorten* that inevitable process of trial and error that all students must experience to be successful and satisfied with their journeys through higher education.

As you read this book, pay close attention to the explanations of how and why the information and experiences presented are helpful. You won't change your approach to learning without good reasons to change. Many books of this kind tell you *what* to do, but not *why*. In this text you'll find references to research and theories about learning. You deserve more than suggestions—you deserve explanations, good reasons to want to change, and the knowledge to help you change.

BECOMING SUCCESSFUL, SATISFIED STUDENTS

Successful and satisfied college students are not born that way; they are willing to take risks, change, learn from their mistakes, and grow. Sure, we all know people who seem to go through college effortlessly. They make good grades, have social lives, seem happy most of the time, and are rarely caught in stressful, last-minute efforts to save one course or another. Some of your peers like to maintain the illusion that they never study. This maneuver is known as **gamesmanship,** the art of "psyching out" or wrecking the confidence of another—a perceived "opponent."

gamesmanship the art of "psyching out" perceived competitors in order to diminish their performance

You can see many examples of gamesmanship in sports and games—blatant "flopping" to get the officials in a basketball game to call a foul on an innocent defender, or a tennis player acting as though an opponent's return has hit out of bounds when it actually landed inside the line. There's always bluffing in poker and other card games. And in chess, a player may make a move very slowly or so quickly that it totally rattles the opponent. Students sometimes take joy in flustering other students. It's a universal pastime, so roll with it, but don't indulge in it.

Get your thinking straight from the beginning! Other students are not your opponents; forget the business about "grading on a curve." You are in competition with yourself, not with others. You may believe that certain students are brighter, luckier, or know some gimmick that other students do not. Stop it! You'll never be content if you continually dwell on the seeming ease of success of others. It's *your* success that you are after. The truth is that in college, despite the seeming hazards of competition for good grades, you are mainly challenging yourself to be a better learner—to grow and to have a successful and satisfying college "career." You are the most important tool you have to work with; you have a lot. However, college is not an experience through which you need to proceed alone.

With yourself as the center of your energy and attention, be fearless; be intrepid, and find others to learn with and from. Remember that you have the power to be successful in college. With requirements for college becoming stricter and more complicated, the admissions office of your school would not have accepted you if you didn't look like a good candidate for success! It is a profound act of your courage and faith in yourself to continue, day after day, to find ways to make learning less oppressive and more effortless and pleasurable. You don't have to be one of those "geniuses" to accomplish all you strive for.

Let's start with the fundamentals. Most high school and community college experiences require the invention of *some sort* of note taking methods, ranging anywhere from copying the instructor-prepared material from the chalkboard, the overhead projector, or the computer display to trying to take down the important points verbatim, or in your own words, in your own system. While some school instructors provide instruction in note taking, many do not.

Note taking is not an end product of your efforts; students take notes to get material to learn, but there are other processes involved. Hearing information, watching the teacher's style of delivery, translating the "teacher talk" and visuals into knowledge in a language that makes sense to you—the whole process is a complex act of learning. Regardless of your level of experience in note taking, one of the attributes of successful, satisfied students is their knowledge of and versatility with a variety of ways to organize and understand all the different kinds of information that college courses offer.

This book begins with strategies for getting and learning course information and constructing meaning from that information. These acts inevitably involve taking notes in class and working with them. One key to managing your information, which is a fundamental skill of successful, satisfied students, is to know how to "decode" or interpret the course outline, or **syllabus.**

> **syllabus** the organizing structure, assignments, required reading, assessments, and expectations for a particular course

DECODING YOUR SYLLABUS

Even before experimenting with note taking, there is one essential "first step" to understanding the intentions of your instructors and their organization, delivery, and evaluation of your grasp of the information. A critical activity on the first or second day of each of your courses will be receiving the course syllabus from the instructor, or receiving instructions for purchasing it at the bookstore or accessing it on the World Wide Web. A syllabus contains the schedule of topics to be covered with dates, assignments, test schedules, course requirements, including required reading, and other rules and standards for the class. It should include the names of your instructors, phone numbers and/or email addresses, and other information on how to reach those "in charge." Most syllabuses include statements warning against academic dishonesty and ensuring accommodations for differently abled students.

A syllabus can be a single page or it can be a small book. Syllabus styles vary as much as your instructors. You can't really judge a course or its

Reading List, 1999

- Big, fat text
- At least 12 novels
- Endless handouts
- *The Wallstreet Journal*

instructor by the syllabus, but there are certain issues you must discover or decode immediately in order to know how to proceed. If some key information is missing, you have every right to get answers to your questions. Figure 1.1 shows an excerpt from a fairly thorough First Year Experience Course syllabus. Notice the order in which the topics are presented and the many ways different kinds of activities comprise the course requirements.

The important dates for dropping a course, changing grading options (from a letter grade to pass/fail, for example), the day of the "Activities Mart" where clubs and organizations have booths to solicit new student involvement, and even the fact that February is Black History Month are all important information. If one or more of your course syllabuses are not as thorough, you may wish to revise them to include important dates and deadlines. In any case, the syllabus is the key to the course. Make sure you read and understand each one you obtain!

FIGURE 1.1   *Syllabus example.*

THE FIRST YEAR EXPERIENCE COURSE:
Learning Strategies for College Students
Curriculum & Instruction T-42
Winter, 1999

SECTION ONE
Lectures: 2:40–3:30 p.m. Tuesday in A&S 41
Discussion Sections: See your Winter Semester schedule.
ALWAYS BRING YOUR TEXT TO CLASS!

Week 1   T 1/21   Lecture: Overview, Administrivia "Listening, Note Taking and Note Learning
                             READ: *Learning in College: I Can Relate* Chapter 1 and Chapter 7
                             SEE ALSO:

          R 1/23   DISCUSSION: Get acquainted

January 27: Attend the Activities Mart in Memorial Union
January 27: Last day to register, add, or change sections
January 27–February 24: Drop classes only

Week 2   T 1/28   Lecture: Managing Your Time and Your Tasks
                             READ: *ICR*, Chapter 5

          R 1/30   DISCUSSION: Assign student interview paper (Handbook, p. 83–85)

February is Black History Month
*** February 3 is the last day to change grading options ***

Week 3   T 2/4   Lecture: Textbooks and Reading Proficiency
                             Read: *ICR*, Chapter 7 and Chapter 12

          R 2/6   DISCUSSION: Student Leader Interview Drafts Due (5 points toward final draft)
                             Activity: Introduction of group projects

---

Week 4   T 2/11   Lecture: More on Notes, Reading and Time Management
                             READ: Handouts provided in lecture and *ICR* Chapter 2

          R 2/13   DISCUSSION: Managing your money
                             Location: Ellis Library auditorium

---

Week 5   T 2/18   Lecture: Essay Tests and other Writing Tasks (Including Midterm Essay Test)
                             READ: *ICR*, pp. 129–138

          R 2/20   DISCUSSION: Student Interview papers due
                             Review for midterm

*** February 24 is the last day to drop a course without a grade ***

Back to note taking. Regardless of your instructor's syllabus, there is no one correct way to take notes or study in your college classes; however, some methods are more effective than others. This chapter describes many different systems for taking notes in class, organizing the notes for efficient learning, and bringing lecture and textbook information together for ease of study and heightened understanding. Options for using writing and drawing as alternatives to merely rereading to learn are also included in this chapter. Finally, you will learn about transmediation,[1] an active learning strategy that involves the translation of information from one symbol system (words in a formula, figures in an equation, or notes in sheet music, for example) into another kind of symbol system (a written translation of the formula, the solution to an equation, musical notation, or an essay that explains a diagram). Transmediation is another alternative to rereading, and this process is very productive in accomplishing some kinds of learning endeavors.

Starting College by Capturing the Lectures: Note Taking and Note Learning

General Characteristics of Good Note Taking

Note taking is not just about producing a product; it is part of a larger, more complex system of getting, learning, and using information. Research on college students' note taking reveals that most students assume they will be tested on the important ideas, so that's the type of information they record; additional studies show that college students record 70 percent of main points and only 38 percent of minor points.[2] Let's conclude, then, that college students typically record 50 to 70 percent of lectures. What if a particular instructor likes to test heavily on details? Getting only main ideas may not be sufficient.

Your instructors' specific instructions or lack thereof about what to record or how to record it will naturally influence your note taking. However, you can't expect a lot of direction about the specifics of note taking from instructors during the lecture. So what should you do? Be prepared to listen actively, to anticipate patterns in the content, and to write, not just record. You will begin to understand and remember as you write. You will remember more through the acts of listening and writing the information. The process of moving "teacher talk" into your own words is an act known as **encoding,** which is an essential skill in college.

encoding the act of translating text or speech into your own written version

Let's face it; your notes are helpful only to the degree that they contain the information you can use in life or on a test. (See Chapter 6 for strategies for getting input from your instructors on the quality of your notes.) Your goal is to create complete, "user-friendly" notes, as suggested in Figure 1.2. Following are examples of different systems that do or do not apply to the guidelines. Which ones make the best sense to you? Which features might best aid your studying and learning?

The "Chaos" System

The person who took the notes in Figure 1.3 has one rule: write something down and deal with it later. These notes are flawed: where are the main ideas? The details? What is the relationship between these random jottings? How would you know what to study and what it means? There is no notation of the date or topic; there is very little here of any value. These notations are nearly worthless. To continue to take notes in this manner would lead to confusion, frustration, and really, really low grades.

FIGURE 1.2) *An efficient note-taking system.*

AN EFFICIENT NOTE TAKING SYSTEM:

- is fast and streamlined; uses dashes rather than numbers or letters, uses your own brand of "shorthand"
- adds "structure" (i.e., numbers and letters) upon initial review of the notes, as soon as possible *after* the lecture
- blends the instructor's wording with your own, avoiding attempts at verbatim transcription. If you can accurately translate lecture material into your own words, it's a good indication that you grasp the concepts and their relationships
- uses the space on the page meaningfully, not haphazardly, in order to easily "see" the areas of related information to study together
- gets all of the discussion, including concepts, definitions, elaboration and the instructor's "real-world" examples; there is an important correlation between course grades and completeness of notes

rehearsal study that involves repetitive use of the material to be learned

- leaves space for later additions so there is less need to recopy merely for neatness
- is designed to compare with other students' notes
- is arranged to insert actual questions to study later
- reflects the instructor's "cues" and "clues"

retrieval study that involves unaided recall of the material to be learned

- sets up a two-tier procedure for study: **rehearsal** and **retrieval** (see Chapter 3 for a thorough discussion of memory)
- marks "confusions" to clarify later
- anticipates additions from the text, the instructor and/or other students, other readings, and so on

---

FIGURE 1.3) *Chaos note-taking.*

Intro to Sociology

BACKGROUND = WEBER OBSERVATION DATA

   Symbolic interactionalism (handshake)
   Marx? The study of groups
   "sociological imagination"
                    C. WRIGHT MILLS

DURKHEIM: SUICIDE

   Reliability & validity (see p. 17)

The "Rainbow" System

This note taker (Figure 1.4) has done a better job with the content; at least there is some physical organization of key topics, but the content is skimpy. The main feature of this method is the plethora of colorful highlighting! According to this system, all the information is important because it's shaded, but what did the student learn from all this coloring? Do the colors mean anything? This example illustrates a common misconception—that highlighting is a learning strategy. This

FIGURE 1.4   *Rainbow note taking*

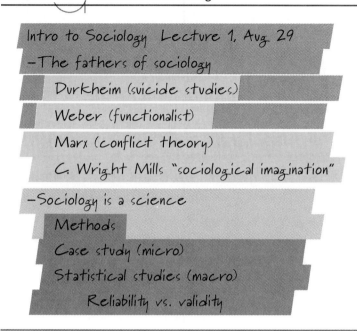

Intro to Sociology Lecture 1, Aug 29
- The fathers of sociology
     Durkheim (suicide studies)
     Weber (functionalist)
     Marx (conflict theory)
     C. Wright Mills "sociological imagination"
- Sociology is a science
     Methods
     Case study (micro)
     Statistical studies (macro)
          Reliability vs. validity

writer needs to go back to Figure 1.2 and find some aspects of note taking that will capture the lecture adequately and set it up for ease of learning!

The Traditional Outline System

This system concentrates on an outlining format which, when used well, shows relationships between and among main ideas, explanations, and examples. Figure 1.5 illustrates a reasonably effective traditional outline system.

The most helpful parts of a traditional outline system are the use of space to create "chunks" of interrelated information and the use of numbers and letters to indicate relationships. However, keeping up with the structure—whether you're on point A or B or #1 or #2—distracts you from getting the important parts of the information, and all that formal numbering and lettering may not be necessary to include while actually taking the notes. You may prefer to use the overall outlining structure. However, you can eliminate the immediate need for attention to numbers and letters by using dashes to indicate the chunks. Then add numbers, letters, and other study aids after the lecture is over when you return to your notes to start learning them.

The Cornell System (Why Is It So Famous?)

Walter Pauk, working at Cornell University, developed "Cornell Notes"[3] from 30 years of experience working with college learners. Pauk views note taking as a device for external storage, but there are also encoding values to this system (Figure 1.6). Pauk's special contribution to the wealth of advice about note taking is his notion of a "recall column," which provides the important means of self-assessment mentioned on page one. As soon as possible after the lecture, the note taker should go somewhere quiet, reread the notes, and create the recall column. Some students try to frame the question as they are taking notes; this is a poor idea because it distracts you from hearing and recording the "teacher talk" and visual aids. Make additions from what you still remember but did not record, and create

FIGURE 1.5 *Traditional outline note taking.*

History 4: American History 1865 to the Present
Dr. Slick Storyteller
Lecture, September 2: Post Civil War Experiences

I. White Working Class—Northern

   A. —America's other civil war because of internal strife between workers and employers. Example - Strike of 1877

     1. Economic downturn, company cut wages and laid off workers,

     2. 10% wage cut was not acceptable by the workers

     3. in Martinsburg, West Virginia, railroad cars were not hooked to locomotives - crippled transportation

     4. workers are forced to work in two ways: private armies and state militias

     5. workers face outright physical attack or jail—General strike

     6. No one works, similar incidents in St. Louis

     7. RR workers and support groups strike

II. Native Americans

   A. White settlers ultimately take over lands

   B. 1860's Great Plains Tribes (Sioux, Arapaho, Cheyenne) are led by Red Cloud

   C. 1868 treaty is signed to keep ancestral lands

   D. 1870 US government uses new strategy

     1. the assault of the buffalo—systematic destruction, a very important commodity for food, clothing and shelter

     2. 1870—15 million buffalo, 1880—nearly extinct

   E. Interest in the Black Hills region—Sioux had been guaranteed rights to this region in the 1868 treaty

   F. US ignores treaty because of gold discoveries

   G. Sitting Bull and Crazy Horse prepare for war

   H. 1876—US Army led by General Custer defeated at Battle of Little Bighorn

     1. increases US military force

     2. land is still taken

   I. Sitting Bull escapes to Canada until 1881, was arrested and put on reservation, special humiliation for him - in 1887

   J. Dawes Act (see text) destroys Native American cultural system and social organizations.

Summary: Some things never change.

FIGURE 1.6   *The Cornell system of note taking.*

History 4: American history 1865 to the Present   Dr. Slick Storyteller
Lecture, September 2   POST CIVIL WAR EXPERIENCES

Recall column (added after lecture	Notes from lecture
	I. White Working Class—Northern
	A. America's other civil war because of internal strife between workers and employers—Ex. Railroad Strike of 1877
Explain the 6 conditions of the northern white working class after the Civil War.	1. Economic downturn, company cut wages and laid off workers
	2. 10% wage cut was not acceptable by the workers
	3. in Martinsburg, West Virginia, railroad cars were not hooked to locomotives—crippled transportation
	4. workers are forced to work in two ways: private armies and state militia
Reasons?	5. workers face outright physical attack or jail
	6. General strike—
	a) No one works, similar incidents in St. Louis
	b) RR workers and support groups strike
	II. Native Americans
	A. White settlers ultimately take over lands
	B. 1860's Great Plains Tribes (Sioux, Arapaho, Cheyenne) are led by Red Cloud
	C. 1868 treaty is signed to keep ancestral lands
	D. 1870 US Government uses new strategy
	1. assault of the buffalo—systematic destruction, a very important commodity for food, clothing and shelter
Explain the 7 conditions for Native Americans after the Civil War.	2. 1870—15 million buffalo; 1880—nearly extinct
	E. Interest in the Black Hills region—Sioux had been guaranteed rights to this region
	F. US ignores treaty because of gold discoveries
Reasons?	G. Sitting Bull and Crazy Horse prepare for war
	H. 1870 US Army led by Gen. Custer defeated at Battle of the Little Bighorn
	1. increases US military force
	2. land is still taken
	I. Sitting Bull escapes to Canada until 1881, was arrested and put on reservation in 1887, special humiliation for him
	J. Dawes Act (see text) destroys Native American cultural systems and social organization.

Summary: some things never change. The powerful AngloEuropeans exploited all other groups including working class whites and Native Americans to control their resources and lives.

questions in the margin to use to aid learning. Finally, summarize the essence of the lecture (from memory) at the bottom of the page. Some know the Cornell method as the upside down "T-form" of note taking because of the addition of the summary at the bottom.

The creating of the questions is not a passive approach such as highlighting. The act of composing good questions and the types of questions you create should prepare you for the way you will be asked to use the information. For example, in Figure 1.6, the questions are a mixture of main idea and detail questions because the test will be both essay and multiple-choice. Notice that the questions even contain the number of points to be recalled about the post–Civil War conditions for each group. The creation of the questions gives you an early understanding of the material. This is rather like the TV shows *Jeopardy* and *Rock & Roll Jeopardy,* where contestants win cash for showing their knowledge by asking the right questions. Therefore, preparing the marginal "test" is a first-order comprehension strategy.

Once you have this testlike situation, study until you can cover up the lecture and answer the questions—both orally and in writing—completely from memory (no peeking!). Working in and out of the questions and the "answers" (the notes) creates that necessary combination of rehearsal (study using the answers) and retrieval (work from memory) studying. Even if the test were to be all multiple choice, your writing from memory consolidates and stores the information you wish to learn. (See Figure 1.12, page 18, for the benefits of using writing as a learning strategy.)

Expanding Your Learning with Different Notes/Book Systems

Let's be mindful of research on strategies of successful college students. To be a successful test taker, your learning must be meaningful and must focus on all the content that is covered on exams. The influence of your notes in your learning and your test taking largely depends on the time between taking them and your schedule for studying them, beginning with an initial review as soon as possible after that class. Whatever system you use for a particular course (different courses necessitate different systems), regular work with course notes leads to deeper understanding for both life use and testing purposes.

Studies show that students who elaborate on their notes learn much more thoroughly than those who do not. Information management systems consist of a combination of instructor-talk and text-talk, plus some personalization, or additions from your own experiences. In this way, by including your own experiences along with text material, you will develop an important "relationship" with all the information that you wish to understand, learn, and remember.

Don't you long for the days when instructors gave you a study guide that included what you need to know and how to know it? College instructors won't do that for you. They offer you what they want you to learn and understand. Their mode of delivery is known as a lecture. However, college tests are a blend of information sources, so think of good notes as a "study guide" to your text. Bringing notes and books together leads to a deeper understanding. Note/book consolidation systems may include features such as "Page-to-Page," as shown in Figure 1.7.

Every Other Line

The bold text in Figure 1.8, page 14, illustrates the notes taken in lecture on every other line of your notebook, leaving space for the later additions, which are shown in nonbold. The additional information was added soon after the lecture by using information from the text to make the notes more complete.

FIGURE 1.7   *Page-to-page note taking.*

Notes from your reading of the text:

American Government: Political Science 1
Dr. Bombast
Book: The American Government

How Are Presidential Decisions Made?
—Executive branch
     13 cabinet positions/agencies
       These make recommendations
       Multiple advocacy: not making decisions
       without consulting each other
Should Presidency be reformed?
       Selection process—some say it should
       be changed—lose first couple of primaries
       and you're done

Chapter II: The Federal Bureaucracy
   —Bureaucratic approach to government
     - clear division of labor
     - hierarchical authority patterns
     - specific job qualifications
     - objective administration of rules
   —What is the Federal Bureaucracy?
     Gov't organization whose staff is non-
     elected and that is engaged in a set
     of specific tasks
     —the bureaucratic approach:
     - Clear division of labor
       -large jobs broken down
     - Hierarchical authority patterns
       -chain of command
     - Objective administration of rules
       -follows rules
Organizations of the federal bureaucracy
   —353 legislators   —1 president
     Appoints 9 Supreme Court justices
   —2,871,000 employees
   —Cabinet level departments
     - 13 cabinets
     - State Dept   - Defense
     - Treasury   - Justice

Notes from lecture:

American Government: Political Science 1
Dr. Bombast
Lecture October 28

Bureaucracy—characterized by
   - Division of labor
   - Hierarchy
   - Specifications
   - rules
Also private bureaucracies:
  —telephone company
  —university set-up
Bureaucracies are necessary:
   1. To handle huge amount of work in an
     orderly fashion
Fears of bureaucracies:
   1. They become disconnected
Worst nightmare of bureaucracies:
   1. People aren't people anymore, just numbers
   2. People are insignificant

Biggest nightmare—losing self-government
Stages of Bureaucracy:
   1. Washington, Adams, Jefferson—they just
     chose each other
   2. All changed by Andrew Jackson
     - Political parties developed
     - Patronage—help the winning side and
       you get an office job
   3. Civil Service Administration
     - Purifies politics
     - Stops/slows down corruption
Ways/Reasons bureaucracies grow:
   1. Expansion of some agencies (EPA, FDA,
     etc.)
   2. Trying to please interest groups
   3. Lawyers are needed to tell what's
     what
   4. Economic reasons

FIGURE 1.8   *Every other line note taking.*

I. Native Americans

   A. White settlers ultimately take over lands

   -started in Jacksonian era—by 1861 the transcontinental telegraph lines hooked the East to the West.

   -1864—Transcontinental R.R.

   B. 1860's Great Plains Tribes (Sioux, Arapaho, Cheyenne) led by Red Cloud

   -U.S. policy to segregate Indians

   C. 1868 treaty is signed to keep ancestral lands

   -"Treaty of Fort Laramie"—Sioux agreed not to make war on U.S. gov't and to move to the Great Sioux Reservations (Black Hills, S.D.)

   D. 1870 U.S. government uses new strategy—to wipe out Native Americans

   1. the assault of the buffalo—systematic destruction, a very important commodity for food, clothing and shelter

   -a totally intentional plan led by federal authorities

   2. 1870–15 million buffalo; 1880—nearly extinct

   -Vermont businessman invents a way to turn buffalo hides into fine leather

   E. Interest in the Black Hills region—Sioux had been guaranteed rights to this region in the 1868 treaty

   -when Sioux fought Custer at Little Big Horn the U.S. gov't negated the treaty so they could mine the Black Hills

   F. US ignores treaty because of gold discoveries in Black Hills

   -So the gov't took 1/3 of the land—the part with minerals

   G. Sitting Bull and Crazy Horse prepare for war

   -"Indians wars" were not started by Indians—Wounded Knee, S.D.–1890–300 of 350 Indians slaughtered

Other Systems of Note Taking

- The note taking technique shown in Figure 1.9 may be better for left-handed students.
- Figure 1.10 shows an example of notes/book summary outlining.
- Figure 1.11 shows a double-entry, or dialectical, journal.

FIGURE 1.9   Notes/recall column note taking suggested for left-handed students.

Notes from the lecture:	Recall questions, added after lecture:
Sociology 1 Dr. Vague	
Lecture: September 10	
Chapter 7: In Groups/Out Groups	
Ex. Blind people—now are referred to as people who are visually impaired or people who are blind—positive adjectives are okay, but not negative	How does labeling create in-groups and out-groups? Give examples.
Ex. Growth of the term "colored" to Negro to African-Americans—people are defining themselves	
—labeling groups is a political process	
Level of groups:	Define, compare and contrast dyads and triads
Dyads (2) Triads (3)	
book refers to the addition of 1—which can make a significant change	
Primary Groups:	
1. Small	Define, compare and contrast and give examples of
2. Know people	
3. Ex. Family or work groups	
Secondary Groups:	- primary groups
1. Can recognize, but not intimately	- secondary groups
2. Ex. Class or a club	- aggregate groups
Aggregate group:	
1. Collections of people	
2. Ex. Group watching a fire; eating at McDonald's	
3. A situation that brings people into temporary contact	
Organizations:	
1. A large group for a special purpose	
2. Planned activities (bureaucracy)	
3. Often affiliated with institution	
Institution:	
1. Patterns of organization	
2. Persist for generations (religion, education)	
3. Relatively large size (except for family)	
Society:	Define, compare and contrast and give examples of an institution vs. a society
1. A nation-state with specific regional boundaries	
2. The government has the monopoly over legitimate power— often economic hardship, ethnic rivalries are caused from artificial nation-states; ex. Africa was carved up in the 1800's; Vietnam was split into North (industrial) and South (agricultural)	

FIGURE 1.10 *Notes/book summary note taking.*

Sociology 1   Dr. Durkheim   Lecture: October 1

Summary, added after the lecture:	Notes from the lecture:
A seemingly harmless, "normal" guy with a sick need to have a following turned into a cult leader	Jonestown Massacre—events leading up to it
	A Sociology professor has interpreted the events from the perspective of Jones' followers:
	* Jim Jones—ordinary, lower middle class white man from Indiana
	* Strongly committed to ethnic equality
	* Integrated congregation in Indianapolis draws criticism
	* Moves to California–Ukiah in the North – about 80 followers
	* Once again—problems—goes to San Francisco
The "people's temple" evolved from a movement to help ethnic minorities and the poor into a "deviant" organizations or cult. How did this happen??	* People's Temple becomes headquarters—in 2 years has 3000 members
	- Not merely an audience; members lived in church-owned apartments
	- Very communal—all money went to group
	- Strong program that focused on injustice, alcoholism, drug abuse and the poor
	* In its heyday was not a deviant organization—Jones was asked to be Chairman of the SF Public Housing Authority

LEARNING THROUGH WRITING TO LEARN, DRAWING TO LEARN, AND TRANSMEDIATION

It's natural to start learning course material by rereading for familiarity. While rereading the information to be learned is a good and appropriate way to begin to rehearse it, true learning is achieved through a cycle of reading and alternatives to reading, not merely through highlighting and reading the highlighted parts. That passive relationship with information will not ensure learning. After a while, the storage part of the brain switches off, even if you're still sincerely eyeballing the material! There are many excellent alternatives to rereading material in order to learn it. They are "pencil-in-hand" strategies that include using writing as a learning strategy, drawing as a way of understanding, and symbol switching (known as transmediation) as a test of comprehension.

Writing to Learn

Writing to learn is not the same thing as learning to write (composition). Using writing as a learning strategy is a natural, powerful way to construct a thorough relationship with your course content. This process begins with your intention to encode or summarize the main ideas of what you are reading. Your goal is to retell accurately the "gist" of the piece, in your own words as much as possible, by paus-

FIGURE 1.11   *Dialectical note taking or journal.*

Sociology 139: The Black Americans   Dr. Dubois
Discussion of An American Dilemma (1944)   Lecture: September 11

Personal notes and responses:	Notes from the lecture:
	The author's, Gunnar Myrdal, perceptions in the book are based on his own mind
Swedish economist—studied race relations in the US.	– to be pro-black is a nuisance to America's idealism and rationale
	example: the New Covenant (Bill Clinton) a sense of morality or concern for our fellow citizens—we are a hopeful and optimistic people (mysticism or romanticism would not be adopted)
Black soldiers returning from WWII expected better treatment after their heroism in the war— Myrdal saw this situation.	The American Creed: This contradiction is a conflict of values with the Negro problem—a belief that all people should have equality and the rights to freedom, justice, and a fair opportunity creates a conflict among whites when the race issue is raised—a conflict between thought and action.
	conflict is not limited to just white Americans
Myrdal observed that the behavior of the Nazi regime would have made Americans more sensitive to the harm caused by white supremacism.	– reflect moral compromise
	– suppression of conflicting attitudes toward blacks
	– and a conscious negative attitude toward blacks on a daily basis
Myrdal was right when he labeled race "an American dilemma."	example: a person who is a bigot, but still believes in the creed
EX: race riots in 1943 in Detroit	Moral Compromise general evaluations are morally higher—view issues in a universal sense—in America group or individual concerns are not handled as well
I agree that "race" has not been handled well in the US.; after 125 years there's a long way to go. Why can't the gov't enforce its laws?	– prejudice or irrational if not universality of mankind
	– tradition, expediency, or utility is how irrational thought is explained

ing to turn away from the original and write what you know. Always begin your reading and/or note review with a serious intention to write your summary from memory, not by merely copying bit after bit of the original. You don't recopy your notes on tests!

This process takes a while to get used to since it's not what students usually do as part of their reading and studying. The time you take to develop and use this approach is well worth it, but in order to reap the benefits of using writing as a learning strategy, you have to take some time to practice your new strategy and stick with it until it becomes familiar, almost second nature. Otherwise, you will be so self-conscious about taking more time and studying differently from the old days that you'll abandon the process before it becomes yours.

The change is worth it! Reading with the goal of summarizing in your own words changes the way you read, think, and remember because you are making yourself responsible for producing (not just reproducing) information. Eventually you will understand, and therefore remember much more of what you read and study. Depending on how often and how extensively you use writing as a learning strategy, you may feel comfortable with it in a few days or a few weeks. The payback in higher grades and lifelong learning will keep you going strong.

Writing to learn is a cyclical process of reading, thinking, and "talking on paper" to rehearse and assess what you do or do not understand. Writing to learn goes very well with using a sound notetaking format, such as using every other line and, as soon as possible after the lecture, filling in the blanks with information you didn't have time to write down in class. Why is taking all this time and trouble superior to trying to learn only by rereading? The following list enumerates the cognitive benefits of writing to learn.

EIGHT GOOD REASONS TO USE WRITING AS A LEARNING STRATEGY

1. Humans aren't equally facile with all ways of using language (reading, writing, speaking, and listening).

2. The ability to discover or explain is a necessary and valuable attribute for learners in all parts of their lives, and writing clarifies thinking.

3. Community colleges, junior colleges, and four-year colleges and universities require competence in composition skills. People learn to write primarily by writing, and to a lesser extent by reading, speaking, and listening.

4. Skill in moving from thought to language enables a person to be understood. This is a process all learners develop over time since thought and language are not the same phenomenon.

5. The key to learning is active rehearsal. While reading is active involvement as well, writing (rehearsing) ensures active involvement in the meaning.

6. In academic settings, writing as rehearsal is superior to oral rehearsal (repeating information aloud) because very few examinations (except for some foreign language exams) are oral. Most college assessment involves print on paper, and you must read, respond, and/or write to display your knowledge.

7. Writing fosters the organization of knowledge and ideas. Organization is essential to learners, for your memory consists of organizational patterns. In addition, organized writing is essential to both the writer and the evaluator since it's easier to give a good grade to a written piece that is easy to follow.

8. Using writing as a learning strategy is not a universal practice among new college students. However, "writing to learn" can be one of the most important ways for you to learn in college. Figure 1.12 lists four benefits to this process that make it superior to more passive rereading.

FIGURE 1.12 *Four benefits of using writing as a learning strategy.*

1. The activity checks your comprehension.

2. Writing to learn aids your comprehension; therefore it improves your memory.

3. This process makes for more active learning.

4. Writing to learn creates a better text for you to study; it's condensed, in your own words, and can contain the best points from the instructor.

Drawing to Learn

There's a wide variety of strategies for understanding and storing information before, during, and after reading. Visual aids, or graphic organizers, include charts, categorization systems, sketches, and other forms, depending on the information to be learned and how instructors expect their students to use the information. Illustrating the relationships between and among ideas is often a more effective way to learn than rereading linear notes. Drawing to learn, then, includes strategies such as memorizing visual or pictorial information, mapping or webbing information, charting information, and transmediation or symbol switching. Figure 1.13 lists some steps in one drawing to learn process.

Using the illustration of the anatomy of the ear below, follow the steps in Figure 1.13 to teach yourself to draw the picture from memory. This is a sample of an exercise that might aid you in an audiology or communications disorder course. Start with an overall sketch of the parts of the inner ear. Once you can reproduce those parts, work on adding the labels spelled and positioned correctly. Remember, you teach yourself to draw figures and pictures not only to be able to reproduce them if required but also to be able to write in an informed way about the figure, its relationships, and its significance.

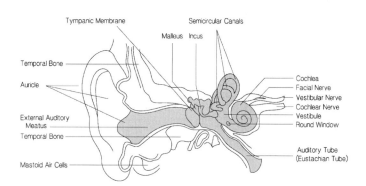

FIGURE 1.13 *Drawing to learn.*

STEP 1
- Put abbreviated title or name of specimen at top of page
- Count numbers of items to be recalled
- Concentrate on spatial relationships and shapes first, i.e., linear vs. round

STEP 2
- Look at specimen, diagram, slide, etc.
- When you think you have "seen" all items:
    Turn away from specimen and make a quick sketch of it
    Use letters, not words, for labeling
- Throw away the sketch
- Look at the specimen again
- Note mentally what you omitted or sketched incorrectly

STEP 3
- Repeat until you have a reasonably correct drawing, including both figure and labels
- Always start at the beginning of the process; spend no time correcting mistakes on your practice sketch

STEP 4
- Wait at least two full hours, then
- Draw the figure and write in the full names of the labels from memory
- If necessary, check with the text

EXAM PREP
- On several occasions before exam, try to reproduce sketch from memory
- Compare reproduction with your sketch
- Make necessary corrections (in color, if you wish)
- Throw away sketches
- Repeat until your recollection is complete

Mapping or Webbing

Mapping or webbing is a way to connect and organize ideas, and to brainstorm ideas and relationships. It can also be used as a post-reading or post-writing activity to check your understanding of ideas by relating general concepts to specific ones. To "web" ideas, follow this procedure:

1. Write a general term or concept in the middle of a blank page.
2. Brainstorm any ideas you associate with the concept.
3. Connect various ideas by drawing lines to connect similar categories.
4. The basic webbing of ideas can be rearranged, expanded, or reduced. Different categories will emerge, depending on the subject area. For example, a particular piece of literature can be webbed according to cause and effect, comparison–contrast, events, characters, and so on.

Figure 1.14 illustrates a webbing technique to brainstorm ideas for an essay about the Vietnam conflict starting with the concept of Vietnam 1947–1975.

FIGURE 1.14   *The Vietnam conflict.*

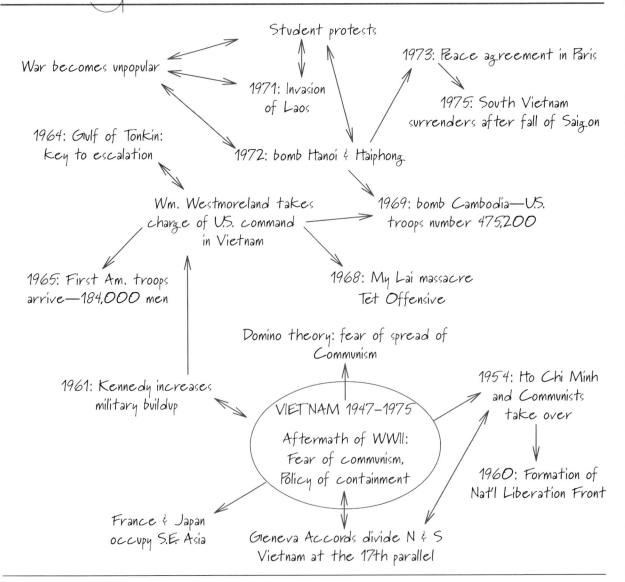

Charting

The procedure for charting is easy. All you need to begin is the set of items to be compared, which become the vertical categories as in Figure 1.15, and the aspects held in common to be compared, which become the horizontal points of comparison. In Figure 1.15, Example 2, the aspects of comparison between the theorists are their theories, their beliefs about group behavior, the unit of behavior, and the particular parts of society that each theorist has investigated. Take another look at Chaos Note Taking on page 8. Wouldn't you rather invent and study this chart than try to make sense of those crummy notes?

Transmediation, or Symbol Switching

Learners of all ages relate what they read and hear to their backgrounds and experiences. Moving text material or notes into another communication system, such as art or the symbolic system of mathematics, will assist you in making new meanings and finding new insights. You may find interrelationships in the text and keys to its structure. After all, what do symbols mean? Charles Sanders Pierce, the father of semiotics, or the study of signs, observed that "A symbol . . . cannot indicate any particular thing; it denotes a kind of thing."[4] In other words, symbols aren't meaning; they stand for meaning. We make meaning of the world by using and interpreting signs and symbols.

FIGURE 1.15 *Charting to learn.*

Example 1

THE STUDY OF LITERATURE
Important Elements of Literature

Author	Theme	Setting	Key Images	Other
Poe				
Hawthorne				
Melville				
Etc.				

Example 2

STUDY OF SOCIOLOGY THEORY

Theorist	Name of Theory	Belief About Behavior	Unit of Behavior	Part of Society
Weber Durkheim	Functionalism	Society is a system	Structures	Organizations
	Symbolic Interactionism	Interaction = Social roles		
Marx	Conflict Theory	Conflict is responsible for social change	Power, ownership	
Etc.				

transmediation a learning strategy that moves information from one symbol system to another in order to aid comprehension

Charles Suhor, in an article in which he hails the power of **transmediation,** observed the following about sign/symbol switching:

> If we think of learners as individuals with the potential for expressing themselves through a variety of signs (such as linguistic, gestural, pictorial, musical, and mathematical signs) and systems of signs, we gain a fresh perspective on both human potential and on the organization of school subjects.[5]

Transmediation, for your purposes in learning, includes all of the following symbol-switching activities.

- Translating a paragraph that describes a chemical reaction into an equation, or translating the equation into a written description of the chemical operation.
- Working a word problem in mathematics.
- Using a solution to a word problem, working backward and writing an appropriate word problem to set up the context for the operations involved.
- Translating sheet music into a concert on a piano or other musical instrument, or writing musical notation to fit the music in your head.
- Translating a long chapter on the lineage of the Tudor family—a ruling family in England from 1485 to 1603—into a diagram of ancestry. This would enhance understanding of the scandal of Henry VIII dismissing of the Catholic Church, divorcing Catherine of Aragon, marrying Anne Boleyn, and fathering Elizabeth I.
- On the other hand, translating the lineage chart into a summary of the Tudor succession would also show that you understand their messy relationships.
- Translating a chapter from a nutrition textbook into a chart that shows similarities and differences among the water- and fat-soluble vitamins, or writing a comparison/contrast summary of the vitamins by using information in chart form.
- Working from a map of Europe and summarizing Hitler's attempts to conquer the European countries, or working from a description of Hitler's early invasions, sketching a map that shows his plan for conquering Europe.

Each of the above examples is an alternative to rereading and gives you ways to be very versatile in how you choose to learn information for college and life. While the suggestions may seem more complicated than reading to learn, the concept of transmediation affords you proof that you truly understand the concepts with which you are working because you can move from explaining in one symbol system to using an alternate symbol system. What might be the implications for using transmediation as one of your many learning strategies? In what courses could you use transmediation to your advantage?

Invitation: Invent Your Own Systems for Learning

There's no one right, best way to learn in college. But there are many choices of ways to learn, ways to relate, and ways to own information. This chapter presents you with a plethora of ways to streamline your learning for school and life. If you had no interest in becoming a more proficient learner, then why are you spending time with this book? Why not grow as you go?

Journal Reflections

1.1 Describe a course situation in which it would be advantageous to learn information by teaching yourself to draw it from memory. What are the steps you would use to learn this process, and why is this procedure a good alternative to rereading to learn information?

1.2 You have a close friend who, frankly, takes terrible lecture notes. Your friend blames this situation on the instructors, who your friend claims all "talk too fast and provide too many visual examples on the overhead projector at the same time." What suggestions could you make to your friend for improving her ability to "capture the lecture"?

1.3 Invent, describe and write a "how to" explanation of your own private system for learning that utilizes, but does not clone, ideas from Chapter 1. Get creative, give your strategy a name, and tell how you'd teach your strategy to a friend.

Experiences

1.1 DECODING A SYLLABUS

Examine and analyze the excerpt on the following page from a syllabus for a Basic Music Skills course (Figure 1.16). Suppose this instructor felt his syllabus was very self-explanatory and did not allow time for questions on the day he distributed it. In a written summary, note what questions you would have about this syllabus in order to clarify the instructor's expectations. You may wish to "decode" this syllabus with a partner or in small groups.

1.2 PERSONAL INQUIRY

If you want to know about college life, ask those who have successfully negotiated the early stages! Find a fellow student who has attended your school for at least a year, someone who has settled into college life and is experiencing success and satisfaction. Interview your chosen subject about how he or she began, as a first-time college student, the process of "learning to learn." What pitfalls did your subject encounter along the way, and what advice does this "veteran" have for you that can help you begin your college adventure? You may wish to write down shared ideas, good advice, and other highlights of your interview. It would be interesting to reread this exchange sometime later, when you qualify as a "veteran" college student.

1.3 DRAWING TO LEARN

Imagine that in five days, in a history or political science course, you will be tested on the impact of American foreign policy after WWII on the long and bloody Vietnam conflict. You decide to teach yourself to draw the map in Figure 1.17 from memory, so you'll be able to sketch, label, and discuss events on the exam or answer a variety of questions on the exam about the American policy of "containment" that legitimized the extended Vietnam conflict.

   Since so much international military action took place in such a small, remote part of Southeast Asia, being able to "see" this area will help you fully understand the complexities of the conflict and the roles of different nations in the situation over time. If you were to combine knowledge of the physical layout with the web construction of the events from 1947 to 1975 as shown on page 20, you would be well equipped to answer a variety of questions regarding the events and the "so what?" about the conflict. Practice your version of "drawing to learn" techniques until you can fully reproduce and explain the relationships of locations and events

FIGURE 1.16 | *Syllabus analysis.*

BASIC MUSIC SKILLS—MUSIC 18, SECTION 2
Syllabus: Winter Term

Instructor: Tommy Tune
Office: Room A, Building B (Phone 555-1234)
Office Hours: M-F 8:00-12:00, and by appointment

Goal: To develop skills and understanding about music and music reading. This includes the study of pitch, rhythm, notation, and structure as well as the interpretation of music through performance on voice, recorder, rhythm instruments, and piano.

REQUIRED MATERIALS:

- *Learning the Recorder through Folksong,* Moore
- *The Melody Book,* Hackett
- Soprano Recorder (Baroque System by Yamaha)
- Music Manuscript Paper

OBJECTIVES:

The student will:

- Perform songs on the recorder and piano with correct rhythm, pitch, tone, and phrasing
- Sight-read songs using the recorder and piano with correct rhythm, pitch, tone, and phrasing
- Demonstrate good singing technique
- Read, write, and perform pitch and rhythmic notation, chord markings, and selected musical symbols with accuracy
- Demonstrate in writing and at the keyboard a basic understanding of scale and chord spellings in both major and minor keys
- Transpose songs for playing and singing
- Conduct with a steady beat in meters of 2, 3, and 4
- Use correct musical terminology to describe music presented aurally and visually

COURSE REQUIREMENTS:

% of Grade

5% Attendance
5% Participation and preparation
20% Homework assignments and quizzes
15% Written Midterm (26 February)
15% Practical Midterm (27 & 28 February—by appt.)
20% Written Final (2 May)
20% Practical Final (7 & 8 May—by appt.)

(Make-up exams will not be given except in the most exceptional circumstances. "Pop" quizzes may not be made up. Points will be lost for late assignments.)

Grading: A 90–100%; B 80–89%; C 70–79%; D 60–69%; F below 60%

FIGURE 1.17 *The Vietnam conflict.*

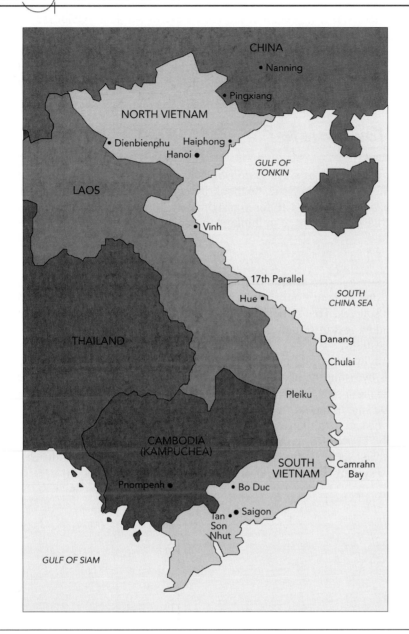

as shown in the figure. Record the steps in the process you use to achieve this learning goal. You may wish to share your procedure with a partner or a small group. Note others' approaches to the same task. Ideally, you would be able to explain why the Vietnam conflict was an undeclared, unwinnable war.

1.4 WEB ACTIVITY

At the Web site fye.sc.edu/syllabi/index.html, pick three of the college and university syllabuses listed for the Freshman Year Experience Course and compare and contrast them. What questions would you have regarding each one? What are their good points? What are their bad points? Which do you find the easiest to use, and why?

1.5 WEB ACTIVITY

Andrew Hicks was a freshman at the University of Missouri–Columbia during the fall of 1985. He wrote a journal of his experiences and placed it on the Web at students.missouri.edu/~ahicks/diary1.html. Read through his experiences for August 1995. How do these compare with your first week of college life? What differences are there?

Can You Relate?

Test your knowledge of ways to consolidate your lecture notes with the important related information from your textbook by composing an answer to the following essay question. Plan to write for approximately 30 minutes. You may wish to time yourself to assess your pace in thinking, organizing, and writing your analysis.

ESSAY 1.1

Select a representative sample of your note taking handling text consolidation system from one of your courses in which you are heavily dependent on knowledge from both sources. This sample should contain at least one entire lecture's notes and corresponding text information. Refer directly to this sample as you answer the following questions.

Explain in detail your note taking system and the ways in which you strengthen your notes by using the textbook in this particular course. How, when, and why do you utilize these strategies? Next, how do you study this information management system? Be sure to include a justification of how this system utilizes components of a "good" system for this particular course.

Finally, be sure to include a critique of this system: How successful has this system proven to be? Which features are most helpful? What modifications may make your system even more powerful and efficient? Be thorough!

Language and Thinking

IT'S READING AND WRITING

LITERACY: READING, WRITING, UNDERSTANDING, REMEMBERING

Chapter 1 focuses on getting the best possible start in creating information management systems and using various ways to study and learn information for college and life. Chapter 2 explores the complex frontier of reading, writing, concentration, motivation, and memory. The topics of reading, writing, speaking, and listening are so related that they must be discussed in connected chapters. Therefore, Chapter 2 tackles the subject of proficient reading and continues the discussion of the ways writing is its complement. Chapter 2 also examines different text forms in different academic disciplines and suggests strategies for reading and thinking critically about the many different print forms college learning utilizes.

We tend to judge our memory capabilities in terms of how well we understand, and as a result remember, different kinds of information. Chapter 2 concludes with a discussion of the relationship of concentration, motivation, and memory and their impact on comprehension, especially reading comprehension. These issues and strategies are closely related, for what is the point of trying to read and write if you can't get started, stay focused, and understand and remember the content? A lack of understanding of these mental processes is a common reason for "blowing off" your books. You've paid a small fortune for your textbooks—use them to your advantage to learn in skillful ways!

Proficient acts of literacy—reading, writing, and thinking critically—produce the power to learn and to grow. Let's look at what an expert, psycholinguist Frank

Smith, writes about literacy: "I should say what I believe literacy to mean—that is, the ability to make use of all available possibilities of written language. By using written language I mean making sense of it, and using it to make sense of the world, as well as producing it . . . Reading and writing can be used for exploration, experience, and discovery."[1] Your college years afford you the best time in your life to develop reading, writing, and critical thinking skills. Are you up to the challenge? It will pay you back for the rest of your life!

The enormous reading loads and the necessity to understand were not as challenging in high school as they are now in junior college or college. Your former teachers probably suggested strategies to launch you into college-level learning. Now it's time to get even more serious and purposeful about reading, understanding, and retaining the information your courses have to offer.

READING: MOTIVATION AND CONCENTRATION VS. BOREDOM

Your goal in reading is to make meaning—to relate ideas, to understand. There are many good reasons why some of your college reading is effective while much of it may not be. You may define reading as "finding the assigned chapter and tracking my eyes over it, left to right, until I finish the last page." That's what reading may look like from afar, but that is not the process of reading for meaning. Any activity without meaning is an invitation to boredom! Boredom kills the possibility of learning.

Frank Smith has also written that "Everyone is equipped with a very efficient device that prevents our wasting time in situations where there is nothing to learn. That device is boredom, and boredom is something all [learners] want to escape."[2] Reading is ineffective—boring—when there is a lack of purpose. Purpose directs and promotes concentration; reading with a purpose fights off boredom. By comparison, therefore, reading can be quite effective, and not boring, if you begin with the setting of purposes, execute those carefully chosen purposes, and devise a plan of attack (active involvement) to ensure ownership of the information and your learning.

Unless you are willing to actively develop good reading strategies, your feelings of boredom and inadequate speed and comprehension may result in frustration, anxiety, and even anger at your instructors for their demands and expectations. According to Martha Maxwell, reading specialist at the University of California, Berkeley, "Reading assignments in undergraduate courses range from 300 pages a night in some history and political science courses to 10 pages a week in mathematics, although math students may spend 20 hours or more on those 10 pages."[3] You can't change instructors' expectations, but you can change your approaches to reading in college.

That solid combination of planned activities is exactly why SQ3R,[4] a reading strategy developed by Francis Robinson back in 1941, is still the most frequently suggested reading strategy in most college survival texts. It's a clearly laid out, focused plan of textbook "attack." The acronym SQ3R stands for *Survey, Question, Read, Recite, Review.* A focus on the purpose for your reading directs your attention and your concentration. Before you attack your textbooks, however, consider the differences between effective and ineffective reading. Assess your current reading strategies—and maybe understand why reading can be boring—by comparing your approaches to the following characteristics.

Effective vs. Ineffective Reading

EFFECTIVE READING:

- Aims at comprehension; therefore, memory is achieved through understanding
- Uses different strategies to get the important information

- Is guided by organizational aids
- Focuses toward well-defined purposes that are established by prereading
- Uses writing as a learning strategy and prepares you to be an informed writer on tests, essay exams, and in real life
- Is practical and prioritized; focuses on reading for main ideas
- Is therefore rapid, attending to larger units of meaning rather than individual words

INEFFECTIVE READING:

- Is slow, focused on individual words, or may not be focused at all (the reader may be tracking over the print only because it has been assigned by the instructor)
- Aims at finding isolated details, perhaps those in boldface or italics, to memorize later
- Is reading for definitions, losing the focus of the phrases in which they're contained
- May consist of merely tracking the eyes purposely through the paragraphs with no delineation of goals
- Is aimed at memory rather than comprehension
- Does not prepare you to write in an informed way about your reading

Which of these characterize your present practices? Do any of these characteristics surprise you or contradict what you believe about reading? Which seem to be reading behaviors that you wish to adopt or discard? It is important to note that there are two terms that many people use interchangeably to describe their main reading techniques, yet there is widespread confusion about the exact differences of the processes of skimming and scanning.

Skimming vs. Scanning

Both are useful alternatives to unfocused slow reading, and they help you determine what should be read carefully and what to breeze through. **Skimming** is a rapid trip through the material to determine main ideas and organizational patterns. It is reading for a foundation of the important concepts and how they relate. Examples of skimming are a quick first read of an assigned chapter before lecture to help you get more thorough notes or a breeze through several articles in your favorite magazine to get the main points and to decide which ones to read thoroughly at another time.

Scanning, on the other hand, is a rapid trip through the material to find and focus on individual details, examples or definitions. Scanning a text is very much like looking for a word in a dictionary or seeking a particular number in a telephone directory. You are "saying" the word or phrase in your head, so when you track your eyes over it, it seems to jump out at you. It may even appear to be in a different style of print because you are concentrating on finding it.

The inclusion of headings and subheadings in textbooks is meant to help you find main ideas and patterns of relationships, while **boldface** and *italics* tend to draw your eyes to the details. You may be drawn to the details in boldface on a first read, but if your background for the material is scant or the material is dense, your first trip through the assignment should be skimming, supplemented with quick summarizing on paper or strategic marking and commenting in the margins. Both skimming and scanning are purposeful ways of getting what you need from your reading, as long as you have made a place in your memory marked "main ideas and important concepts" before you scan for details.

When scanning for particular terms, the index of the textbook may be more efficient to use than whizzing through page after page in hopes of discovering the terms you seek. Indices are wonderful yet underutilized parts of textbooks. Regardless of your primary reading strategies, "knowing all the words" is not a true mark of a good reader. Because of all our life experiences with written language, we can be better readers than we think we are.

We Are All Better Readers Than We Think

Many people think they are poor or at least inefficient readers. What does that really mean? Some suggest that it's a problem with their eyes, but reading is only incidentally visual, proven by the fact that blind people read and make meaning from symbols. Our brains govern our reading; our eyes go to and focus on what the brain seeks. Becoming a better reader requires a modification of how we use our brains to guide our senses and perceptions.

Additionally, we all are language users, and we have a good set of rules in our heads about how language—including written language—works. Watch young children with books; they know how to hold them, and even if they are "play reading" they know that those symbols say important things. When they "read," *they* are saying important things as they learn to experiment with written language. More experienced readers understand even better how written language works, and can often make sense of it even if they don't "know all the words." The "nonsense example" in Figure 2.1 is borrowed from Kenneth Goodman, reading researcher and Professor Emeritus at the University of Arizona–Tucson.[5] It illustrates the notion that we can understand written texts better than we may think, because we consciously and unconsciously "know" how our language works, and **context** helps us make sense when we read. Read the story all the way through, then try to answer the questions that follow, using the language clues in the story.

context the surrounding print, pictures and other features, including socially constructed meanings, with a written form

Goodman explains his story in terms of how we can make sense out of seeming nonsense: "This nonsense is so much like English that you have the feeling that it ought to make sense to you. The problem is that you are culturally disadvantaged. You've had little experience with being *fraper.* You don't know what happens to a *mardsan* when it is *denarpen,* or the preferred way to *plimp a mardsan binky.* And certainly if you don't know what makes a *mardsan binky* a *crouistish* one, it will be difficult to make sense of this sentence and story.[6] If you are able to answer any of the questions, you've proved that readers use language patterns to get meaning. If you think about it, by comparison the nonsense story may make your college reading assignments look possible to tackle!

FIGURE 2.1   *Language in context.*

A Mardsan Gilberter for Farfie

Glis was very fraper. She had denarpen Farfie's mardsan. She didn't talp a gilberter for him. So she conlated to plimp a mardsan binky for him. She had just sparved the binky when he jibbled in the gorger.

"Clorsty mardsan!" she boffed.

"That's a crouistish mardsan binky," boffed Farfie, "but my mardsan is on Stansan. Agsan is Kelsan."

"In that ruspen," boffed Glis, "I won't whank you your giberter until Stansan."

1. Why was Glis fraper?
2. What did Glis plimp?
3. Who jibbled in the gorger when Glis sparved the binky?
4. What did Farfie bof about the mardsan binky?
5. Why didn't Glis whank Farfie his gilberter?

Source: Goodman

What do all readers know about? Two systems of any language that work together to enable readers and writers to make meaning are **syntax** and **semantics.** The above example illustrates the notion that because we internalized these structures as we learned to read and write, we can make "sense" out of what we read and write. Even if there is seeming "nonsense" (unfamiliar words and structures) in the text you are trying to read, by relying on your background of experience and your abilities to predict, or substitute what makes sense, you can get the gist of the text. That's a very good start to reading to understand, and therefore, to remember.

syntax the order of words that construct sentences

semantics the meaning of words used to construct sentences

Vocabulary Development

In the earlier days of college reading instruction, materials included loads of drills and practice with word cards and word lists in order for students to "know more words," presumably so they would become better readers. This kind of artificial transfer of information sounds like a good idea, but it doesn't happen. Sound reading techniques are linked to the requirements of specific course content. Don't treat the expansion of your vocabulary as separate from the improvement of your reading comprehension.

You may wish to maintain a list of words important to the understanding of your subjects, especially those that relate to your major course of study, but don't spend your time poring over word lists that have nothing to do with the content of your courses. You will also improve your vocabulary naturally through the relationships you have with language—acts of reading, writing, speaking and listening. (Figure 2.3, page 35, illustrates a way to keep track of new words you encounter in your reading.) Become a collector of new words, even a lover of new words, but not a slave to them. Life's too short . . . .

A Simple Reading Format (Not SQ3R!)

When we read, our reading process consists of the acts of *predicting, confirming,* and *integrating,* as illustrated in Figure 2.2.[7] Notice that reading is a complex, interactive cycle rather than a step-by-step, one-way linear process. With this in mind, here's a formula for textbook reading that is easy to modify and use for specific kinds of reading requirements:

1. *Predicting.* Preview the text by skimming the following:
   - Title and introduction
   - Chapter objectives
   - Visual aids: charts, graphs
   - Key concepts, noting how they are related within the headings, subheadings, and summary

   Now set purposes for your reading:
   - Devise questions to answer as you read
   - Enter the text with a plan to capture the main ideas and important concepts

2. *Confirming.* Read the text:
   - Skim; sample from the print, look for answers to your questions; confirm or discard your predictions and inferences and predict and infer again
   - Pause and restate important points in your own words
   - Think about how the information fits together as you read and how you would summarize it

3. *Integrating.* Make the text your own:

FIGURE 2.2)   *The reading process.*

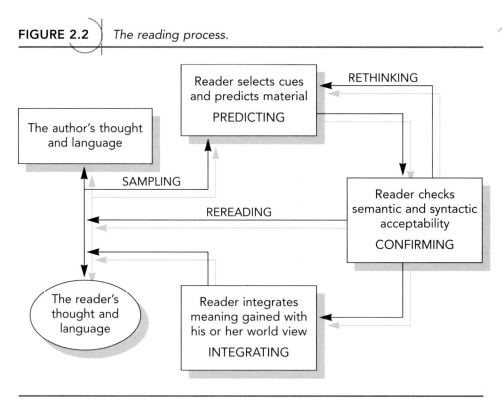

Source: Adapted from Goodman, Watson, and Burke

- Write a quick summary, in your own words as much as possible, using the writing to learn approach (see Chapter 1)
- Compare your reading/summarizing with both the book and your lecture notes
- Brainstorm the best strategies for managing the information (refer to Chapter 1) to prepare for the test: What should you do next with the information?
- Discuss your interpretation of the reading with one or more of your classmates. You'll know you understood your reading if you can explain it to others. This will also help you connect with other students (see Chapter 5).

To Mark, or Not to Mark, the Text

Some students automatically associate reading with highlighting or elaborate systems of text marking. Highlighting or copious marking in texts may be highly overrated. They may seem satisfying, but they can be skimpy substitutes for more active learning. If the information is marked or highlighted in the book, you may not have really had a relationship with the information, and there's no guarantee that it's in your memory system! Highlighting is a very passive association with print material. After studying how college students highlight and annotate their textbooks, S. L. Nist made five recommendations:[8]

1. Throw away the yellow highlighter and use a pen so [you] can write in the margins
2. Think in terms of test preparation
3. Annotate during reading
4. Underline after reading and annotating
5. Review annotations regularly

Nist also recommends that underlining should be "the last step, not the first step that students usually take."[9]

Rampant highlighting is not all it's cracked up to be, and the above list of strategies will be more useful to you in the long run. Nist's suggestions produce active involvement. The above discussion may also explain why writing and drawing in order to own information *may be,* depending on your background for the material, far superior to marking words and passages that you might make sense of sometime later, or you may choose to never look at again. If you are going to spend time in a textbook, why not have something to show for it (in your brain and on paper) when you have finished your reading? Why not work to be a better reader every time you read?

GETTING TO BE A BETTER READER—A PRICELE$$ SYSTEM

Personal reading improvement is a wise, natural project for anyone in (or not in) college. The long-term benefits of your reading improvement will pay you back with more time, which everyone can use, and heightened understanding and retention. You've got all those expensive books—why not teach yourself to read them more efficiently while you are tackling them for your classes? Nist maintains that students who understand the nature of the reading process and current theories of memory and retention will show greater improvement than those who merely engage in paced practice.[10]

Your goal should be improved learning, not just increased reading speed. It is also important to know that reading more slowly does not improve comprehension either; in fact, the more dull and difficult the material, the faster you should read it the first time through. Your own reading improvement program will prove most beneficial when it uses your current course material and/or material relevant to your major and career goals. For fun, you can add recreational reading.

Procedure: Reading Improvement

1. Pick your target textbooks. These are the books you'll need to spend a lot of time with to be successful in a particular course or courses where the readings are crucial. This includes textbooks you may have to read more than any other books during a particular term because they're for a course in your major. Depending on your familiarity with the material, choose a preliminary strategy for reading the chosen text for reading improvement:

   • *Prereading* sets the process of reading in motion. It is a skimming activity to stimulate your predictions (see Figure 2.2); you use the key cues from the text to plan your purposes for reading. Prereading is often a "first read" activity. Lack of familiarity with the material will make prereading a necessary first step. You may preread material before a class to facilitate better note taking, or you may preread a novel or set of assigned readings to be informed for an initial class discussion.

   • *Extensive reading* is reading various sources to gain a broad background for the most important topics of the lesson, chapter, or unit. This is a cycle of skimming and scanning. Extensive reading is an intermediate step from the initial sampling of prereading to the highly focused and precise intensive reading. Reading several different sources to prepare for essay exams, as in history or philosophy, are examples of extensive reading.

   • *Intensive reading* is a close, analytical reading of a single text source. You need a good background in the information to read intensively. Dense texts such as physics books and medical texts may require this approach. Intensive reading is the part of the process in which you are ready to incorporate the details and examples into the basic framework that you constructed through your prereading and/or extensive reading. The goal of intensive reading is a good understanding of the material. This is when the main ideas and the details come together.

2. Based on your chosen strategy from above, time your "casual" reading for a chapter or section. Write down your beginning time, turn the clock face away so you won't obsess over the time you are spending, read, use "pencil-in-hand" strategies, then write down the time you finish the section. Note how long it takes to finish a chapter or section.

3. Keep a personal reading improvement log (see Figure 2.3) of the time it takes to complete your chosen reading tasks, your response to the reading, and perhaps a few new words you encounter in your reading.[11] Keep striving to move quickly for a good, basic understanding.

4. Your goal is to increase your casual reading speed over time, as you develop your comprehension strategies. Devise a system to move your current speed up to your "stress speed," along with a writing to learn (see Chapter 1) approach.

- Use chapter objectives to guide your reading;
- Use headings or subheadings, depending on the density of the reading;
- Use the summary as an introduction to, rather than the end of, your reading;
- Use lecture notes as a preview, if possible, before or along with your reading;
- Set goals for reading and recording key information. Every day, try to take less time to accomplish the same amount of learning;
- Write or sketch quick summaries as you read section by section, from memory as much as possible. Keep your summaries (in your personal reading improvement log) with your lecture notes.

5. Keep a long-term record of the amount of time you need to cover comparable parts of the text. Over time, strive to write less but remember more from your reading improvement work.

6. Add other texts and assigned readings to your reading improvement work.

7. Work on evoking your stress speed in your regular day-to-day reading.

8. Strive to summarize or draw more completely and quickly as your reading improvement progresses. If you are serious about increasing your reading efficiency, you will notice a big improvement in the *quality* of the time you spend with your textbooks, and how much more you understand and remember.

Though the student who wrote the reading improvement log shown in Figure 2.3 did not get very *deeply* into an analysis of her reading, she at least has a written record of the main ideas, key words, and her own response to the material. Keeping a reading log can increase learning and give you a good source to review without returning to the original article.

A WORLD OF READING MATERIALS, A WORLD OF RELATIONSHIPS

A college experience will offer you more kinds of reading material than you could ever imagine! You are right if you believe that college reading is challenging, especially as you find that different disciplines, subjects, and different written forms (a poem vs. a research article vs. an historical novel vs. a physics text, for example) present unique features and reading challenges. It will help you to know that there are different ways of relating to different kinds of texts. Writing styles in each of the many academic disciplines have both universal characteristics and special requirements for your understanding in each unique reading situation.

FIGURE 2.3   *A personal reading improvement log.*

Personal Reading Log June 18, 1990

I read "Reagan's America: A Capital Offense" by Kevin P. Phillips, New York Times Magazine, June 17, 1990, p. 26+.

Comments: Phillips analyzes the effects on U.S. citizens of Reagan's economic policies. He basically states that the rich got much richer, the poor got much poorer, and that the middle classes were having a very difficult time making their money stretch to cover everything they needed. I certainly agree with their premise, because I have felt this personally. I get very upset when I see people sleeping on the streets or rummaging through garbage cans for food and know that we could be doing better in all areas of social welfare.

Time: 15 minutes (this is 5 minutes faster than my last entry)

New words: "entrepreneurism"—meaning (from context): belief or practice of being an entrepreneur —a starter, a gambler, innovator in business area.

Adapted from Kroeker & Henrichs

Another way of describing your reading is to say that you will have different relationships with different reading requirements. The difference between reading "just for the facts" and reading for some personal response to the facts is an important distinction to know when reading—whether it's academic, professional, or for personal enjoyment.

"Efferent vs. Aesthetic" Reading

Louise Rosenblatt, a reading theorist who is a Professor Emerita at New York State University, noted that people read texts for different purposes, and each reader interprets the texts and makes meaning of them for one or more purposes. This "transactional theory of reading" describes a two-way interactive relationship, a "transaction," between a reader and a text. While all reading is an active process, readers interact with a text by choosing a purpose or "stance."[12]

A reader's *purpose* for reading is of critical importance; without purpose, the reading is aimless and unproductive. One purpose for reading is to obtain information, as in reading a recipe to create a meal, the sports page to check scores and the progress of your team, or the page of directions for assembling a bicycle. This practical reading for specific facts is called **efferent** reading—from the Latin *efferre,* "to carry away." Years of schooling have taught most readers to read textbooks in order to "carry away the facts" because facts are what instructors and tests ask for, right? However, another reading stance develops a different relationship with the text—a more lived-through, **aesthetic** reading that will "fuse the cognitive and the affective elements of the consciousness—sensations, images, feelings, ideas—into a personally lived-through poem or story."[13] It means that you are reading not only with your head but also with your senses, your imagination, and perhaps your heart.

Why in the world should college readers care about this transactional theory of reading, anyway—or any theory of reading, for that matter? Because Rosenblatt,

efferent
a way of reading that is primarily focused on the taking away of details

aesthetic
a way of reading that values text as a "lived through" holistic experience

the creator of this theory, and later Ken Goodman and Frank Smith were on to some important and little understood ideas about reading. In an enduring article with the heavily ironic title, "What Facts Does This Poem Teach You?", Rosenblatt laments that in our culture, it's reading for facts—the important stuff—that gets praise in homes, schools, and universities.[14] School teaches us to be like Sergeant Friday on *Dragnet* and go for "just the facts, Ma'am!", but college learning is much more than an accumulation of facts.

Authentic learning is a careful construction—an interwoven relationship—of main ideas and the facts, details and data that support and prove them. This notion is the underlying theme of the first four chapters, and really the entirety, of this book. A discussion of memory systems later in this chapter (pp. 46–49) explains why overloading your memory with a large amount of unrelated details, without the main ideas to connect them, will not work. The human brain does not work that way.

The implications of Rosenblatt's, Goodman's, and Smith's years of investigating reading are a way of understanding **critical thinking** and **critical reading.** Sir Francis Bacon observed around 1620 that "Some books are to be tasted, others to be swallowed, and some few to be chewed and digested." While "tasting" sounds like a discrete sampling or "taking away," "digested" suggests a deep and thorough relationship and understanding. Critical reading must include the weighing of the facts and a personal response to the text by the reader. In critical reading, the reader will taste parts and digest parts, and will ultimately have knowledge of the content as well as personal reactions to the piece.

For example, in reading Alice Walker's 1982 Pulitzer Prize-winning novel *The Color Purple,* you are moved by Celie's letters to God, and you may be horrified at the systematic rape of Celie by the man she thinks is her father. Later, however, it is a deep revelation to both Celie and the reader when she finds out that her children are not her sister and brother after all, and that "Pa not Pa." Walker's novel evokes a reader's critical thinking about what it must have been like to be Celie, and how very difficult the lives of women like Celie must be.

Critical reading is inseparable from critical thinking, and critical thinking can be stimulated by any kind of material. In the example of a reading improvement log in Figure 2.3, the student retells an article about Ronald Reagan's economic policies, and then she moves quite naturally into a personal response in her writing about the piece. She is acting as a critical reader. Recording her personal response helps her understand and remember the article.

Different texts will convey meanings and evoke responses in different ways. According to Figure 2.4 (Goodman, Watson, and Burke), reading has four functions for all of us in daily life: environmental, recreational, occupational, and informational.[15] Each plays a part in reading in college—and in the rest of life. In any or all of the four functions of reading, for any course, discipline, or reading endeavor, certain functions of reading enable critical thinking in a variety of print forms.

No matter whether you are reading environmental, recreational, occupational, or informational sources, you are reading for a blend of main ideas, details, and a personal response. Using material and ideas from Frank Smith and Goodman, Watson, and Burke, and Rosenblatt's notions about ways or "stances" in reading, explore the world of college reading materials and the demands that these materials make in terms of critical reading and thinking.

This is an invitation to explore both the materials and the insights that you may derive from each form. Part of becoming a critical reader is a personal process known as questioning and weighing the facts and thinking about the content of your reading in multiple ways, to understand both the concrete and abstract, the familiar and the unfamiliar in whatever we need and want to read. You should always construct a relationship between the "facts" in the reading and your personal responses and associations to the information. Each college discipline has its own obvious and not-so-obvious requirements for understanding its written forms.

critical thinking
close observation of information or a problem, followed by an informed, organized analysis and response

critical reading
reading in order to facilitate critical thinking

FIGURE 2.4   *The four functions of reading and their sources.*

	BOOKS, MAGAZINES, NEWSPAPERS	RESEARCH/ PROBLEM-SOLVING SOURCES	ALPHABETIC & NONALPHABETIC SYMBOLS	PRIMARY SOURCES
Environmental	Coupons Advertisements Book jackets	Telephone books Recipes Directories	Labels, signs Daily schedules Menus, posters T-shirts, graffiti	Messages Lists Bills Price tags
Recreational	Literary genres Cartoons, comics Poetry Movie critiques Book reviews	Guinness books "How-to" pamphlets Video game guides Model-building instructions	Musical notation Word puzzles Games Jokes and riddles Computer games	Tickets Scrapbooks Theatre and sports programs
Occupational	Want ads Stock reports Job-related articles Job-improvement articles	Professional literature Bibliographies Portfolios Web sites	Blueprints Graphs Manuals Eye charts Computer keyboards	Memos Autobiographies Prescriptions Checks Written reports
Informational	Weather/health/ sports reports Biographies Nonfiction News stories	Definitions Encyclopedias Dictionaries Medical charts Guidebooks	Maps, diagrams Toy boxes Photo albums Computer menus Calendars, Clocks	Birth announcements Receipts Invitations

Source: Goodman, Watson, Burke

Humanities/Literature Texts

If you've ever attended school, then you've been exposed to the humanities (mythology, the classics, religion, women's and ethnic studies, philosophy, art and music history) and literature (poetry, drama, prose, fiction or nonfiction, short stories, collected essays, etc.). No matter what your choice of major, part of your further education will include humanities and literature texts.

The lineup of superstars may have included William Shakespeare, Boris Pasternak, Emily Dickinson, Mark Twain, Euripides and Homer, Toni Morrison, Isaac Bashevis Singer, Alice Walker, Miguel de Cervantes, Lord Byron, Athol Fugard, E.B. White, Sylvia Plath, Black Elk, Charles Dickens, Arthur Miller, or Amy Tan. Whether your prior schooling offered a wide array of international and native authors and multiple themes and **genres,** or a limited and outdated study of literature, reading literature and humanities texts has been part of your academic past. You may have come from classrooms where, in the time-honored texts of choice, the **plot** was the basic thing to know—who did what to whom, the nature of conflict and its resolution. Perhaps the names of the characters and setting were also quiz questions. Maybe you read the piece to answer the questions that followed it in the book; that approach would have been an "efferent" reading for the facts—a reading to carry away the facts.

On the other hand, maybe you've been blessed with a rich background in the study of the humanities and literature from many cultures. Perhaps you have had teachers who loved humanities and literature and gave you provocative essay questions to challenge your abilities to interpret and make connections and to learn to

genre a category or style of composition in literature or the arts characterized by similar forms or content

plot the "story line" of a work of literature: who did what to whom, and why

appreciate reading and writing about these forms. Either way, making sense of the humanities and literature texts in college requires some adjustments in your reading and responding.

Metaphor, figures of speech, imagery, character, theme, plot, setting . . . ah, the language of the study of humanities and literature! Your past experiences with these prose and verse forms have shown you an important point about reading such works: The symbolic or figurative language of poetry—all literature—works to compare *this* to *that.* A key to understanding readings in literature and the humanities is seeing comparisons of *this* to *that.*

According to essayist Owen Barfield, literature and the humanities always operate on several simultaneous levels: "The poet [any writer of humanities or literature] says *B* but he means *A.* He hides *A* in *B. B* is the normal everyday meaning that the words so to speak 'ought' to have on the face of them, and *A* is what the poet has to say to us . . . ".[16] When Robert Burns wrote, "My luve is like a red, red rose . . . .", what did he mean? He was drawing comparisons between his significant other and the elegant beauty of a flower; he didn't mean she spent too long in a tanning bed! When Harper Lee named her 1960 novel *To Kill a Mockingbird,* what in the story was like the sin of shooting a mockingbird? She did not mean the shenanigans of Jem and Scout; she meant the persecution of the accused rapist Tom Robinson. In Arthur Miller's play, *The Glass Menagerie,* there really is a collection of glass figures. What in the play is like a glass menagerie? If the menagerie is *B,* what is Miller's *A?*

Here is a checklist of eight points to consider when reading these kinds of written forms.

1. Why are you reading this piece? How will you be required to display your understanding? What level of understanding does the instructor expect?
2. What are the literal meanings (such as character and plot) of this piece? Does this piece remind you of other readings, films, or other presentational forms? (That is, does it relate to some other works that you know well?)
3. What themes do you think the author is conveying beyond the literal level?
4. How does the author achieve his or her intentions?
5. Does your instructor have a solid interpretation to suggest, or does the instructor invite multiple interpretations? If you have your own interpretation, what specifics of the piece justify your interpretation?
6. If the piece is elusive, dense, or confusing, upon what sorts of outside sources about the author and the work can you draw to gain fuller understanding?
7. How is this assignment related to other assignments in the course?
8. What is the "bottom line" on this particular course? That is, how should you use this reading to make new knowledge for yourself?

Social/Behavioral Science Texts

Psychology is the study of individual behavior, while sociology is the study of group behavior. Both disciplines begin with theories about behavior and illustrate the conclusions of those theories with real-world situations and examples. Students often enjoy reading these sorts of texts because they explain how and why people do what they do. The trap, however, is that since these sorts of theories and real-world examples about behavior are interesting and reasonably familiar, students breeze through these texts, soak up (memorize?) a fair amount of the terms, and feel as though they truly understand the content. We understand the familiar.

The social sciences also include history, political science, anthropology, family studies, education, and economics. These texts are about people and how they live and work as families, tribes, communities, states, or nations. Unfortunately, behavioral and social science texts "set you up" to do assumptive reading and studying—that is, you assume you truly understand the concepts because discussions about people's lives fall into the realm of what feels familiar to us as readers. Be careful with these kinds of texts—the textual cues of boldface and the use of italics present an alluring invitation to read in order to memorize the terms, but the tests won't be vocabulary tests! The lessons we learn from studying people's past experiences are intricately woven themes and patterns, only pieces of which are names, dates, and/or places.

The unique challenge to reading history texts is that the content may come from **primary** or **secondary sources.** Whether you are reading primary sources such as the slave narrative of Frederick Douglass or early versions of the Constitution such as the Articles of Confederation, or secondary sources such as the history of the plague in Europe or scholarly interpretations of the British colonization of Africa and India, your personal involvement through reading and writing will help you understand and interpret the past.

primary source
original works, such as diaries, letters, documents, or texts

secondary source
sources that utilize, analyze, and discuss primary sources

Many students dread having to read primary sources. High school history books tend to retell and interpret rather than offer primary proof. Sometimes readers just want to know the facts and not have to work too hard to find them. For example, even now that you are in college you may prefer to read about the Constitution rather than read the actual text. Do not avoid or dismiss primary sources; they contain the "facts" or data, written from multiple perspectives, including the perspectives of those who lived through the actual events, that help us interpret the past with those informed personal points of view.

An instructor's version of history is based on an interpretation of primary data. A political scientist or historian might mention in lecture that the Constitution is an amazing document because of what it has been able to maintain for over 200 years with the need for only 35 amendments. Why not investigate the original source or sources and develop your own historical perspective? What do the first 10 amendments guarantee? What events caused the need for the successive amendments? Which are your favorite amendments? History books are full of some scholars' conclusions about the past. Why not construct your own conclusions based on the primary evidence? The ability to interpret primary sources is a mark of a critical thinker.

Foreign Language Texts

Foreign language texts are rather workbookish. Their main purposes are to:

- Teach you the meanings of words in another language;
- Teach you how these words work together to make meaning;
- Teach you ways to read, write, speak, and listen successfully in another language, often by comparing the ways this language does or does not work like English;
- Help you understand another culture through a study of its language and other aspects of that culture; and
- Help you become sufficiently proficient in another language so that you can communicate well with its native users when appropriate.

How can you work with your foreign language text and the course content to achieve the above goals? In Figure 2.5, taken from a French I text, the authors have kindly provided a visual schema—a real-world framework, based on the familiar arrangement of a classroom, to help associate vocabulary words to classroom objects. This visual is helpful, yet the page layout leaves the learner at a bit of risk. Notice that the vocabulary words are organized alphabetically by category (verbs vs. nouns), and most are not included in the picture. If organization by alphabet

FIGURE 2.5   *A sample foreign-language text page.*

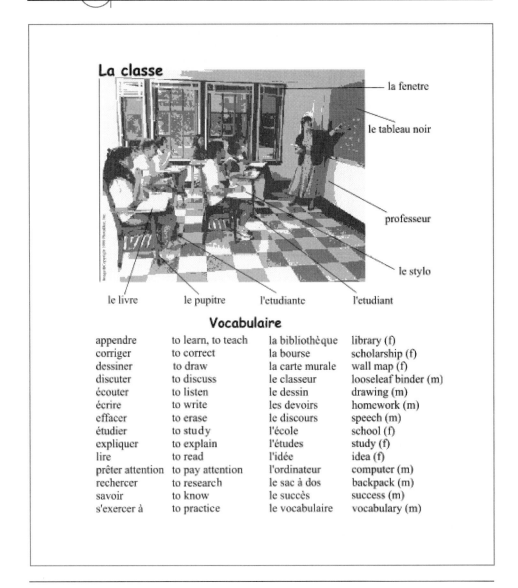

La classe

la fenetre
le tableau noir
professeur
le stylo

le livre   le pupitre   l'etudiante   l'etudiant

Vocabulaire

appendre	to learn, to teach	la bibliothèque	library (f)
corriger	to correct	la bourse	scholarship (f)
dessiner	to draw	la carte murale	wall map (f)
discuter	to discuss	le classeur	looseleaf binder (m)
écouter	to listen	le dessin	drawing (m)
écrire	to write	les devoirs	homework (m)
effacer	to erase	le discours	speech (m)
étudier	to study	l'école	school (f)
expliquer	to explain	l'études	study (f)
lire	to read	l'idée	idea (f)
prêter attention	to pay attention	l'ordinateur	computer (m)
rechercer	to research	le sac à dos	backpack (m)
savoir	to know	le succès	success (m)
s'exercer à	to practice	le vocabulaire	vocabulary (m)

Source: Khojasteh

works for your memory system, then this page is laid out for ease of study. It just may be, however, that this page merely represents the scope of words to learn in this chapter, and the rote memory of words in alphabetical order may not be the best technique for your own memory system.

In what other ways could you organize the content? Might you wish to sketch your own version of a classroom to include the key words? Sketching and associating may be good learning strategies here. Also, if you could move the vocabulary lists into correct sentences that use the words, the inclusion of the words in context will certainly help you learn them.

The main point is that you can and should rearrange, reorganize, and perform learning-centered acts with the content you need to understand and remember. There's no rule that says you must use your text sources exactly as they appear. Rewrite, reorganize, or sketch material from your books to take advantage of the way you learn most effectively!

Mathematics Texts

If you think about it, mathematics texts are very similar to foreign language texts, and the study of mathematics is a very similar cognitive process to the study of a foreign language. How can that be? Both foreign language and mathematics texts are explanations of the rules of a particular language; mathematics is the symbolic language of problem solving and relationships between and among physical phenomena. This discussion of mathematics texts is especially thorough because many students get bogged down or lost in reading them!

Types of Math Skills You Might Need

Math skills are becoming more important in this world of increasingly complicated technology. Your level of math knowledge will affect all areas of your life. The level of competency that you need will vary depending on your specific career goals and objectives, but everyone will need at least a minimal amount of skill. These skills can be broken down broadly into the following areas: logical thinking and reasoning, arithmetic, algebra, geometry, probability and statistics, calculus and differential equations, and higher math. Many students avoid their math books even more than other kinds of texts because they do not know how to use them. The following discussion, contributed by Doug Clark of the University of Missouri–Columbia,[17] is included to demystify the world of mathematics and its different texts.

Reasoning and Thinking Logically

The single most important skill that math teaches you is the ability to think logically and critically. Math is, at heart, a problem-solving discipline. The ability to think logically and to solve problems is crucial in everyday life. You need to think logically in deciding how to plan your day, where to eat, what to eat, how you will drive your car, and so on. Logical thinking involves two types of reasoning: **inductive reasoning** and **deductive reasoning.** Although mathematics seems to develop skill primarily in deductive reasoning, it is actually created through a process of both deductive and inductive reasoning.

   Inductive reasoning, or induction, means determining a generalization from a list of specific events (example-to-idea thinking). For example, if you see 30 men in a row wearing red shirts, you might conclude that all men wear red shirts. In mathematics, induction is often used in determining what a statement or theorem might be. However, it requires proof of some sort before an induction is considered valid. In the instance above, you would need proof before concluding that all men wear red shirts.

   Deductive reasoning means applying a general statement to a specific instance (idea-to-example thinking). For example, if you were told that all fish are goldfish, and you had a fish in a tank, you could conclude it must be a goldfish. Using deduction requires caution, however, because when applying any generalization you need to know whether the generalization is in fact true (which, in the above instance, it is not). This is especially necessary in such fields as sociology and psychology.

   Another factor in reasoning is the ability to *estimate*. In 1989, the National Council of Teachers of Mathematics recognized the importance of estimation skills in their publication, *Curriculum and Evaluation Standards*

(continued)

inductive reasoning
forming a generalization by examining a set of specific events or ideas

deductive reasoning
applying a general principle to a particular situation

for School Mathematics. In these standards, the NCTM notes the use of exploring estimation strategies, recognizing when estimation is important, using estimation to determine the reasonableness of results, and applying it in working with quantities, measurement, computation, and problem solving. Estimation involves both inductive and deductive processes. The ability to use estimation effectively will save you time and effort in solving many real-world problems.

Arithmetic

Many of your everyday tasks require arithmetic. Arithmetic consists of numerical computations such as addition, subtraction, multiplication, and division. It also includes handling decimals, fractions, ratios, and proportions. Examples of where these skills are used are:

- Paying the correct amount on a bill and seeing that you receive the correct change
- Calculating tips in restaurants
- Balancing your checkbook
- Comparison shopping at grocery stores, clothing stores, etc.

Algebra

A knowledge of algebra is needed almost as frequently as arithmetic. Many times you figure out problems without consciously realizing you are using algebra. Some situations where algebra shows up are:

- Computing interest on credit cards, loans, etc.
- Figuring your GPA
- Cutting or enlarging cooking recipes
- Solving problems in areas such as geology, biology, anthropology, chemistry, nursing, physics, and astronomy
- Determining efficient travel plans

Algebra involves determining an unknown value using known values. For example, if you want to make 100 cookies and have only enough flour for three batches, you might use algebra to figure out how many cookies would have to be in each batch: $3(x) = 100$, where 3 is the number of batches, x is how many cookies, and 100 is the number of cookies desired. Through algebra you can find that x = 100 divided by 3, or approximately 33. Therefore, you need a cookie recipe that makes about three dozen cookies.

Geometry

Along with algebra, geometry is the most needed math skill in everyday life. The most important uses of geometry occur in determining areas and volumes. However, geometry problems occur in many other forms. Examples of places geometry is found in your life are:

- Determining the amount of paint needed to paint a room or a house
- Determining what size heater or air conditioner is needed for a room or a house

(continued)

- Determining how much punch you should make for a party
- Determining how closely you can pass a car
- Buying and arranging furniture and appliances
- Packing luggage—for instance, when you pack a suitcase for a trip, in your head you are calculating the size of the different items you will put in the suitcase, adding them up, and determining whether they will fit inside the space determined by the size of the suitcase.

Probability and Statistics

A knowledge of basic probability and statistics is needed to understand the relevance and importance (or lack thereof) of the overwhelming amount of statistical information we are deluged with from the media. Without some knowledge in these areas, you are unable to evaluate the usefulness of such information. For example, if a woman reads breast cancer statistics, her statistical and probability knowledge can help her determine what her chances are of developing breast cancer, and how certain precautions can diminish those chances.

For some careers, such as actuarial or genetic science, a strong background in probability and statistics is crucial. Some areas of business, economics, and engineering also require such skills. In fact, even journalism majors are required to take courses in statistics.

Calculus and Differential Equations

Calculus and differential equations are needed in most engineering fields, business and economics, physics, and astronomy. Any problem in which a rate of change is needed involves calculus and differential equations. Many problems that involve work, water pressure, and areas and volumes also use calculus.

Higher Math

There are some fields and careers in which a high level of mathematics is required. Linear algebra occurs in some business areas and industrial engineering. Abstract algebra appears in computer science and physics. Other careers that require even further mathematics are theoretical physics, economic research and, of course, mathematics itself.

Certainly not every student will need to master calculus or linear algebra. The basics, however, will be of use to everyone.

The Mathematics Textbook

Math textbooks seem to add an extra level of difficulty for many students. The ability to read a math textbook is a skill that must be developed. Do not expect to read mathematics in the same way that you would read literature, history, or psychology.

Reading math is often a time-consuming process. When reading a math book, try keeping a pad of paper with you. As you read slowly, take special note of the examples. If steps are left out, as they often are, work them out on your pad. Draw sketches to help visualize the material as you read. Do not

(continued)

move on until you understand the example and how it relates to the reading. The examples provide keys in working the homework.

Also note what formulas are given. Consider whether these formulas are important; recall whether the instructor emphasized them. Be aware that in some classes you are responsible for all formulas, while in others, the instructors will provide them to you. Look over your lecture notes and see how they compare with the text. After you read the section(s), then you are ready to attempt the homework.

Source: Doug Clark, Learning Resource Specialist in mathematics, University of Missouri–Columbia Learning Center. Doug is a veteran teacher of a first-year orientation course.

Science Texts

The world of science and the texts that explain it attempt to portray an increasingly complete and coherent version of the universe. The explanations—the theories—in science are a product of the interaction of the human mind and the physical phenomena of nature. Scientific methods drive toward constructing theories about the nature of the universe, and each different discipline in the sciences has its own kinds of questions, ways of investigating the questions, and recording, illustrating, explaining, and interpreting the results of the inquiries.

Scientific philosopher Henry H. Bauer has observed the following distinctions among the sciences:

> . . . Whereas astronomy and biology and geology are fundamentally and inherently concerned with large-scale change that seems always to have gone in the same direction, chemistry and physics are not. Astronomy has to deal with the evolution of the universe, the birth and development and death of stars; biology and geology seek to account for the evolution of living things and of the Earth. But physics and chemistry share no such concern with inherent, directional change: they delight, by contrast, in the discovery of permanent relationships, and they do experiments in which time is just another controllable factor. Again, astronomy and biology and geology are, by and large, observational sciences, studying whatever nature presents them with, whereas chemistry and physics, by and large elemental sciences, can decide what to study, within increasingly wide limits—to the extent of making materials and arranging conditions that nature never before knew.[18]

Scientific writing does not describe linear start-to-finish steps; instead, science texts describe a cycle of activities and relationships. Facts and data are the details in science, much as names and dates are the details of history and characters and plot are the stuff of literature.

Many experts in science writing compare the sciences to poetry and painting. Jacob Bronowski, another scientist/philosopher, notes in his book *Science and Human Values* that order, likenesses, and symmetry in the universe are "beauty," the same phenomenon that Louise Rosenblatt calls "aesthetics." Bronowski wrote that "All science is the search for unity in human likenesses . . . science is nothing else than the search to discover unity in the wild variety of nature . . . Poetry, painting, the arts are the same search."[19]

The implications of Bronowski's comparison of science to the arts may have value for you as a reader. Just as reading to understand is based on prediction and confirmation, science itself is based on prediction and confirmation of notions about the universe. Understanding scientific relationships is much the same cognitive process as understanding a play or a painting. Science has large ideas and specific languages to articulate causes and effects and other relationships; literature, the humanities, foreign language, history, the behavioral sciences, and the writing in all college disciplines work in similar ways.

Therefore, if you love novels but dread biology, use what you know about reading fiction to help you form strategies to read, write about, make sense of, and understand your science reading. For example, reading Michael Crichton's *Jurassic Park, The Andromeda Strain,* or even Randy Shilts' *And the Band Played On,* a chilling chronicle of the AIDS epidemic, are certainly exercises in reading scientific information. "Whodunits" by Agatha Christie and international political thrillers by Tom Clancy also require the same thinking processes as do your science textbooks. Release yourself from science anxiety by using what you know about reading other prose forms. We are better readers than we think.

Collected Essay Readings

Regardless of the course, if you are required to read essay collections, they are no doubt short pieces by a variety of authors who have different ways of illustrating the important course concepts through stories, anecdotes, or short summaries of others' research on the topics. Depending on the course, these essays may be intended to illustrate the lecture or supplement the textbook, or they may be rather "freestanding" pieces over which you will be tested.

It's very important to know how your instructor intends you to use the information from these essays. A safe way to handle essays is to keep a record of the title, author, topic, or concept, the main points and real-world applications, and the tie or relationship of each essay to what the instructor says or implies about its relevance. You may wish to add this record into your notes if the essays are closely related to the content, or in a separate but easy to find set of writings. For example, if you are reading a text of collected short stories from an assortment of international writers, you may wish to keep a log from your reading of each story. Later you can add what the instructor or classmates observed about the works in class discussion.

Paperback Novels

Find out the instructor's intentions and expectations. If the paperback has chapter titles, use each chapter title as a guide for your reading. If you can explain the title, you've unearthed the central issue or events of the chapter. You may wish to summarize each chapter right in the book, at the end of each, or keep a separate reading log where you leave a trail of your reading each time you read. That written trail will become invaluable when it's time to review the book or for a quiz or exam. Resist the urge to run through the book with highlighter in hand!

Journal Articles

Again, start with the instructor's intentions and expectations. How, when, and to what extent might you use the information from such articles? What degree of detail will your instructor expect you to know? What examples should you jot down to learn along the way? What other sources on the "information superhighway" can help you understand the topics? Journal articles may be theoretical, aimed at a main idea, or loaded with data to substantiate the main point. In either case, let the instructor's intentions be your guide, but do not concentrate on the details to the exclusion of the main ideas.

Newspapers and Weekly Magazines

More and more instructors are incorporating current events into their courses. *The Wall Street Journal* is now part of many courses' reading requirements, especially in economics and business courses, and even in political science. Reading with the goal of keeping a notebook or log of current events that relate to your particular courses is an excellent way to stay informed and to be a good discussant. Using writing to learn strategies can be especially useful if your instructor expects students to discuss current events and how they illustrate the course concepts. Instructors *notice* and *remember* students who are well informed and willing to share their ideas in class.

Electronically Retrieved Print Sources

The world of electronically delivered, retrievable print sources is beyond the scope of the imagination. Many instructors will expect you to do research on the World Wide Web, and they may or may not suggest Web sites for you to visit. Figure 2.6 is an introduction to Web searches, contributed by Sabrina Friedman, a junior journalism major at the University of Missouri–Columbia.[20]

MEMORY SYSTEMS

Is this topic unexpected here? It should be no surprise: Why discuss memory in a chapter about reading? Unless you are reading for fun, a universal lament of readers, whether they are college students or not, is "I can't remember what I read!" or "I've just wasted three hours reading, and I don't understand any of it!" While retaining the particulars of an office memo, the front page of a newspaper, or the details of a murder mystery may seem easy, there's too much to read in a college career to even attempt to remember it all! Much is made of the differences in "information" and "knowledge." Which do you wish to retain? Why? With the

---

FIGURE 2.6   *Web searches.*

HOW TO SEARCH THE WEB . . . THE EASY WAY!

First, select a search engine:

Yahoo!	*www.yahoo.com*
Excite	*www.excite.com*
Infoseek	*www.infoseek.com*
LookSmart	*www.looksmart.com*
Lycos	*www.lycos.com*
SEARCH.COM	*www.search.com*

- To go to your selected engine, go to File, then to Open Location.
- Type in the Web address (e.g., *http://www.yahoo.com*).
- To search for your topic, narrow it down to *key words!*
- For instance, type in: Megan's Law AND registered sex offenders:
  or: Megan's Law, registered sex offenders
  . . . replacing these key word phrases with your topic.
- You will then be given a list of Web sites that contain your key words, along with a short description of each one. Choose one and surf it; if it doesn't meet your needs, just click Back (or the back arrow) to return to the list of Web sites, and try another.
- If you've explored all the options provided on your particular search engine and have found nothing, or if you're just ready for a new search, go back to File and Open Location, and try a different search engine.

advent of the information superhighway, is our whole society at risk of losing the ability to read and remember because machines can store and find information for us at the touch of a button? Let's hope not. In any event, we all would benefit by becoming better readers, for school and for life.

Therefore, an examination of the systems of memory and how they work, together or at odds, will help you understand how and why you will or will not remember what you read, hear, observe, taste, touch, or smell. Memory is based on understanding what we take in through our senses, and how we choose to use and store that information. There are three related memory systems: sensory, short term, and long term; each plays a key role in remembering. The father of American psychology, William James (1842–1910) observed a simple concept concerning memory: "All improvement of memory consists of one's habitual methods of recording facts." For a student or anyone who is by nature a "lifelong learner," this means that how you approach studying and storing information means everything.

Sensory Memory

Sensory memory consists of what humans take in through their five senses. Sensory memories include the sight of a movie, the smell of the popcorn, the soundtrack of the movie, and the touch of your date's arm on your shoulder during the mushy scenes. These images come in directly through the senses and are stored or discarded, depending on their relevance to your life or how you store the information for later use. For example, the first time a child touches a hot stove and his parent yells, "No! Hot!", that child learns and will remember the concept of "hot" and the label for it through a combination of a memorable sensation and the language used to express it.

Information that comes in through the sense of smell, for some psychobiological reason, stays recorded in the memory longer than impressions from any of the other senses. It's unfortunate that you can't "smell your way" through college! Oh well . . . .

Visual—or iconic—memory and auditory—or echoic—memory, are the two sensory memories most used in schooling. Unfortunately, sight and hearing aren't our sharpest senses, so humans had to invent storytelling, and later writing, reading, and memory devices to keep all the information about the world in some sort of organized system.

Short-Term Memory

Short-term memory is a limited space with a limited time (30 seconds or less if the information is not rehearsed in some way). It consists of what we encounter and acknowledge *right now*. Cognitive psychologist A. D. Baddeley refers to this system as the "working memory."[21] For example, you may look up a telephone number and dial it successfully, but if you don't call that number frequently, you'll have to return to the telephone book over and over again. On the other hand, if that telephone number connects you to your significant other, the importance of the relationship and your frequent use of the number will push it into long-term memory.

Baddeley asserts that there are three parts to working memory[22]:

1. The "articulatory loop," which is a speech mechanism
2. The "visiospatial sketch pad," which functions to rehearse visual images
3. The "central executive," a "switch" that makes decisions about whether the visual or the auditory memory should be activated to best store information

In some interesting research, Baddeley "has provided evidence that one of the deficits associated with Alzheimer's disease may be an ineffective central executive."[23] This memory loss phenomenon may serve to explain the confusion manifested by Alzheimer's patients—their brains don't register on the appropriate perceptual field (hearing vs. seeing) when they encounter information.

The good news for learners is that in the process of working to understand information, your memory for specific tasks can be improved as you study, but the memory does not generalize from one learning task to another. Therefore, you need to be versatile in your study techniques to improve different kinds of remembering. The strategic uses of the four language systems—reading, writing, speaking, and listening—are means of memory development.

Long-Term Memory

Long-term memory is a permanent storage system. There is enormous interest in the way long-term memory works, for it's the memory system so critical for success in school and all of life. Learners can improve their memories only by learning material thoroughly in the first place; thus much of this book describes and explains strategies for learning in college. So you should think of this text as a user's guide to memory and understanding, explained through a system of relationships.

There are two kinds of long-term memory systems:

1. Episodic memory: When or where (episodes and their chronology). Some "school knowledge" is stored in episodic memory; for example, your older instructors can undoubtedly tell you exactly where they were and what they were doing the moment they heard that President John F. Kennedy had been shot. Probably you weren't around in 1963, yet the assassination of a president is certainly a part of history. You may know about that grim day in Dallas because you memorized the facts, but you probably know about the open convertible and all the rest because the information is part of our culture's collective episodic memory.

2. Semantic memory: Think of it as a spiderweb; it is a network or system of categories. It includes causes and effects, concepts, rules, and directions. Semantic (of meanings) memory engages a constructive process and relies on elaborate rehearsal and retrieval activities. (See Chapter 1 for a discussion of rehearsal and retrieval.) Semantic memory is the memory for ideas; it is the holding bin for "school knowledge" and much of what we all "know" in life. For example, semantic memory is where you have stored the concept of what an "assassination" (from the above example) is, and how it is different from a "death" of a president or other public figure. The challenge for all learners is to find multiple ways to successfully move information into their long-term memory systems. Chapters 1 and 2 are especially generous in offering you reading, writing, and thinking strategies that will help nourish your long-term memory.

Figure 2.7 shows one way Frank Smith explains the relationship among memory systems.[24] This is not literally a one-way linear process. Information is taken in through the eyes, goes into a pool of sensory storage, and may or may not go into short-term memory. Use, or rehearsal, of the visual (or any other sensory) information will determine whether it will disappear from short-term memory or whether it will be moved and stored into long-term memory. For example, if you recite or write information, such as the steps in the process of photosynthesis in biology or the results of the 1954 Supreme Court case *Brown v. Board of Education* from memory, your use, or relationship with the information, will help you understand and store it.

The challenge in all learning is determining the best ways to move certain sensory information into short-term, and if important, long-term memory storage.

FIGURE 2.7   *Relationship among memory systems.*

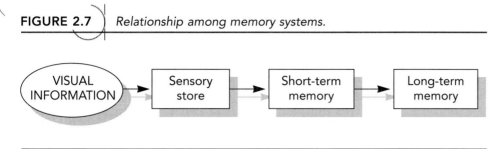

Source: Smith

According to Frank Smith, "Whether or not we can retrieve information from long-term memory depends on how the desired information is organized. The secret of recall from long-term memory is to tap one of the *interrelationships*."[25] Strategies in this book are aimed at using interrelationships to build understanding and memory.

Another way to think about the relationship among memory systems is to think of short-term memory not as a separate system or holding bin for what may become long-term information, but as a part of long-term memory that we tap into from time to time. See Smith's alternative representation of the memory system in Figure 2.8.[26]

Either explanation of the memory systems shows you that understanding and memory are not the same phenomenon. They are both complex, yet achievable aspects to your process of learning. Both explanations point to the roles of active rehearsal and retrieval and the necessity for distributed practice (regular review) in order to retain that which you wish to remember in school and in all of life. In other words, there are ways to reduce *forgetting*—the great nemesis of all lifelong learners. (Whoever wanted to be a lifelong *forgetter,* anyway?) A good rule for remembering, then, is "Use it or lose it!"

Forgetting

Most forgetting, in reading and all learning, is caused by interference from other information. That is, what you may be reviewing some Thursday night after *ER* or some other favorite TV show may be bumped out by the work you do with another course later. That's why the best study is short, intense, frequent, and focused. In that way, you will be able to "cycle back" to previously studied information in order to use it again and to move it into long-term storage.

FIGURE 2.8   *Representation of memory systems.*

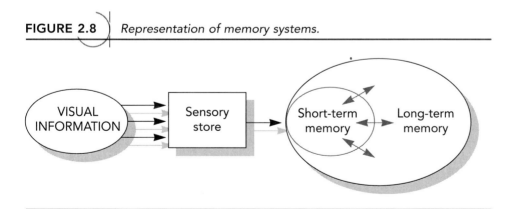

Source: Smith

Additionally, there is no true cause-effect relationship between *time, learning,* and *forgetting.* You see, time does not cause forgetting; it's what happens during a particular stretch of time that determines whether you will retain or lose that which you are studying. Other points about forgetting include:

- We especially forget controversial material. Why might that be true?
- Remembering what we've heard is harder than remembering what we've read. Why might that be true?
- We forget more when we are listening to a discussion than to an organized talk. Why?
- There are two kinds of "forgetting":
  - *"You never had it"* forgetting means you never really understood or learned the information in the first place.
  - *"Mental blur"* forgetting means you are trying to rely on incomplete learning, perhaps passive rereading until you think you "know" the information because it looks familiar.
- Most forgetting begins a short time after learning ends. What are the implications for your learning schedule?
- Without actively using our learning through rehearsal and retrieval strategies, we can actually weaken our memories.

However, there is good news. Using a wide variety of learning strategies can improve one's memory. What are the implications of this for you as a learner?

Remember, how well, how long, and what you do or do not understand and remember are all governed by your perceptual and learning styles. Chapter 7 discusses learning styles, teaching styles, and their important classroom connections. You will gain more insights into how you learn and how your particular memory systems can work most efficiently for you.

Memory and Comprehension Improvement

Many college orientation books devote a lot of pages to memory devices. The very best way to remember information is to *understand it.* Memory tricks are very good to use when there is no cohesive meaning or organizing structure for what you wish to remember. For example, there is a chunked jingle, the "Alphabet Song," to remember the order of the characters in the alphabet, because the alphabet has no inherent meaning. It's a great example of a memory device; it's chunked into bits of three or four letters, and it rhymes. How else would we ever locate anything in a dictionary?

By contrast, much of what you have to learn in college has natural associations by meaning. It's every student's responsibility to look for meaning in what she wishes to understand and remember. For example, the Bill of Rights contains 10 amendments, and a list of 10 unrelated items is too long to commit to rote memory. However, the 10 amendments have internal connections—they are related to one another and grouped by topic, beginning with individual rights and moving to matters dealing with bearing arms, quartering soldiers, and court (due process) procedural issues. The subjects of the amendments set up an organizing structure, so there is less to learn and the information makes better sense and is easier to retrieve.

But hold on—there is plenty of information in college that you need to know that is not internally related. Invented, contrived relationships between items to be learned are known as mnemonic devices. The challenge to learners is knowing when to use mnemonics and when to use meaning-based approaches to learning—so the trap for students is knowing when, and when not, to use memory devices.

Often students invent elaborate and complicated mnemonics when better learning strategies would make learning easier. For example, why would you try to remember all 50 states by alphabetic order when you can visualize the U. S. map and use the associations of its natural regions: New England, the Southern coastal states, the Midwest, and so on?

Mnemonics that create external associations often rely on visualization, and visual images are often easy to create, store, and retrieve. They are good to use when meaning-centered approaches to learning are not effective. Mnemonics are systems that create rhymes, jingles, phrases, and even new words that are easy to recall and that will trigger the complex information for which the memory invention stands. The most widely used mnemonic devices include the method of loci, use of first-letter mnemonics, narrative chaining, pegword method, and chunking, each of which is discussed below.

The Method of Loci

This memory technique has endured from the ancient Greeks, who strove to recall a long list of items or parts of a story in their correct order. To use this system you establish a strong memory of an exact route, pathway, or journey. Then you associate the items or part of a story with particular objects or locations along the path. (Figure 2.5, using visual associations to study a foreign language, is an example of this method.)

It has been said that the Greek and Roman storytellers and orators traveled great distances to spread their tales and deliver their speeches, so they took advantage of associating information with items they encountered on their long walks. Depending on the size of your campus and the distances you need to cover, you may wish to use this system very similarly to the Greeks' approach.

Here's an example: On a long walk from your residence hall or apartment to your psychology or biology class, you intend to memorize the hierarchy of matter found in nature. The hierarchy, ranging from the smallest to the largest unit of life, contains 11 items which do not lend themselves to other methods of memorization. So you mentally place each item along the familiar trail from home to school.

- The door by which you leave is a *proton.*
- The bicycle rack outside the door is a *neutron.*
- The fire hydrant at the beginning of the sidewalk is an *atom.*
- The group of students you pass is composed of *molecules.*
- The gymnasium is full of *organelles.*
- The math building is full of *organisms.*
- The student union is full of happy *families.*
- The building in which your class meets is a *community.*
- The classroom, full of eager students, is a *society.*

If the route to class does not lend itself to association by location, you can place objects to be remembered around any familiar setting—in your house, along a familiar road trip, or along any stretch of space that is highly familiar, second nature, really, to you. The Greeks had the right idea!

Use of First-Letter Mnemonics

The anchor for the memory in this memory aid is the first letter of each item to be recalled, as in two examples for recalling the names of the nine planets in their order from the sun.

One sentence is **M**ary **V**ery **E**arly **M**ade **J**ohn **S**end **U**s **N**ews **P**ronto. Another version is **M**y **V**ery **E**ducated **M**other **J**ust **S**erved **U**s **N**ine **P**izzas. Either mnemonic should unwrap Mercury, Venus, Earth, Mars, Jupiter, Saturn, Uranus, Neptune, and Pluto. There are plenty of well-known mnemonics in our culture, ranging from one involving knuckles as incidents of the number of days in a month (not really a mnemonic), to "**E**very **G**ood **B**oy **D**oes **F**ine" to represent the five lines in a music staff, and FACE for the spaces in the staff. And so it goes . . . .

Use mnemonics only when there is complex information to be learned that has no internal organizing structure. This technique works for remembering the planets because their names are in a random order.

Narrative Chaining

This system is a form of mnemonics that takes the concepts to be learned and weaves them into some sort of memorable story. A story using chaining might incorporate the parts of the brain, in order from the front to the back: "John got into his car, turned on the very large *motor,* and drove to a restaurant. The smells sent him into *somatosensory* overload, and his *auditory* reaction startled all those within *visual* range."

Pegword Method

Similar to the method of loci, this method involves visually relating new terms and concepts to a series of images already stored in long-term memory. However, the method of loci requires that you unroll the whole list of items to be learned in order, so retrieving the ninth item would require a lot of recall to arrive at number nine. Therefore, this method would not be the best way to memorize the Bill of Rights. The pegword method is better for vocabulary.

The pegword method allows access to any item learned without the necessity of repeating the whole sequence. For example, a very well-known pegword uses rhyming to capture a list of words:

- One is a bun; two is a shoe;
- Three is a tree; four is a door;
- Five is a hive; six is sticks;
- Seven is heaven; eight is a gate;
- Nine is wine; ten is a hen.

Some think this pegword method is more trouble than it's worth, but there may be some applications for it in school, work, and life.

Good Old Reliable Chunking

(See the definition of chunking in Chapter 4. See also the sets of note taking styles in Chapter 1 for more examples of uses of chunking.) Chunking may be the most useful memory device. While not a mnemonic, chunking organizes information into manageable "chunks" through either internal or external relationships of information sets.

Seven is an important number in memory, for the human brain best recalls seven, plus or minus two, bits of information. Think about how we use chunking in our culture. The alphabet is chunked, as are phone numbers, social security numbers, student ID numbers, and even auto license plate numbers. All these sets of numbers are chunked for ease of remembering because they have no intrinsic meaning.

However, unlike mnemonics, chunking is a terrific way to remember sets of information that are related by meaning. Using the Bill of Rights as an example, the amendments could be chunked according to topic and order:

- Amendment 1: This amendment ensures civil liberties—freedom of speech, press, assembly, and the right to petition the government.

- Amendments 2–4: These enumerate issues about armies (militia), the right to bear arms; no more keeping soldiers in your home (quartering); no illegal searches and seizures.
- Amendments 5–8: These set up rules for the court system.
- Amendment 9: The people retain their rights.
- Amendment 10: Powers not specifically given to the federal government go to the states.

By reviewing the chunks of the Bill of Rights, it is easy to understand the issues that most concerned the drafters of the document—personal freedom and safety, court procedures, and matters of jurisdiction (states' rights vs. federal rights). Chunking, then, reduces the number of items the memory must hold, while at the same time shows interrelationships of issues and ideas. Try it!

Be Selective in Your Approaches to Learning

There are many, many approaches to reading, writing, understanding, and remembering. Just as you would not read all print sources in the same way for the same purposes, you want a variety of approaches to understanding and remembering information. This book contains endless invitations for you to expand and refine your strategies for learning—not merely by remembering, but by owning what you work with and study every day. A challenge to you as a learner is to become *strategic, versatile, efficient,* and *selective* in your day-to-day practices. There is no need to cling to former practices that will not serve you well in college settings, the workplace, and the rest of your life.

Go for it! Invent! Experiment! Explore! Learning Equals Growth! **Grow!**

Journal Reflections

2.1 Frank Smith states that "There is widespread concern about how the 'language arts'—reading, writing, speaking, the comprehension of speech, and the appreciation of literature—should be integrated into the [college] curriculum. But there is a more fundamental question of how these different aspects of language must be brought together in the learner's mind. The problem is not one of defining terms (it is hard enough for an instructor to say what precisely constitutes reading, writing, and so forth, except as particular activities in classrooms), but of relating the activities that go under these labels to everything else the learner can understand and do. Unless the various aspects of language . . . are integrated into the learner's understanding, then there will be no useful learning in any case."[27] Reflect on this passage in your journal. What would be some benefits to you if you more regularly combined reading and writing activities to enhance your learning? How could you achieve this goal through your daily reading?

Experiences

2.1 SELECTIVE READING

Each of the following statements describes a college reading situation and the material to be read. Read each statement, discuss it with other students, and decide which choice (A, B, C, or D) is most appropriate. Justify your choice in the space provided.

A = Read the material completely
B = Read parts, skip parts
C = Skip most of the material
D = Other strategy

1. You are reading an historical novel assigned as a supplement to an American history class. Your instructor suggests you read it to better understand what life was like just prior to the American Revolution. You come to a long, detailed section on the architecture of the period. How should you read the section? Choose A, B, C, or D and justify:

   ....

   ....

   ....

   ....

2. You are reading a chapter in economics. You know you will have a quiz on it next week, and the quizzes are always very thorough. How should you read the chapter? Choose A, B, C, or D and justify:

   ....

   ....

   ....

   ....

3. You are studying a chapter on genetics that you first read two weeks ago. You're going to have a comprehensive final exam next week. You have already had a quiz over this chapter, for which you answered 9 out of 15 questions correctly. How should you read the chapter? Choose A, B, C, or D and justify:

   ....

   ....

   ....

   ....

4. You are writing a research paper for a political science class on U. S. presidential elections. You have found a fairly lengthy but very interesting book on the history of elections up to 1900. How should you read the book? Choose A, B, C, or D and justify:

   ....

   ....

   ....

   ....

5. You have just attended an English class where the instructor lectured on *Paradise Lost,* but she kept making important references to the Bible. You are not really familiar with the Bible and didn't recognize her references. What should you do? Choose A, B, C, or D and justify:

   ....

   ....

   ....

   ....

6. Tomorrow you will be attending a lecture in biology on the nervous system of vertebrates. You feel that you don't know anything about the subject or any of its terminology. How might you read the chapter in the textbook? Choose A, B, C, or D and justify:

....

....

....

....

....

7. Your teaching assistant in psychology gave your class a list of 15 terms taken from a chapter in your textbook. You are expected to know them for a lab quiz tomorrow. How should you read the chapter? Choose A, B, C, or D and justify:

....

....

....

....

....

8. You have been procrastinating for three weeks, and there's an essay test tomorrow on six chapters of art history. You haven't read any of them. How should you read the chapters? Choose A, B, C, or D and justify:

....

....

....

....

....

9. You received a D on your first anthropology exam. When you reviewed your test, you discovered that you studied the wrong material; you expected the test to be over the lecture, and nearly all the questions were based on the textbook or the assigned paperback. Your next exam will be in 10 days. How should you be reading your books? Choose A, B, C, or D and justify:

....

....

....

....

....

10. Your lecturer in chemistry thinks everything he says is terribly important. He also wrote your textbook, and his lectures follow the chapters very closely; he even uses the same examples on his overheads. When studying for next week's exam, how should you read the book? Choose A, B, C, or D and justify:

....

....

....

....

....

2.2 PERSONAL INQUIRY

Interview a fellow student in or an instructor of a class with a particularly challenging reading requirement. Find out how your informant approaches reading in that discipline, whether it is history, psychology, calculus, French, graphic design, or rocket science. Summarize the advice about reading in a specific discipline. Then share your summary with a partner, small group, or as a whole-class activity. You and other students may be able to collect and compile some very useful "hands-on" suggestions for efficient, proficient reading in a wide variety of academic areas!

2.3 WEB ACTIVITY

Pick a front page news article from the *New York Times* Web site at www.nytimes.com/yr/mo/da/ (replacing 'yr', 'mo' and 'da' with current dates) to read completely, taking notes. Summarize the article. What, in your opinion, is important about the article, and why? What questions did the article leave unanswered?

Can You Relate?

ESSAY 2.1

As a challenge to your creative thinking, choose one of the following quotations from Frank Smith about thought and language. Interpret the meaning of the passage, then apply the author's views about language and learning to your own recent experiences, drawing on information from Chapter 1. Read, think, and plan before you write. Share your essay with a partner or in small groups to get a flavor for how other students have responded to Smith's ideas.

1. "Reading, writing, speaking, and understanding speech are not accomplished with four different parts of the brain, nor do three of them become irrelevant if a student spends a 40-minute period on the fourth."[28] What do you think Smith is saying? What does his idea have to do with learning in college?

2. "My [metaphor] is that the primary, fundamental, and continual activity of the brain is nothing less than the creation of worlds. *Thought* in its broadest sense is construction of worlds, both "real" and imaginary, *learning* is their elaboration and modification, and *language*—especially written language—is a particularly [effective] but by no means unique medium by which these worlds can be manifested, manipulated, and sometimes shared. My metaphor pictures the brain as an artist, as a creator of experiences for itself and others, rather than as a dealer in information."[29]

   How might you conceptualize your brain as an artist? How would your thinking be different if you viewed your brain as a "dealer of information"? In which of your courses should you think like an artist? An information "dealer"? Why?

Language and Thinking

IT'S LISTENING AND SPEAKING

THE LISTENING–SPEAKING CONNECTION

Let's frame this discussion by looking again at language. Our species has developed four wonderful systems of communication: writing, speaking, reading, and listening. Speaking and writing are *expressive* systems, concerned with the giving of information. Listening and reading are *receptive* systems, concerned with the receiving of information. Andrew Wilkinson coined the term **oracy**[1] in the 1960s to relate speaking and listening, which have to do with oral forms of communication, and to distinguish them from the **literacy** systems of writing and reading. Chapter 2 explored reading and writing—those most revered language systems related to print and so obviously crucial to college success. However, speaking and listening are also crucial. Frank Smith points out that "speech and print are not different languages; they share a common vocabulary and the same grammatical forms."[2]

The oral tradition flourished as the communication medium of choice centuries before spoken and written languages began to evolve side by side about five to ten thousand years ago. Migratory storytellers, troubadours, and wandering minstrels spread the classics by telling, listening, singing, and retelling. In the past, then, most listeners were also storytellers as they internalized and mentally illustrated the stories they heard, and as they in turn passed the stories along. Those exchanges of stories were powerful acts of comprehending and remembering. We owe those ancient speaker/listeners a great deal for the heritage they worked to preserve. How else could we still have *Beowulf* and Greek, Roman *(The Iliad, The*

oracy
activities and experiences that involve the spoken word: i.e., speaking and listening

literacy
activities and experiences that involve the written word: i.e., reading and writing

Odyssey), and Norse mythology? How else would we have the American oral tradition of tall tales and humor? How else would we be able to understand Native American cosmology?

Today, speaking and listening, while often taking a back seat to the mastery of print forms, deserve their own examinations. As students advance through grade level after grade level, their opportunities to use oral language sadly diminish. However, these uses of oral language enhance print-related learning and in their own right are skills to be consciously and rigorously cultivated.

In *The Adult Learner: A Neglected Species,* adult learning theorist Malcolm Knowles observes:

> No educational institution teaches just through its courses, workshops, and institutes; no corporation teaches just through its in-service education programs; and no voluntary organization teaches just through its meetings and study groups. They all teach by everything they do [and say], and often they teach opposite lessons in their organizational operation from what they teach in their educational program.[3]

Using information always precedes really learning it, and we can learn a lot if we are strategic listeners. We can be better understood if we are strategic speakers. Oracy, then, deserves its due.

College life is one endless barrage of dialogue, whether it's a required oral report in a history class, an inspired greeting to new students by some sincere high-level campus administrator, or a private conversation with a significant other. In life and school, we could all be better listeners and speakers. "Listening is actively making sense of what you hear, while speaking is an active process of naming the world. When two or more people meet and are involved in making meaning, the relationship is called 'dialogue' or 'intercommunication,' which *is* the listening–speaking connection." [4] This chapter explores the listening–speaking relationship and shows the connections of oracy to literacy.

THE FUNCTIONS OF ORAL COMMUNICATION

Active learning requires a two-way, back-and-forth dialogue, and all dialogue is socially constructed. It's a myth that Socrates enlightened his disciples by orating eloquently, on and on, until they got it. His disciples originally asked him questions, recorded his answers, and he questioned them back so they could benefit from finding their own answers rather than by merely soaking up Socrates' wisdom. This way of learning translates into many of the strategies for learning suggested in this book. We learn language and about language by using it.

Some authors suggest that the authentic uses of oral communication in college should include more than persuasive speaking—speaking in college should include more "informal and interpersonal goals"[5] that are relevant to learners of all backgrounds, grade levels, and cultures, even bilingual cultures. These goals include:

- *Controlling:* communication in which we seek to influence others or respond to the controlling communication of others (e.g., bargaining, refusing)
- *Sharing feelings:* interaction that expresses our feelings or responds emotionally to others (e.g., getting angry, showing support)
- *Informing–responding:* messages we use to give information or respond to information given to us (e.g., explaining, questioning)
- *Ritualizing:* communication that seeks to initiate or maintain social contact (e.g., greeting, using small talk)
- *Imagining:* communication that deals creatively with reality through the use of language (e.g., storytelling, fantasizing)

IMPEDIMENTS TO ORAL COMMUNICATION: COMMUNICATION APPREHENSION

1. This phenomenon is about an abnormal fear of communicating, not about stage fright or having a bad day. It's about communication, not about one's level of intelligence or personality. **Communication apprehension** (CA) is a very serious problem.

communication apprehension the fear of speaking in front of people

2. Vast research has revealed that one out of every five students is "communication apprehensive" and that between 10 and 20 percent of all college students and adults suffer from severe communication apprehension.[6]

3. Instructors are often not conscious of the problem in particular students; therefore, CAs are at risk of being misjudged and falsely evaluated in classroom and out-of-classroom settings. Instructors and students need a chance to help CAs overcome their fear of communication.

4. Communication apprehension is a debilitating condition. Its symptoms include withdrawal from communication and interaction, avoidance of eye contact, a hesitancy to join clubs or organizations, and a choice of seating in classrooms that helps the sufferer avoid classroom interaction. CAs may have fewer friends and have difficulty connecting with their instructors. None of these symptoms are helpful to a learner. Many students who choose to leave college before completion are communication apprehensive.

5. Communication apprehension begins early in the family; it does not begin in classrooms. Research has pointed to family size as a contributor to people's positive or negative attitudes about communication. The more children in a child's environment, the less time, attention, and positive reinforcement the individual is likely to receive.[7]

6. Instructors have a direct effect on students' levels of communication apprehension. Students fear instructors' biases, yet in postsecondary settings, students must take control of the situation to diminish the problem. For example, if you feel anonymous in the classroom, there is little chance that the instructor and other students will get to know you unless you take the initiative, and that process can be very intimidating. (See Chapters 5 and 6 for strategies for working with peers and instructors that can help communication apprehension both in and out of the classroom setting and make your relationships in college more positive and fulfilling.)

PURPOSES OF LISTENING

Listening as a language art has been "ignored" and "neglected" despite the fact that students spend up to 60 percent of their classroom time listening.[8] A group of first-year students prepared a list of uses of listening in college life; see Figure 3.1.

The Listening–Reading Connection

Both listening and reading are receptive uses of language. However, words themselves don't make meaning; *people* make meaning. Some students tend to avoid speaking in class, but who could or would avoid listening? Listening and reading are more internalized uses of language—they are not overt, so they do not call immediate attention to the student. Yet many researchers believe that listening problems are as serious as reading problems.

A comparison of listening and reading reveals some important relationships and many similarities.

FIGURE 3.1   *Uses of listening in college.*

ACADEMIC	ACADEMIC/SOCIAL	SOCIAL/INTERPERSONAL
hearing the lecture	participating in study groups	listening to friends, showing sympathy
hearing homework assignments	listening to others as a gauge to how you sound yourself	listening to your parents, family
hearing other students' questions—and the responses	listening to other students to find those you might want to meet or study with	listening to music, sports, TV, radio, movies
listening practice in foreign language labs		makes you look sincere and attentive

1. Listening (like reading) is a purposeful reconstruction of meaning, not a duplication of it.
2. Listening (like reading) is an interactive process and requires a relationship between the listener and the *information,* but not necessarily a relationship between the listener and the *speaker.*
3. Listening (like reading) must be aimed at more than the facts to be carried away. To be effective, it should blend the main ideas with the details that support them.
4. Active listening (like reading) is enhanced by the *desire* to listen, and is informed by the listener's personal experience, so that listening (like reading) involves the prediction and confirmation of ideas.

Getting to Be a Better Listener

Getting to be a better listener begins with developing an open mind. Developmental theorists claim that new college students often have a two-valued orientation, one that may determine the nature of a spoken communication event (acceptance or rejection). This is a way of seeing everything in terms of "good vs. bad" or "black vs. white," which is an especially troubling and counterproductive way of categorizing the world. Milton Rokeach of Michigan State University has suggested that there are four ways a listener can react in a communication.[9] These represent the four choices of reaction to anything you hear, whether it's in lecture or an out-of-class encounter:

> You may accept the speaker and accept his statement: *This instructor is cute, funny and smart; I believe him, hang on his every word, and will try to write down every word he says.*
>
> You may accept the speaker but reject her statement: *This woman is attractive and self-assured, but I don't think I like her politics; she seems way too conservative, so I'm not going to go overboard with my notes in here.*
>
> You may reject the speaker but accept the statement: *This instructor must have his mother pick his clothes and his socks don't match, but I believe he really knows his field and I will try to learn from him.*
>
> You may reject the speaker and reject his statement: *This instructor talks down to or never calls on women in the class; I'm not going to pay any attention in here. Maybe I'll read the book.*[10]

Have you ever responded to a high school teacher or college instructor in one of these ways?

According to Rokeach, a "closed-minded person" is able to have only the first and last reactions, while a more "open-minded" person is able to have the more complex second and third reactions. Rokeach discusses "belief systems" and "disbelief systems," and concludes that "to be open to information about the disbelief system is to have an open mind."[11]

A challenge for college learners is to evolve from closed-minded to more open-minded listening orientations and to decide on the basis of evidence, rather than emotion or the appearance of the instructor, what parts of all they hear to accept and reject. The cultivating of an open mind is more important and conducive to learning than the need to like everything about the speaker in order to hear, record, and believe what she says. This business of liking or disliking, and therefore accepting or rejecting, teachers rather than ideas is a rather immature, high-school way of looking at learning. One of the marks of an efficient, proficient learner is the ability to consider and "see the differences among the various things you do not believe in."[12]

Other Tips for Listening

Really listening in a lecture means giving up the urge to record the teacher talk verbatim and instead to understand it and translate it into meaningful notes.

Active listening is a skill to be developed, whether or not you are writing while listening. Skillful listeners:

- Receive the message being sent.
- Notice nonverbal communication.
- Stay with the speaker through eye contact.
- Don't interrupt the speaker, and don't project what might be said next.
- Know when to write down parts of discussions to consider later, but in lectures, resist the urge to take notes verbatim and try instead to capture the essence of the information.
- Use visualization techniques and may sketch mental pictures of what is being said.
- Are prepared at any moment to react to the speaker in meaningful ways. In college, the roles of speaker and listener may change at any given moment, without much notice.
- Suspend judgment until the entire message is received—as important in listening as it is in reading.
- Know that listening, to be most effective, requires some meaningful follow-up, such as talking, writing, or drawing the information to make it their own.

To Tape or Not to Tape

All right, let's deal with this conundrum. Should you tape your instructors' lectures—especially if you have one or more who talk really, really fast? What would you do in class while the machine is on? What would you do with all those hours of the best-of-Professor So-and-So on tape? It takes roughly three to four hours to transcribe by hand a 50-minute lecture. Do you really want to get into that? No, you don't. That's a waste of your time. Good listeners may own and use tape recorders, but they don't turn off their brains when they turn on their machines!

Use the following guidelines to make the best use of a taped lecture.

1. Start recording, then forget that the tape player exists. Take notes as though your notes were going to be the only source of the lecture available to you. A

tape recorder is *not* a viable substitute for active listening at the time of the listening event.

2. As soon as possible, listen to the tape *while following along in your written notes.* Make strategic corrections and additions, and resist the urge to turn off the tape to transcribe verbatim.

3. A very disciplined approach would be to use only the pause button, and then only occasionally, when you have discovered a gap in your notes.

4. Plan to spend no longer than 90 minutes on this process.

5. This is very important! Rewind the tape after you've completed the above process, and tape over the current recording with the next lecture. In other words, keep using the same tape over and over, thereby forcing yourself to stay current with the recordings. This way you won't have endless hours of taped lectures for which you will never find the time and energy to use to your advantage.

6. Every time you both listen to and look at the information you wish to learn, you are making the learning process easier and more efficient. Combining the auditory with the visual (or tactile or olfactory, which is the sense of smell), can really heighten your knowledge ownership!

PURPOSES OF SPEAKING

When asked to brainstorm a list of the uses of speaking in college, a group of first- and second-year students produced a long list. These uses can be categorized loosely as *academic, academic/social* and *social/interpersonal,* although some of the distinctions are a bit arbitrary. Figure 3.2 shows a compilation of their ideas about speaking.

The Speaking–Writing Connection

Both speaking and writing are expressive functions of language. However, words don't *mean;* people *mean.* Saying something isn't the same as communicating it. Even if you are the quiet type, you cannot escape communicating in a classroom or any other environment, so get used to it.

FIGURE 3.2 *Uses of speaking in college.*

ACADEMIC	ACADEMIC/SOCIAL	SOCIAL/INTERPERSONAL
communicating with your instructors	collaborative studying, job interviews	communicating with friends
presentations, class discussions	discussing grade changes	communicating with parents, family
public-speaking classes, getting noticed by instructors	working in campus organizations	ordering and paying for food
Expressing yourself/Understanding yourself		
staying awake in class! improving grammar	getting your point across	communicating with old friends from high school
mastering a foreign language	improving memory and vocabulary	facing your fears, meeting new people
talking to yourself as a learning strategy	improving telephone skills	displaying your sense of humor
talking to yourself as a rehearsal for writing	skillfully disagreeing networking	venting, relieving stress

FIGURE 3.3   *The speaking–writing connection.*

SPEECH	STYLE	WRITING
Whispering sweet nothings; joking about old times	*INTIMATE*	Journal writing; passing notes in class
Family conversation; party talk	*CASUAL*	Friendly letters; some contemporary fiction (e.g., Richard Brautigan)
Business talk; teacher talk	*CONSULTATIVE*	Business memos; journalistic writing
Keynote speeches; public lectures	*FORMAL*	Academic essays; technical manuals
Parliamentary debate; diplomatic policy statements	*FROZEN*	Legal documents; scientific reports

Students can profit from experiences spanning the full range of speaking and writing styles.

Source: Rubin and Kantor

Rubin and Kantor[13] suggest that both speaking and writing can be categorized along the same dimension of "intimate" to "frozen" styles; see Figure 3.3. Each of the above speaking or writing styles has a place in school and in life. Which of the above styles is most appropriate in which kind(s) of communication?

"Interactional Scaffolding": A Classroom Strategy for Dialogue

Focused, guided classroom interaction, when everyone "has a turn" in the discussion, has a direct connection to students teaching students, as participants "inch" toward the right answer. This group movement toward new insights and answers is known as "interactional scaffolding" (Cahir and Lucas, 1981).[14] The image of scaffolding relates to the building of knowledge among learners who are reaching for a mutual understanding. Powerful classroom discussion takes some work; it's no accident! We usually think of the relationship between language and thought as a one-way street:

Have a thought or idea ⟶ Express the idea in language

However, classroom dialogue may be seen as a conversational "ladder" with different persons contributing different rungs, as in this modified version in Figure 3.4.[15]

In postsecondary classrooms, knowledgeable students may be able to add more to the ladder of meaning than does the instructor. College-level discussions should afford students many opportunities to find their own answers, with very little direct input or prompting from the instructor.

The challenge to you as a college learner is to be an active participant in the building of knowledge through discussion, as both an active speaker and an active listener. Become an observer of classroom talk, and begin to find ways to make the discussion more valuable for all those involved. Authentic "turn taking" in conversation absolutely requires that you listen to what is being said, instead of ignoring the speaker while you think of something insightful to say when you get a turn. Don't you hate it when some show-off dominates a potentially good classroom discussion just to get noticed and maybe score a few points with the instructor?

FIGURE 3.4   *Interactional scaffolding.*

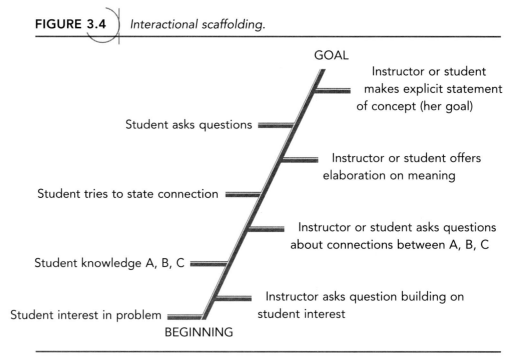

Source: Staton

Getting to Be a Better Speaker

The word for "communication" comes from a Greek word meaning "to make common." Good speaking involves the controlling of message variables as described in the following passage from Hurt, Scott, and McCrosky's *Communication in the Classroom*[16]:

MESSAGE VARIABLES

In general, verbal and nonverbal messages that contain those elements which increase attention are more likely to be accurately processed. Let's briefly examine some of the more common elements relating to message content and arrangement which teachers must deal with when determining the content to be taught and the size and order of instructional units.

Organization. Most of us would expect that the organization of a message affects its comprehension and processing. Research, however, indicates that this is not always the case. If a message is moderately well organized, it usually produces the same level of comprehension as an extremely well organized message. Only when a message is extremely disorganized does detrimental information-processing occur. The order in which important points are placed in a message does, however, affect processing and recall. In general, material presented first or last in a message is better remembered and understood.

Message sidedness. Research has shown that two-sided messages are more persuasive than one-sided messages. A two-sided message presents opposing views and sometimes refutes them. This produces greater retention and comprehension, because attention and perceptions are increased by the contrast, change, and novelty introduced by the message strategy. This type of message structure is particularly important when a [student] is concerned with affective learning.

Language intensity. Language intensity refers to the extent to which a source's position deviates from neutrality. Many teachers feel that intense language facilitates learning; and, to a certain extent, it does in that it increases students' attention levels. If students' anxiety levels are increased by the intensity of the language, however, then it becomes difficult for them to discriminate among critical aspects of the message. After a while, information processing of the message will be terminated.

    Concreteness and ambiguity. Teachers usually expect that the more concrete (or specific) their language and examples are, the better they will be remembered and processed. For the most part, this is correct. The difficulty in accurately processing ambiguous language cues comes from the fact that lack of specificity in a message will often cause students to distort the message to fit their own past experiences, attitudes, and needs.

To summarize, effective speakers adhere to the following guidelines:

- Remember that the order of presentation of the information is the key to effective communication.
- Give time and attention to both sides of the issue to increase the effectiveness of your message.
- Be intense; be passionate about your subject and your delivery.
- Be specific and relevant, and give examples. Avoid ambiguity, as it confuses the receiver of the message.

Other Tips for More Formal Speaking

Effective speakers, in discussion and especially in presentations, know how to:

- Plan for the presentation by assessing the constraints of the assignment and the characteristics of the listeners. Empathizing with the listeners is a key component of effective speaking.
- Incorporate visual aids and other attention-getting devices such as props, jokes, and human-interest stories. Illustration is a key component of effective speaking.
- Challenge the listeners to really work with the material of the speech or presentation by using a startling fact or a paradoxical situation. Generating questions in the mind of the listener is a key factor in effective speaking.
- Organize the material in a thought-provoking order. Information presented first and last tends to be remembered and understood best.
- Stay within the time constraints of the speech or presentation.
- Get meaningful feedback or responses from the listeners and strive to develop powerful speaking strategies.

FINAL OBSERVATIONS ABOUT LISTENING AND SPEAKING

Think about these related issues as you strive to be a more effective oral communicator:

- Vocal behavior tends to arouse stereotypes about instructors and students. Listen to the message beyond the sender's dialect, accent, nasality, and other potentially distracting vocal patterns. Many schools have actual courses that can help you work on your voice and articulation. You certainly may work on your own verbal idiosyncrasies, but forgive others theirs.

- Dialects are different ways of saying the same thing. Dialects can be regional (a southern drawl) or social (classroom lecture style vs. interpersonal, idiomatic, slang-laden). All of us move in and out of different dialects, depending on time, place, and relationship of the participants in the dialogue. This "code switching" is a natural part of conversations, just as different styles of writing are appropriate for different audiences and purposes.

- Talking and listening, if they are going to contribute to a grade or a promotion in the workplace, *are* harder to evaluate than reading and writing. Find out your instructors' expectations and standards for oral tasks; don't assume anything.

- The rewards system (the perception of competition for discussion credit/class participation) in classrooms can sometimes cause unnecessary gamesmanship in class discussions. Don't fall into the "my recitation and brain are greater than yours" syndrome. Keep your oral communications genuine. Everyone can spot the wise guy by the degree of show-off he acts like. You know the type—people sigh audibly when a class big mouth gets ready to monopolize the discussion. That's not what dialogue is for.

- Body movement, gestures, and eye contact in oral communication are all very important. Teachers use eye contact to gauge who is ready to add to a discussion; some instructors like to call on those who avoid eye contact. Eye behavior makes a difference. "One social scientist has estimated that there are over 700,000 physical signs capable of stimulating meaning in another person. For example, there are 23 distinct eyebrow movements, each capable of stimulating a different meaning."[17] Mannerisms, together with vocal behavior, say much about the speaker to the receivers of the communication.

- Be self-conscious; be aware of what your eyes and body are saying because, whether consciously or not, people will judge you on these nonverbal forms of communication regardless of whether the overall effect of your message is accurate. At the same time, become an observer of those around you to increase your sensitivity to others' nonverbal communication. In other words, don't judge an instructor by his weary stance alone—you may be in his third lecture of the day. Also, don't assume that because certain classmates are usually silent, they have nothing worthwhile to say.

- Please don't think that greater skill with print language than the spoken word is the final mark of success in college. More and more instructors have discovered, or rediscovered, the value of "dialogue." As you find your way through your college experience and as you enter the workplace, people will judge you on your listening and speaking as well as your reading and writing. The challenge to move toward excellence in oracy is yours!

- Want a way to judge who your better instructors are? "They encourage students to capture the conversational and expressive qualities of speech in their writing, as well as adapt the vocabulary, diversity, and planned qualities of their writing to their talk."[18] In other words, good teachers engage you in meaningful ways of using one function of language to enhance the others. Think about the possibilities.

Journal Reflections

3.1 After completing Experience 3.1, on the following page, write about a time in grade school when you experienced "communication apprehension." Where were you, what were you supposed to be doing, and what caused the apprehension? How did you handle the situation? Next, discuss a much more current episode of "tongue-tiedness." What sorts of situations render you reluctant to engage in a discussion, and what steps can you take to overcome any current communication apprehension?

3.2 Have there been occasions when you have been guilty of prematurely judging an instructor or student by his dialect, accent, intonation, or other quality of speech? Think back to a time when you may have been guilty of stereotyping through listening. Ultimately, what steps did you take to overcome your rush to judge based on the way another person sounded? Examine your listener stereotypes; are you still guilty of such errors? What steps can you take to overcome the barrier of stereotyping on the basis of speech?

3.3 Discuss ways that you could work toward being a more productive discussant in your classes. Have there been times when you had good ideas to contribute but did not speak up? Why?

Experiences

3.1 PRCA: DO YOU HAVE COMMUNICATION ANXIETY?

The following instrument called the Personal Report of Communication Anxiety, or PRCA,[19] is composed of 20 statements concerning feelings about communicating with other people. Indicate the degree to which the statements apply to you by marking whether you (1) strongly agree, (2) agree, (3) are undecided, (4) disagree, or (5) strongly disagree with each statement. Work quickly; just record your first impression.

* .... 1. While participating in a conversation with a new acquaintance, I feel very nervous.

.... 2. I have no fear of facing an audience.

.... 3. I look forward to expressing my opinion at meetings.

.... 4. I look forward to an opportunity to speak in public.

.... 5. I find the prospect of speaking mildly pleasant.

* .... 6. When communicating, my posture feels strained and unnatural.

* .... 7. I am tense and nervous while participating in group discussions.

* .... 8. Although I talk fluently with friends, I am at a loss for words on a platform.

* .... 9. My hands tremble when I try to handle objects on the platform.

* .... 10. I always avoid speaking in public if possible.

.... 11. I feel that I am more fluent when talking to people than most other people are.

* .... 12. I am fearful and tense all the while I am speaking before a group of people.

* .... 13. My thoughts become confused and jumbled when I speak before an audience.

.... 14. Although I am nervous just before getting up, I soon forget my fears and enjoy the experience.

* .... 15. Conversing with people who hold positions of authority causes me to be fearful and tense.

* .... 16. I dislike using my body and voice expressively.

.... 17. I feel relaxed and comfortable while speaking.

* .... 18. I feel self-conscious when I am called upon to answer a question or give an opinion in class.

.... 19. I face the prospect of making a speech with complete confidence.

.... 20. I would enjoy presenting a speech on a local television show.

SCORING PROCEDURE

Add scores for items with asterisk.

Add scores for items without asterisk.

Complete the following formula: PRCA Score = 66 – Total 1 + Total 2.

INTERPRETATION

Students with scores above 72 are probably highly communication apprehensive. Students with scores between 61 and 72 are moderately apprehensive.

3.2 PERSONAL INQUIRY

Interview an instructor in one of your courses (not public speaking) that involves discussion. Find out how the instructor evaluates students' discussions and whether the evaluation is a formal part of the course grade. Next, extend your discussion to a more philosophical plane—how does this instructor see dialogue as part of her classes? In what ways can the class dialogue add to a student's understanding of the material and its relationship to other parts of life?

3.3 COMMUNICATING WITH INSTRUCTORS

Use information from Chapter 6 to devise a plan to diminish any communication apprehension you may have in regard to instructors. At what point in the term do you feel safe enough to connect with your instructors? Are you willing to make contact before your first exams? Would it be easier to wait until you've taken an exam to approach an instructor?

3.4 COMMUNICATING WITH CLASSMATES

Use ideas from Chapter 5 to devise a plan to diminish any communication apprehension you may feel in regard to other students in your classes. At what point in the term do you feel safe enough to approach other students with the purpose of learning together? Are you willing to make contact before a first exam, or would you feel more comfortable suggesting partner or group study after a first exam?

3.5 WEB ACTIVITY

On August 28, 1963, Dr. Martin Luther King, Jr., delivered a famous civil rights speech in front of the Lincoln Memorial in Washington, D.C. A recording of the speech can be found at *www.audioarchives.ml.org.* Listen to the speech (you will need the Real Audio plug-in, which is available free at the site, to listen) and take notes. Using what you've learned about listening and speaking in this chapter, discuss the purpose(s) of Dr. King's speech. What characteristics make his speech effective or ineffective?

Test your understanding of the importance and many uses of listening and speaking to enhance your learning and communication skills.

Can You Relate?

ESSAY 3.1

Your mission in writing is both to show that you understand strategies for listening and that you understand the relationships between and among reading, writing, speaking, and listening for school and life endeavors. Brainstorm ideas with partners or small groups as a warm-up to writing. After brainstorming, you may wish to create a web of ideas or a chart (see Chapter 2) to help you work through your ideas about the functions of language. After your preliminary work, plan to write for approximately 30 minutes. You may wish to impose a time limit on your writing as practice for writing timed in-class essays.

Questioning and Conquering the Exams

4

TESTING,
TESTING

GETTING THE CUES: WHAT TO STUDY

"Holy Smoke! There's too much to learn!" "There's not enough time!" Now settle down and get a grip. Testing will always be part of your reality if you are scaling the walls of higher education. There are ways to narrow your focus as you regularly cope with all that material to be learned. You *can't* learn everything, nor would you want to! In your regular day-to-day studying, narrow your attention to these categories of information (many may overlap, which would be both helpful and comforting).

- Topics prominent in the syllabus
- Handouts from your instructor
- Examples presented by the instructor during class
- Verbal cues from the instructor, e.g., "This is really important," "Let me repeat . . . "
- Topics referenced in both lectures and the textbooks
- Prolonged, multiple examples of a concept or set of concepts
- Topics explored in discussion or recitation sessions
- Sets of related topics as prepared in study guides
- Summaries in your textbooks
- Figures, tables, and charts from text or lecture

chunks sets of interrelated information, organized by meanings or positions, which facilitate learning and memory

- Concepts (not the questions themselves) that played prominently in your instructor's past exams
- Topics of discussion from a post-class visit with the instructor (see Chapter 6)
- **"Chunks"** of topics from your lecture notes

Format-Specific Preparation Strategies and Tactics

Well-informed, regular, practiced, and versatile study strategies, along with stress reduction (see Chapter 10) are learnable test preparation skills. Some students believe that they can coast along day to day, then entirely change their approaches to learning right before tests and receive high grades for last-minute valor. There aren't certain pills to swallow or acts of magic to perform at the onset of exams. Certain basic strategies are appropriate for smart test preparation, regardless of the specific test format or kind of material. Chapters 1 and 2 describe these processes. If you are looking for all the answers here, you may need to review those chapters along with this one.

It is impossible to separate the acts of preparing for and taking tests, because certain kinds of study are the best practice for taking exams. Research on high-scoring college students conducted in 1980 revealed that high scorers have two strategies: they "know the material well enough to go through the test very quickly; or they go through the test very slowly, checking, changing, and verifying each answer. Either seems to be an effective approach."[1] You will be able to take tests successfully if you are well practiced at recalling and using the information.

A 1983 study[2] showed that A students "anticipated answers to more questions than did the low-scoring students . . . In addition, they were more likely to analyze and eliminate incorrect alternatives to help determine the right answer . . . The A students skipped more questions they were unsure of." Again, these strategies are possible to use in tests if they are familiar behaviors.

Objective Tests

Objective tests are "objective" because there is assumed to be one correct answer, and all you have to do is find it or provide it. Believe it or not, when preparing for objective tests, students who ultimately make the highest scores study as though they were preparing a more subjective short answer or essay test. Why? A basic learning process is involved here: it is easier to master details if they are related into a framework of larger concepts. Also, it is easier to answer multiple choice and true/false questions if you know enough about the topics to be able to write about them from memory. Therefore, as explained in Chapter 2, the cognitive implications are that you should study the big ideas first, then gradually fit in the details, as though you were constructing knowledge the way contractors construct buildings, from the foundation upward. If that seems to be an unfamiliar system for you, think about the following.

- The course is taught for a purpose. What is that purpose?
- The syllabus has a plan, like a blueprint for a building. What is that plan?
- The instructor has a purpose. What is the instructor trying to bring out in all this information?
- What are the foundations—concepts and important related information for each concept—that your instructor seems to value most?
- What are the specific examples and terms that illustrate the course foundations?

Answers to these kinds of questions will provide you with a blueprint for study. Details follow main ideas. Remember, details are just that—details. They are important, but not the most important aspect of the course. Don't overlook the forest for the trees! If you know in advance that you will be held responsible for the recall of a multitude of details, you will be tempted to start right in—memorizing. This is the worst possible approach. Do this: study the big ideas first, then fit in the details. (Is there an echo in here?) Learning is knowledge building, not knowledge borrowing.

Multiple-Choice Preparation

To put this discussion in perspective, consider the difference between a "high school level" multiple-choice question and a "college" version of the same question:

1. **High school M/C:** According to the Constitution, which person or group is most "in charge" of American government?
    a. the President
    b. the Congress
    c. the Supremes (Court)
    d. the people
    e. all of the above

2. **College M/C:** Of the following, which best describes who has the last word, i.e., sovereignty, in the American government system?
    a. The President when he issues an executive order.
    b. According to the process used to ratify Constitutional amendments, the groups that perform this task.
    c. The Congress as it passes legislation, the President as he enforces the law, and the Supreme Court as it interprets the law.
    d. a and c

The fundamental questions are the same, yet the added complexity of the college version includes these layers of mystery, intrigue, and confusion:

- Much wordier questions and answers;
- Plausible, yet incorrect distractors that you may have read while you were studying (item c in the college example does say what each branch of government does; unfortunately it's the wrong answer);
- More complex multiple-multiple choice items (as in the case of choice d in the second example);
- "Predictable" questions cast in unfamiliar wording—different from either your class notes or your books—so recognition of the "right" answer may be impossible; and
- "Unpredictable" questions—those for which you did not prepare at all because your notes did not include the information, you didn't study the book appropriately, and/or you crammed like crazy the night before, missing the information in your haste to overload your short-term memory.

Multiple-choice tests are very much reading tests, and in college, a basic rote memorization of terms in order to *recognize* the right answer will fail you—it is an insufficient way to prepare. If you memorize definitions, several of the "distractors" (the official name for the incorrect multiple choices) will seem plausible. This is the "I know just enough to be dangerous" test preparation approach, which will lead to the "Gosh, I couldn't pick the best answer" test-taking experience. In the above example, could you have chosen the correct answer to the college-level question by memorizing the functions of the three branches of government or by memorizing the definition of *sovereignty?* Maybe, but it would have been a stretch!

Multiple-choice exams rarely require only the knowledge of definitions of terms. Instead, they require an understanding of the significance and relationships among sets of terms and discrete factors that require judgments such as the best, the most, the least, or which item in the series does not belong with the set. For example, an analysis of a 50-item multiple-choice examination for an Introduction to Political Science course revealed this breakdown of kinds of questions on the exam:

BREAKDOWN OF THE 50 ITEMS	COUNT	PERCENT
Term or "definition" questions	6	12%
Situational or "apply to an example" questions	13	26%
Significant point of a member of a set of terms	28	56%
Important people in political science	3	6%

You can imagine the scores of the students whose study strategies were primarily to memorize the definitions of the individual terms!

Multiple-choice preparation strategies. Multiple-choice preparation strategies consist of good information management systems and a good time/task management system that include:

- Notes/book recall column study for recall (see Chapter 1)
- A regular cycle of rehearsal/retrieval study activities (see Chapter 10)
- Alternatives to rereading to learn (see Chapter 2), such as charting, webbing, transmediation, and, of course, writing to learn approaches.

Multiple-choice tactics. This format utilizes the successful strategies of high-scoring students.

- Read the question only. Cover the answers if you need to.
- Trigger your stored information about the topic—you have been studying to recall rather than to attempt to recognize something familiar. Reach for recall.
- Underline the topic of the question, and look out for and mark qualifiers—those sneaky little words that radically alter the aim of the question, such as *always, never, best, least, except, not, may* vs. *will,* and so on.
- Upon entering the answers, use a process of elimination by comparing what you have already recalled in your mind to the choices presented on the page.
- Leave a "trail" of your thought processes by marking on the exam. Eliminate options you know to be wrong, irrelevant, or "cute"—so you will not waste time rereading them.
- Get what you know out on the page where you can see it—use those "pencil-in-hand" techniques—draw or write from memory if needed.
- Over time, note whether changing answers helps or hurts you. Study how best to use your time. Do you reread unnecessary parts of the question or answers?
- You may mark in the margin items that you cannot answer in one or two attempts, go on with the exam, and return to them later.
- Recognizing cues, or "testwiseness tips" ("When in doubt, mark answer B"; "The longest answer is often the correct one"; "One of two opposite answers is correct") should *not* be a primary test-taking strategy. As you take more and more multiple-choice tests, you *will* get better at recognizing the less plausible distractors, and taking risks and guesses. Your experience with the language of college tests will enable you to get better at taking them.

You will need to practice taking tests and doing homework problems in test conditions (in a time limit, without the help of notes, books, or peers) to improve your performance. Instructors don't give grades for your ability to highlight what seems important, nor will they test you in ways that allow you to use your notes for assistance. Therefore, there is really no way to get better at taking tests than to regularly practice the thinking processes and pacing required to successfully complete your actual college exams. Other kinds of objective tests require only slight modifications in your test-taking strategies.

True–False Preparation

True–false tests in high school were not fun, but they were not very complex, either. Consider the differences between "high school" and "college level" true–false items:

1. **High school T/F:** John F. Kennedy was assassinated in 1963. *[Notice that there is a single subject, JFK, and only one item to consider. Because you have only one fact (the date) to consider, there is only one proposition to judge: whether he was assassinated in 1963.]*

2. **College T/F:** John F. Kennedy, the 35th president of the United States, was shot in an open convertible in Dallas, Texas, on November 22, 1963, and died immediately. *[In this version, the question poses at least six separate propositions:]*

   1. *Was he the 35th president?*
   2. *Was it a convertible?*
   3. *Was it open?*
   4. *Is the location correct?*
   5. *Is the date correct?*
   6. *Did he die immediately? (This is a tricky question.)*

Even if you've seen the movie *JFK*, never mind the conspiracy theory. The best way to handle a loaded college-level T/F question is to underline each separate proposition, and then to consider each idea separately, as in the example of T/F tactics below.

True–false tactics. The key to success in taking true/false exams is separating and marking all the different **propositions** imbedded in the sentence to be considered and judging each individually. *John F. Kennedy, the 35th president of the United States, was shot in an open convertible in Dallas, Texas, on November 22, 1963, and died immediately.* By underlining each part to consider, it's easier to keep reading until you can find one proposition that you know, positively, to be false. Even if you're not sure about the exact dates, if you keep reading and thinking, you can mark this item "false" if you are patient enough to wait until the last proposition: *"he died immediately."* This example illustrates the point that in T/F items, it's often easier to find "falses" to be false than it is to absolutely believe the "trues" to be true.

proposition a statement or idea in the form of a sentence or sentences

Matching Items Preparation

There is no special secret to studying if you will be matching items on an exam. Matching involves recall and an organized process of elimination, much like the processes you should master in order to be successful on multiple-choice items. The biggest differences between the two forms of testing are the larger number of choices to choose from in matching and the lack of context derived from the wording of the question that you do get in the multiple-choice format, but do not have in the matching format.

FIGURE 4.1 *Matching items.*

Make the *most likely* match between the numbered and lettered items (5 points per answer); numbered items used only once.

.... a) Dredge	1. Hallucinogens
.... b) Wolff	2. Indonesia
.... c) Knauft	3. Homicide
.... d) Phillips	4. London
.... e) L'Armond	5. East Africa
.... f) Harner	6. Vasodilation
.... g) Robbins	7. Mongols
	8. Tobacco
	9. France
	10. Rape
	11. Detroit
	12. Palermo
	13. Coca

Matching items tactics. When answering matching items, concern yourself with two procedures—recall and the process of elimination. Figure 4.1 is a matching section taken from a cultural anthropology course.

This instructor kindly added the helpful phrase, "numbered items used only once." Such a cue reduces a great deal of uncertainty when trying to match answers. Also note the "trap." There are 13 alternatives for 7 items. The best strategy in preparing for matching items is to prepare as though the format was to be short answer. Again, if you know the information well enough that you could write it from memory, your accuracy in "matching," or actually eliminating extraneous choices, will increase dramatically.

Practice Objective Items

Try your objective test strategies on the items in the practice test in Figure 4.2[3]. Note how much "testwiseness" does or does not help you choose the correct answer. You'll find the answers at the end of this chapter.

Subjective Tests: Are They More Difficult than Objective Tests?

Writing What You Know and Winning Over Your Audience

It's often much easier to predict what you may be asked on essay tests than on objective tests. Successful essay exam writing depends heavily on how you prepare. High-scoring students have reported using the following strategies in essay tests: "quoting books and articles, rephrasing arguments several times, rephrasing the questions [and] the most common strategy was that of expressing opinions similar to those of the instructor."[4]

Taking an essay test should be a very similar experience to the preparation for that exam. Actually, writing an essay test should feel as close to the preparation as

FIGURE 4.2 *Practice Objective Quiz*

1. Name both the Chief Justice of the *Dred Scott* decision, who was defied by Abraham Lincoln during the Civil War, and his successor, an ambitious Lincoln Cabinet member with aspirations to the Presidency.
   a) John Marshall, Roger Taney
   b) Roger Taney, Salmon P. Chase
   c) Salmon P. Chase, Morrison Waite
   d) John Marshall, Oliver Wendell Holmes
   e) Louis Brandeis, Charles Evans Hughes

2. Which of the following are allowed in residence hall rooms?
   a) Computers
   b) Waterbeds
   c) Microwave ovens
   d) Toasters
   e) Candles

3. Given the three statements below, which of the following is true?
   A. For any real number a, |–a| = a.
   B. For any real number a, –a is negative.
   C. For all real numbers a, –(–a) = a.
   a) A only is true
   b) B only is true
   c) C only is true
   d) All three are true
   e) Two of them are true

4. The stage of mitosis in which the chromosomes separate is known as:
   a) Prophase
   b) Metaphase
   c) Interphase
   d) Anaphase
   e) Telophase

5. Which of the following are psychological models?
   a) Psychophysiological
   b) Psychodynamic
   c) Behavioristic
   d) Psychometric
   e) Cognitive

For the following, match the correct definition with the term it defines:

.... 6. Republic
.... 7. Democracy
.... 8. Oligarchy
.... 9. Theocracy
...............10. Aristocracy

A. A government in which power is vested in a minority consisting of those believed to be best qualified.
B. A government in which supreme power resides in a body of citizens entitled to vote and is exercised by elected officers and representatives responsible to them and governing according to law.
C. A government of a state by immediate divine guidance or by officials who are regarded as divinely guided.
D. A government in which a small group exercises control.
E. A government in which the supreme power is vested in the people and exercised by them directly or indirectly through a system of representatives.

Source: Clark

an opening night performance is to a dress rehearsal of a play. There are no notes to lean on, and you're even better because you want to please your audience, even if it's only an audience of one who is also a critic!

Essay Exam Preparation

Essay exam preparation is a matter of prediction and practice. Essay questions are designed for you to show what you know by constructing an argument, which is a proven point of view about main themes and concepts. A good way to begin to predict areas of questioning would be to find patterns of important topics in the syllabus and in your notes. Figure 4.3 shows an excerpt from an American history syllabus; it's easy to see the instructor's pattern of topic development. This particular instructor teaches history by examining the roles of family structures, work (who does it, where, and to what end) and the domestic impact of war. In fact, his syllabus very clearly states that his way of investigating history is through the themes of "family, work, and war." With that in mind, it's easy to flush out possible areas from the notes and books to prepare to frame, write, and illustrate a point of view as rehearsal for the examination.

This instructor's course organization and his mention of "themes" he values in the study of history enable his students to "see" the likely areas of questioning on his essay exams. There are clearly "family, work, and war" themes in his syllabus, and luckily, his lectures deliver what he has planned and indicated on his syllabus. Not every course that includes essay exams as evaluation are this easy to "read"—that is, to predict what may be asked. However, in courses that include essay writing, this "predicting" procedure certainly reduces the uncertainty of which areas to review and write as preparation for the exam.

The next step after predicting areas of questioning for essays is to develop and practice writing them. Your practice is aimed at producing a sound, well-illustrated argument, not to memorize what you plan to write. There are two very good reasons

FIGURE 4.3   *Finding "themes" in the syllabus.*

THEMES IN AMERICAN HISTORY (1600–PRESENT)   (This column not part of syllabus)

Date	Topic	Family, War, or Work
Thur Feb 18	First Hour Exam (On text to p. 15 and lectures)	
Tues Feb 23	Victorian Family Life, 1820–1890	Family
Thur Feb 25	Victorian North and South: Conflicts in the National Consensus	Family
Tues Mar 2	The Civil War: Crisis and Reaffirmation of Victorian Values	Family
Thur Mar 4	Industrial Capitalism: The Dominant Culture	Work
Tues Mar 9	Industrial Capitalism: The Subordinate Cultures	Work
Thur Mar 11	Crisis and Regeneration: The Meaning of Imperialism	War
	—spring break—	
Tues Mar 23	The Decline of Victorianism, 1890–1920	Family/Work
Thur Mar 25	Over Here: WWI and American Culture	War
Tues Mar 30	Efficiency for Profit: The Degradation of Work in the 20th Century (Review Session same evening)	Work
Thur Apr 1	Second Hour Exam (On lectures, text pp. 1–358, Sinclair and Gilman)	

not to memorize an essay answer. First, you won't know the exact angle of the question until you see the test, so you need to have a wealth of main ideas and details in your head that you can use to shape the answer. Second, even if you know ahead of time what the actual questions will be, rote memorization of an answer could fail you. What if you forget part of the answer and lose your way? You may go blank and blow the exam.

The structure of a good essay is basically the same, whether you write it in or out of class. The main differences between in-class and out-of-class essays is how you use your writing time. Figure 4.4 shows that on an in-class essay, you spend less time on an introduction, get down to the thesis quickly, and spend less time in the conclusion summarizing the essay, while you should always end with some statement of the significance or broader meaning of your answer.

Typical Patterns of Essay Development

No essay should ever be written in a random, haphazard order. Remember, you are out to persuade and impress a reader who needs structure to follow your argument. Essay exam preparation—all essay writing—requires a consideration of the content to be used and the most effective way to present it. The first requirement is to state the **thesis,** or main idea statement, which introduces the essay and lays the groundwork for what follows, serving as a map for both you as writer and your reader.

thesis statement
the "map" or main idea statement indicating what a piece of writing is discussing or proving

The following examples illustrate thesis statements that set up some of the most basic and useful organizational patterns of essay construction. The challenge of the essay in question is to explain the gradual and horrifying shift from white to black slavery in the United States beginning around 1619. In each case, the thesis statement is designed to state the purpose of the essay while supporting the organizational pattern (in boldface) to be followed.

FIGURE 4.4   *Basic structure of an in-class essay.*

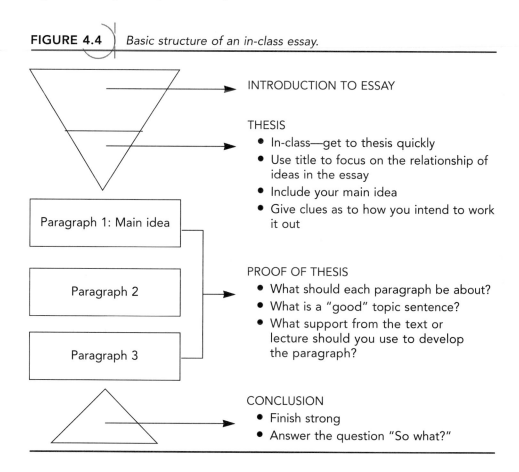

INTRODUCTION TO ESSAY

THESIS
- In-class—get to thesis quickly
- Use title to focus on the relationship of ideas in the essay
- Include your main idea
- Give clues as to how you intend to work it out

Paragraph 1: Main idea

PROOF OF THESIS
- What should each paragraph be about?
- What is a "good" topic sentence?
- What support from the text or lecture should you use to develop the paragraph?

Paragraph 2

Paragraph 3

CONCLUSION
- Finish strong
- Answer the question "So what?"

- *Chronological.* The year 1619 is often referred to as the beginning of black slavery in the United States, when a Dutch warship disposed of 20 black slaves at Jamestown. The travesty was legally (but not actually) ended by the passage of the Fourteenth Amendment in April 1866.

- *Spatial (in this instance, geographical).* Black slavery was not merely a southern phenomenon. Black slavery in the United States began with the delivery of 20 black slaves to Jamestown, Virginia, but by the end of the century the black population had spread through the southern colonies as well as into the northern states, such as New York, Connecticut, and Rhode Island. Black populations also grew in major seaport towns.

- *Cause–effect.* The failure of indentured servitude, or white slavery, together with the rise of the plantation system, caused the need for another, more manageable group to use, and opportunistic European mercenary traders quickly began to raid Africa to use its people to sell into slavery in America.

- *Problem/solution.* The shortcomings of white labor, such as limits on terms for indentured servitude, the massive numbers of runaways, lack of incentives to work hard, and riots spawned by former "servants," all resulted in the increasing importation of Africans to use as labor on the plantations and in the homes of white Americans.

- *Most to least.* The reasons for burgeoning black slavery in the United States are many. The failure of white slavery, the ease of kidnapping Africans, the changes in the tobacco market, and the restrictive trade regulations imposed by England forced small farmers out of business. The growth of the plantation system increased the need for cheap, manageable labor, and the helpless Africans filled that need.

- *Least to most.* The changes in the tobacco market and restrictive trade regulations that forced small farmers out of business, the resulting growth of the plantation, the need for a huge pool of cheap, manageable labor—all were contributing factors to the massive kidnapping into slavery of hundreds of thousands of helpless Africans.

- *By type or category.* The evolution from white to black slavery in America occurred due to a blend of economic, social, and political reasons.

- *Question–answer.* What were the many causes of the introduction of black slavery into America? The evolution from indentured white servitude to African slavery occurred through a confluence of economic, social, and political forces.

Do you see how easily you can cast the same issue from many different molds or frame a written argument in different ways to achieve the same end?

Essay Exam Tactics

It's time for all that work and preparation to come together!

- Take a minute and a deep breath and make a rough outline. This is your planned "performance." Essays are arguments—proven points of view. Take the role of the expert.

- Give the main idea of your essay in the first sentence or the first paragraph. Now you and your reader have an understanding about your intentions.

- Use new paragraphs to answer the different parts of the question. Paragraphs are groups of sentences focused on the topic of the first sentence of each group. An essay written in one huge, endless paragraph, even if the information is brilliant, will not get the same high marks as an answer organized into several paragraphs. It's too hard for your reader to determine your main points unless they are clearly in separate paragraphs.

- Use good, illustrative supporting details in each paragraph. Generalizations alone don't get A's. Proof is essential in all successful arguments, in the classroom, workplace, or court of law.
- Use transitional words *(additionally, however, next, finally)* and phrases between sentences and paragraphs to help your reader follow your argument. She can't read your mind.
- Use your strongest, most persuasive ideas, reasons, or explanations first.
- Check the flow of your essay with the original question to make sure you haven't strayed from the point. Starting the essay with the thesis statement is a good way to stay on track.
- Save time to proofread for mechanics, illegible words, misinformation or a lack of examples and proof. You are out to impress your reader, not confuse her.
- Avoid pointless padding—this isn't high school, and your grader will hate it! However, it's better to scratch out an irrelevant point or to insert an unused key idea than to leave a neat but incomplete answer.
- Watch your writing time and pace yourself appropriately to give the most important parts of your answer the most discussion.
- End your essay with a restatement of your main point, then go beyond summarizing to relating your answer to a broader context: If you've just written about your interpretation of the main causes of the Civil War, give your reader a punch line. Answer the great college question: "So what?"

Fill-in-the-Blank and Short-Answer Preparation

The compelling feature of fill-in-the-blank and short-answer exams is that you must provide accurate information from memory. Though you do not have to write sustained text, the cognitive processes required are the same. Unlike an essay exam, where if you write enough your instructor may give you the benefit of the doubt about what you're trying to convey, precision and correctness are essential for success with these exams. The same strategies that are so powerful for any other kind of test will serve you well to prepare for these formats.

Fill-in-the-Blank and Short-Answer Tactics

1. Review the suggestions for essay exam preparation. If you can write a well-informed essay about a topic, you should be equally successful with these kinds of tests.
2. Review the suggestions for preparing for multiple-choice exams on page 74. Note that these guidelines refer you back to Chapters 1 and 2 of this text.
3. Stress writing to learn as you prepare. Why would you prepare to provide answers in writing by just rereading information?
4. You might want to find out if a particular instructor will deduct points for misspelled terms. If you are a poor speller, you may need to review the spelling of important terms, particularly those with obscure spellings. A few misspelled words in an essay are forgivable, but some instructors are real sticklers for correctness on FITB and SA tests.

CONQUERING TEST ANXIETY

Test anxiety is not your mind playing tricks on you; it's very real! Researchers have identified two factors that contribute to test anxiety: emotionality and worry. Emotionality is a level of psychological arousal that, at a certain level, helps test performance. Worry, on the other hand, manifests itself as internal messages that wreck test performance.

FIGURE 4.5   *Test Anxiety Scale (TAS) items.*

Directions: Answer the following questions as truthfully as possible. Circle the T if the statement is *generally true* for you and the F if the statement is *generally false.*

1. While taking an important exam, I perspire a great deal.   T   F
2. I tend to panic when I have to take a surprise exam.   T   F
3. During tests, I find myself thinking of the consequences of failing.   T   F
4. After important tests, I am frequently so tense that my stomach gets upset.   T   F
5. While taking an important exam, I find myself thinking of how much brighter the other students are than I am.   T   F
6. I freeze up on things like intelligence tests and finals.   T   F
7. If I were to take an intelligence test I would worry a great deal before taking it.   T   F
8. During course examinations, I find myself thinking of things unrelated to the course material.   T   F
9. During course examinations, I frequently get so nervous that I forget facts that I really know.   T   F
10. If I knew I was going to take an intelligence test, I would feel confident and relaxed beforehand.   T   F
11. I usually get depressed after taking a test.   T   F
12. I have an uneasy, upset feeling before taking a final.   T   F
13. When taking a test, I find my emotions do not interfere with my performance.   T   F
14. Getting a good grade on one test doesn't seem to increase my confidence on the second test.   T   F
15. After taking a test, I always feel I have done better than I actually did.   T   F
16. I sometimes feel my heart beating very fast during important examinations.   T   F

Source: Sarason & Ganzer

How test anxious are you? Sarason and Ganzer created the Anxiety Scale shown in Figure 4.5[5] to help identify those most at risk for test anxiety. Wark and Bennett recommend a cutoff score of 11 or above as an indicant of test anxiety.[6] How do you fare?

Although research indicates that 20 to 50 percent of students report test anxiety, much of the anxiety is a symptom of their awareness of insufficient study strategies. If you modify your day-to-day study habits and your test preparation techniques, you are likely to experience much less test anxiety—that is, you'll have positive emotionality and reduced worry. Think back to a time when you experienced a serious bout of test anxiety. What was it like? What did you do to overcome those feelings? Were you truly prepared for the test?

While there is no surefire remedy for test anxiety, the following are some suggestions for minimizing test anxiety.

• For starters, if you have access to old tests, use them wisely to help you prepare. Use them for real, timed test-taking practice; don't just memorize those old questions and answers. The wording of your exam will be different, and your memory will fail you. Do not make working with old exams your first priority in test preparation; your reliance on old tests will make you more anxious when you see the real thing.

• Do not study late into the night before the exam. New learning replaces the previously stored information. You're much better off getting a good night's sleep.

• Focus. Manage your worries. Arrive at the test site early, but do not visit with others; you may inherit their anxiety. Instead, indulge yourself in positive messages: "I've been doing successful work with material that this test will require; I know this material and can use it effectively!" You can say this to yourself with *real confidence* if you have a regular, proficient system for learning. Practice a quick stress reliever (see Chapter 10 for a discussion of stress reduction).

• Know that a certain degree of nervousness is healthy and productive. You are creating energy to recall and accurately use information.

• You may actually wish to visit, before the exam, the room where you will take the test. Go to a test site to study and do active work with the material you predict will be on the exam, and work with it near or at the place you will take the exam. This process "desensitizes" you to the testing site and will make the actual testing situation more familiar and comfortable.

• Manage distractions and use your emotionality in a positive way. Once in the exam, begin with success by answering an item you are sure of, even if it means skipping to a later part of the exam or a different type of question.

• Unless you've been specifically told not to mark on your exam, strategic underlining and marking parts of the questions can help you focus and reduce confusion. Also, it's vital to get what you know "out in the world" where you can see and use it. If you draw or write fleeting bits of pertinent information as you proceed through the exam, you create a record of what you have recalled, and you can use this information to answer the questions. Somehow students think it's strange to write on tests, especially multiple-choice exams. You can be prepared to leave "trails of knowledge" only if you have practiced this strategy as a regular part of your study cycle.

• Manage the test conditions. That is, deal with or shut out disruptions, such as surprise questions or problems to solve, the number of test items, a lack of choices of essay topics, distractions from the proctor, or even the temperature of the room. You have the power to concentrate on the information you have learned and truly understand. Concentrate on what you *know* you know.

LIVING THROUGH FINAL EXAMS

A student-prepared "advice for finals week" handout written for a final group project for a large Midwestern university orientation course begins with the following introduction.

> Finals week is designed to create the most stress and general havoc on the most students in the shortest possible time. What finals week really does is help the police department determine if there are any axe-wielding, homicidal maniacs out there. If you can get through finals week, you can accomplish almost anything.

Is the student author joking, or what??

No, he's not joking; he may be exaggerating about the stress level you and others may experience the first time you encounter the final exam period, but finals week just is not business as usual! Honestly, nothing from your high school years prepares you for this part of your college experience. How does it work? Ordinarily a week is set aside at the end of each term for final exams; some "finals" will be only a last exam over the remaining, untested sets of topics covered in the course. Some others will cover "best-ofs" from prior tests while focusing on more recent material. Other final exams, especially in science, problem-solving, and foreign language courses, will be comprehensive tests that assess your knowledge of all the material covered in the course.

Instructors use finals in a variety of ways: to test your total knowledge of the course, to make the final decisions about your grades, and even to evaluate their own teaching effectiveness. Often, finals are longer and harder than prior tests in the course. This testing period is intense! You may be preparing simultaneously for anywhere from two to five examinations and/or writing final papers during the same time period. The computer labs are full, the collective anxiety level of the campus is at an all-time high, and the whole ordeal may seem unbearable. Even some seniors still "go to pieces" during finals. After all, this is the last shot at influencing those grades! Can you imagine what the world of learning could be like without the tyranny of tests?

Preparing well for finals is very possible, especially if you have dismissed the mythology or hype about the process, if you have sound study strategies, and if you are ready and willing to start your serious exam preparation at least two to three weeks ahead of time. There is a world of misconceptions and a ton of well-intentioned bad advice out there about final exams.

Debunking the Myths About Final Exams

Some instructors or TAs do offer final review sessions; however, they are not intended to be the keys to the final test questions, and they are held within a few short days before the exams. It is your responsibility to determine the material you should study well in advance of the review. Instructors do not always prepare thorough reviews; some are prepared to answer questions, and if there are no questions from students, there's not much of a review. Go to exam reviews with questions, big or small.

Let's debunk a few more myths with these truths:

cramming a last
minute attempt to
learn material by
"cramming" it into
short-term memory

- Studying old exams is *not* sufficient preparation for finals.
- **Cramming** for a final, no matter how intense and sincere, is not sufficient preparation. All-nighters are *not* worth the loss of sleep.
- Caffeine, sugar, and other stimulants do *not* enhance learning; they wreck it.

Since most students are on the border between grades at the time of their finals, serious study *is* worth the time and trouble. It is never wise to "blow off" or sacrifice one exam in the hopes of greater success on the others. Why is this true? You should be able to manage appropriate preparation for *all* your finals!

Even though your exams fall in a particular order during the exam period, it is *rarely* wise to study for them in the order in which they occur.

Not all finals are equal in their effect on your grade. Finals may be worth as little as 20 percent of the total points, while others may be worth 50 percent. Be sure you know the value of each final exam.

Truths About Strategies for Final Exam Preparation

Studying for final exams in the order in which you will take them is rarely a good idea. For example, your first exam may be in history, a three-hour elective course in which you have a solid A. However, your last exam is in a five-hour mathematics course that is a prerequisite for your chosen major, and the final exam will determine your grade.

You wouldn't wait until all the other tests are over to start to prepare for math—there's too much at stake. You should be protective of courses that grant more credit hours because of their impact on your grade point average. You should be more careful with examinations that are comprehensive; they take more preparation because they cover the whole term.

Certainly, you'll want to be very attentive to courses in your major and courses that may impress potential employers. However, if your total preparation is effective, you need not *flush* one exam for the sake of the others. Effective finals preparation is a cycle that moves in and out of studying for different courses, in a variety of ways, over time.

All that you have learned about time management, test preparation strategies, and working with peers and instructors (see Chapters 5 and 6 for more information) will work to your advantage during the final examination preparation weeks. *Weeks? All this takes longer than a week?* Yes, it does. In the best of circumstances, preparing for exams is, at the very least, a three-week, three-part process. A countdown to finals might include the timeline and strategies offered in the box on the following page.

STANDARDIZED TESTS

Standardized tests are an unrelenting part of academic life. You really can't be a stranger to them; they exist for every grade level, starting with kindergarten and looming at the doors of graduate and professional schools. Some students are just better test takers than others, some are willing to seriously prepare for the tests, and others just grit their teeth and take them.

Myths About Standardized Tests

Standardized testing, a life-altering assessment from the cradle to the grave, is a multimillion dollar enterprise. American College Testing (ACT) is a self-proclaimed not-for-profit corporation with its headquarters in Iowa City, Iowa; the most important part of its program is the ACT battery of four tests—English, math, reading, and science reasoning.

It is no myth that the scores you receive on a standardized test will be sent to the colleges and programs to which you apply, and the college financial aid offices will use the scores to determine your eligibility for scholarships and other kinds of financial aid. The scores are important and the stakes are high. It is no myth that there are hundreds of test preparation manuals, preparation courses and CD-ROM exercises available for big bucks to help people get ready.

One particular preparation guide for the ACT discusses a concept known as "the myth of final judgment,"[7] explaining that fear of the ACT (or any other standardized test) as a final judgment of your merit as a student is "created by a group of mistaken beliefs or impressions that work together to create the greater anxiety." Among the attempts at myth debunking in a typical preparation manual related to such tests are these:

- Standardized tests are not written by "superpeople."
- ACT scores are not as precise as people think.
- Standardized testing services set testing dates, fees, locations, and the conditions under which you take the exams, but the test-takers are not powerless.
- Scores aren't everything—in fact, you can retake any standardized test in the hope of raising your scores.
- The ACT and SAT do not measure intelligence. (Then what *do* they measure, anyway?)

BOX 4.1 | COUNTDOWN TO FINALS

THREE WEEKS PRIOR TO FINALS WEEK:

- Find out day, time, scope, and format of all finals. Is there a test review? If yes, when?
- Reread the syllabus for any hints or directions for your preparation.
- Target all the accumulated information that is "fair game" for the exams.
- Divide the information into manageable "chunks"—a note set with additional book information. This is what you'd study at one sitting, for 30–90 minutes, and is a complete "unit" or set of related information.

ONE WEEK PRIOR TO FINALS WEEK:

- Same as above, but begin to integrate newly acquired information into your study.
- Do not rely on final "review session." (See earlier comments on exam reviews.)
- Review older information while you "work in" the newest. You may be acquiring new content until the day before the exam!

FINALS WEEK:

- See sample finals week schedule.
- Plan your week. Prioritize your time, considering the following:
  - Your current grade in the course
  - The percent of the total course grade the final contributes
  - The number of credit hours the course contributes to your total for graduation
  - The "good impression" value of the course grade
  - Whether the course is elective credit or an important part of your major sequence
  - The time and day of the week for which the final is scheduled

OTHER HELPFUL ADVICE:

- Remember the principle of distributed vs. massed practice: The best study is short, intense, but frequent (more than once a day).
- You should not be studying totally "new" information during finals week. If you encounter totally unfamiliar information too late in the preparation process, you'll start to convince yourself that if you don't recognize part of your notes, you must not know *anything*, and you'll start to lose confidence.
- Never underestimate the power of study groups and visits with your instructors.

Defining the Common Standardized Tests

Here is a rundown of standardized tests that you may have experienced or that may await you in the future:

GED (General Educational Development). This is a high school equivalency test. Students take this exam if they do not have a high school diploma but wish to go on to postsecondary education. Its subtests include:

- Writing, 75 minutes
- Writing Part 2, 45 minutes
- Social Studies, 85 minutes
- Science, 95 minutes
- Literature and the Arts, 65 minutes
- Mathematics, 90 minutes

ACT (American College Testing). Many experts say that this test is the best predictor of college success. Its subtests include:

- English, 45 minutes (no writing; just multiple-choice)
- Math, 60 minutes
- Reading, 35 minutes
- Science Reasoning, 35 minutes

SAT (Scholastic Aptitude Test). This is the other college entrance test of choice in the U. S. It is three hours long and consists of a verbal and a mathematics section. Some say it is harder than the ACT; 75 percent correct is considered a good score.

MAT (Miller's Analogy Test). This test is designed to test your verbal reasoning. It supposedly tests your understanding of the analogies, or relationships, among words. Here are two examples of mock analogy items taken from the SPLAT[8] manual:

1. *Media : Reality*
   a. night: day
   b. astigmatism: 20/20
   c. criminal: testimony
   d. cartoon: photograph
2. *Congress : Action*
   a. pothole: road
   b. flypaper: fly
   c. constipation: colon
   d. hairball: drain

GRE (Graduate Record Exam). This is a common requirement for college and university post-baccalaureate study. This three-and-one-half-hour multiple-choice exam gives what its authors claim to be a standardized measure for students from varied undergraduate backgrounds. Most items in each subtest are arranged by difficulty, so if it feels like the questions are getting harder—they are. Worry about accuracy rather than speed. The subtests are:

- Math (Arithmetic, Algebra, and Geometry)
- Verbal (Word problems, not grammar or writing skills)
- Analytic (Analytical Reasoning and Logical Reasoning)

MCAT (Medical College Admissions Test). This one is a 5.7 hour multiple-choice and essay exam consisting of four general sections:

- Verbal Reasoning, 85 minutes
- Physical Science, 100 minutes
- Writing, two samples, 60 minutes
- Biological Sciences, 100 minutes

LSAT (Law School Admissions Test). This exam, unlike many others, is not a test of field-specific knowledge such as chemistry or literature. It consists of 175 minutes of multiple-choice questions and a 30-minute writing sample.

GMAT (Graduate Management Admissions Test). This exam has verbal and quantitative sections and two 30-minute essays, for a total of 225 minutes of testing. Students interested in pursuing advanced degrees in certain areas of business are required to take this one.

CLEP (College Level Exam Program). This set of 34 exams is used for advanced placements in college courses. These are especially useful for those students who have been away from college for a while and would like to get credit by exam for certain courses. If you are a returning and/or nontraditional student, find out if you can CLEP your way into some added hours toward your degree.

Standardized Test Strategies

Standardized tests are difficult, stressful, and frustrating, and their scores open or shut doors to learners. Some realities about them include the following.

• There are some good sources, such as books, CD-ROM materials, and practice exams, for preparation and practice for standardized tests; there are even rather expensive courses that some people have found to be worth every dime—they work for some and not for others.

• The test preparation books and CDs for purchase can be extremely useful if you use them systematically, over weeks or months. This is like getting ready for a marathon! No test preparation work will be useful if you start at the last minute.

• There is no law in the world of testing that says you cannot eat during the testing experience, although there may be a test site rule; check with your instructor. If the exam is longer than an hour, and these all are, take some food to fuel your brain. Granola bars, fruit juices or water, a pre-peeled orange, or an apple and/or some easy-to-eat source of protein will really benefit you during the exam. Thinking burns up an enormous amount of energy. Just don't take items that are hard to eat so that your refueling interferes with your test taking.

• It is true that you can retake standardized tests. If you plan to retake an exam, be mindful of your previous scores. Work on improving the scores on both your highest and lowest subtests for maximum gain.

Do not be intimidated by these tests. Yes, there is a lot at stake when you take them, and even though the writers try to prepare "culture free" test items, there is no such thing as a totally "culturally neutral" exam. Our knowledge is derived from our cultures. Take a deep breath, pull up your socks, and do the best you can!

Journal Reflections

4.1 Think back to a time when you were hit with a serious case of test anxiety. Didn't you want to express your feelings about the test? According to past studies, students gain a lot of insight by writing or talking about their experiences with and feelings about taking tests. Take a deep breath, and, drawing on as much as you can remember about an awful test experience, get out your feelings: What would you have said to the instructor immediately after the test if you had been given the opportunity to comment? You may want to grab your journal if you have another exam catastrophe!

4.2 What have been your experiences (positive and negative) with standardized testing—whether it was The Iowa Test of Basic Skills in grade school, the ACT, SAT, GED, or any other standardized test? What sort of attitudes did you (do you) have about having taken such tests?

Experiences

4.1 ESSAY TEST PREPARATION

You have a friend who has never taken a college essay test before, and her first one is in a week. She is too timid to visit her instructor, so you decide to write a guide to prepare her for the exam. Your directions should include, but not be limited to, the following.

- When to begin to study
- How to choose what to learn
- How to practice writing to learn
- How to manage time during the study cycle
- How to impose time into test preparation

4.2 USING OLD EXAMS

Explain three different ways to use old exams (yours or others) from courses to help you in studying/preparing for future tests in those classes. How is each different set useful? Hint: Memorizing the questions and the correct answers is *not* a recommended practice!

4.3 ESSAY EXAM KEY WORDS

With a partner or in small groups, discuss and invent the real meanings of the key words or "command terms" used in essay exam questions. Your list should include terms such as *compare, contrast, explain, critique, define, demonstrate, discuss, evaluate, illustrate, justify, list, outline, summarize, support or refute,* and *trace.* Remember, none of these terms means "tell all you can remember about . . ." or "fake your way through an answer about . . ." anything! You may wish to refer to the patterns of essay development on page 80 to determine which term corresponds best to which organizational patterns.

4.4 WEB ACTIVITY

Review the information in this chapter, especially regarding essay, objective, and problem-solving exams. Compare it to the information found at the following Web sites:

- *www-slc.uga.berkeley.edu/CalREN/TestsGeneral.html*
- *www-slc.uga.berkeley.edu/CalREN/TestsProblems.html*
- *www-slc.uga.berkeley.edu/CalREN/TestsObjective.html*
- *departments.colgate.edu/diw/essayexam.html*

Can You Relate?

Test your knowledge of ways to prepare for and take college tests by drafting an answer to one or more of the following questions. After preparing, plan to write for approximately 30 minutes. You may wish to time yourself to assess your pace in writing the essay and to work on your essay production strategies.

ESSAY 4.1

Some students believe that taking objective tests is easier than essay exams because they involve a different kind of study than does the writing of an essay test. Therefore, many students believe that they should prepare for objective vs. essay tests in very different ways. Using information from your text and your own experiences, construct an essay in which you compare and contrast the strategies for preparing for essay vs. objective tests. After brainstorming and planning, your procedure is to take 30 minutes writing your answer.

ESSAY 4.2

Developing your metacognitive skills (your thinking about thinking) will aid you in analyzing the demands in each of your courses so that you can prioritize your studying. Follow the steps below to gather and evaluate the information needed to analyze the syllabus, professor's teaching style, textbooks, and other readings for each of your courses. Attend two to three days' classes, take notes on what you observe, and then record the information in the course demands analysis (use one per course) shown in Figure 4.6.

- Analyze your syllabus to identify major assignments and other ongoing demands during the semester (e.g., papers, projects, quizzes, recitation, homework, etc.) What should be your timeline for keeping up?

- Analyze the instructor's style and how it will make it easier or harder to take good notes. How does he or she let you know what's important? What note-taking problems might you encounter? Identify any of the following characteristics and describe them in detail: speaks rapidly or slowly; speaks loudly or softly; does or does not use board, overhead, or other visuals; is organized or disorganized; follows book or does not; and so forth.

- Identify positive factors concerning the instructor's teaching style that you can use to your advantage.

- Analyze each major textbook to determine what learning aids are available to you: e.g., glossary, questions, summaries, objectives, appendice, and important visual representations that may help you comprehend the material. Also analyze any other characteristics of each book that would make it easy or hard to read and use. What about assigned paperbacks? How would you use each book in conjunction with the lecture notes?

Remember, you are making preliminary judgments about your classes and how to strategically handle each one. These plans should be modified and refined as you proceed through the semester. This process is what efficient, proficient learners do each new term or semester.

Use the information gathered in your course demands analysis to write an essay in which you compare and contrast the demands of your different courses. The essay should serve as an analysis and summary of your entire course load this semester. What conclusions do you draw from this analysis? What similarities and differences do you see between and among your different courses?

FIGURE 4.6   *Course demands analysis (reproduce if necessary).*

Course #1 Title: ....

Day, Time, Location: ....

Instructor(s): ....

Syllabus Analysis: ....

....

....

Teaching and Testing Style Analysis:

....

....

....

....

Text(s) Analysis:

....

....

....

....

Initial plan for approaching and mastering this course:

....

....

....

....

Modified plan for approaching and mastering this course:

....

....

....

....

Answers to Practice Objective Quiz

1. B	6. B
2. A, C, D	7. E
3. C	8. D
4. D	9. C
5. A, B, C, E	10. A

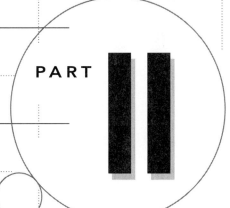

PART **II**

Relating with Peers and Instructors

LEARNING AND UNDERSTANDING

CHAPTER 5   Socializing Your Learning with Peers:
Within the Zone

CHAPTER 6   Relating with Your Instructors:
Meeting of the Minds

CHAPTER 7   Catching On to Learning Styles and
Teaching Styles:
The Essential Classroom Connection

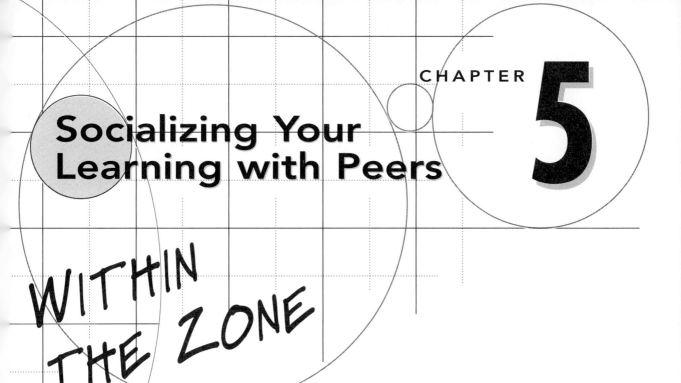

Socializing Your Learning with Peers

WITHIN THE ZONE

BRINGING TOGETHER THE ACADEMIC AND THE SOCIAL

Part I of this text deals with the most fundamental and necessary processes and strategies that college students need to get off to a successful start in college. These processes include managing information sources, managing time and responsibilities, using solid reading, writing, speaking, and listening strategies for learning in college, and preparing for and taking all kinds of tests. Whew!

You'd think that mastering all the above strategies would be more than enough to take you successfully through your college experience, but it covers only your *individual* relationships with ideas and information, and they're not the only critical relationships you will form during your college years. In order to "soar" or "sail" through college you must establish meaningful, working relationships with your peers as study partners or in study groups; you may have occasions to work with tutors; and you *must* actively cultivate valuable relationships with many, perhaps most, of your instructors.

The relationships you form with other students and with your instructors are a blend of the academic and social aspects of your college life; they will make your experience more complete. Part II of this text, therefore, explores the many ways in which you can connect with other students (Chapter 5) and your instructors (Chapter 6) to enhance your learning through these relationships. Chapter 7 investigates learning styles, teaching styles, and their relevance in making the important classroom connections between how and what is taught and how you learn different kinds of material.

If you think about all that you know and how and why you know it, you'll see that, really, all learning is social. You didn't learn to talk, walk, cook and eat, read, make jokes, and get along this far in life all by yourself. Language and thinking are perfect examples of *socially* constructed systems. Therefore, any reading, writing, speaking, or listening strategy can be modified to become a group learning strategy. Chapter 5 in particular gives guidelines and reviews several ways to work with other students; however, it is not meant to be a complete, exhaustive primer to collaborative learning. Consider this chapter to be a "starter" to the world of learning with your peers.

THE "ZONE OF PROXIMAL DEVELOPMENT" (THE WHAT?)

Before noted Swiss psychologist Jean Piaget (a name you will encounter in many college courses) was studying how children learn individually, a Soviet psychologist in the 1930s, Lev S. Vygotsky, studied the stages of intellectual development of children as they worked together with their peers. Piaget gained much fame from his work on individual cognitive development, and Vygotsky's research eventually gained much attention from educators because it proved a very basic and powerful premise: that social contact among learners stimulates higher-order thinking and is a necessary condition for learning.

Vygotsky demonstrated that "directed thought is social"[1] because he focused on shared learning. In other words, he looked beyond individuals working alone to establish that thinking and learning are social activities, and that trying to understand concepts and their relationships comes more easily when working with others who are equally invested in their learning. In a groundbreaking work translated and first published in 1978, Vygotsky described a "zone of proximal development"[2] wherein learners of different ages and levels of experience work productively together. He found that within the "zone," sharing ideas and working together enhanced the group's or "learning community's" understanding of the shared material.

Think about what "being in the zone" means if you're Michael Jordan or Mark McGwire. They aren't just isolated superstars; their teammates support and aid their success. Now think about all those other students seated in your classrooms who would love to make their learning easier! There is a potential untapped "zone" of learners of different ages, levels of experience, and orientations toward learning in every one of your classes. Why not share the load of college learning with a few of them?

Consider how much of your prior schooling was spent working alone in a busy classroom. Somehow, the American educational system has overvalued the work of the "rugged individual," perpetuating the notion that we learn more or better by ourselves. The notion of the "zone of proximal development" creates a peer-operated system where learners develop relationships among ideas as well as with each other. Research by Ann Ruggles Gere has confirmed that "when groups form voluntarily, authority originates from the original members who choose, for reasons of friendship, solidarity, respect or need to give, temporarily at least, authority over their [learning] to others".[3] Sharing course commitments, tasks, or problems makes knowledge something that students create together. Our species has survived and advanced through shared knowledge.

FORMING STUDY GROUPS

Many students *think* that they hate study groups and are more productive alone, while most students *swear* they hate group work. For the sake of argument, let's agree that both ways of working with other students have the potential to be very,

very helpful. Now, the ways to form study groups vary, so a little reconnaissance is necessary. Unlike some group work where the groups may be assigned or imposed by the instructor, for the most part study groups are voluntary and self-selected. Your instructors are very likely to leave this endeavor up to you. Remember, you're not shopping around for a date or a party pal or a lifelong partner here; you're looking for people with whom you can learn.

Look around your classrooms. Who among all those students seems to be involved in serious note taking? Who asks good questions? Who even speaks up at all? Whom in the class do you know already? Does he or she fit the requirements? After the first exam, who has a reputation for making high grades? Is there anyone in the class who has had the instructor for another class and knows about the teaching and testing styles you are likely to encounter? With whom could you stand to spend regular time and effort? The requirements for membership in a study group also include, on the part of each member:

- A willingness to set times to meet and a reliance to be there for the group
- A shared belief that a study group is as important as individual efforts
- A shared investment in coming to the group prepared, including whatever preparation is necessary in terms of reading, note taking, additional research efforts, and so on
- A common sense of group purpose, a tolerance for "rules," a sense of humor and good will, and respect toward others' ideas and learning styles
- An individual understanding of how each can best serve the group (leader, organizer, stabilizer, recorder, bouncer)
- Patience to go through the initial "bumpy" stages necessary to achieve a lasting, effective working group

Remember that in most schools you have the flexibility to enroll in courses with students that you know, if you plan accordingly. In general education courses, and certainly once you are in your major course of study, you may wish to arrange your classes to maintain a good study group over several terms, or even over several years. Good study groups, like all lasting relationships, take time and work. They're also as priceless and rare. Strive to make good study groups flexible and durable parts of your college experience!

Interacting in Study Groups/Group Projects

The forming of study groups and the assigning of group projects stem from the assumption that at times, groups have more learning potential than do individual efforts. Your instructors may have never heard of the "zone of proximal development," yet they understand the power of collaboration. In many colleges and universities, students are intentionally enrolled in the same courses and assigned living space together in the residence halls in order to enhance their learning potentials. Group assignments are well-intentioned efforts to help you learn. We often do better for others than we do for ourselves. As a member of a study group or group project, you have certain obligations to others, and that's good, because you may find it easier to keep working when the outcome will affect more than just you alone.

Teamwork in sports has many obvious advantages. Employees working together to solve a problem in the workplace save time, money, and their private "gray matter." Group work is intended to empower students to learn together by sharing, comparing, wrestling with, and making sense of course content. Box 5.1 lists some well-known and some less obvious requirements for individual and group behavior in group work.

BOX 5.1   MAKING GROUP WORK A SUCCESS

1. You need to be serious about your group work, but if the group is tired, confused, frustrated, and feeling a bit overwhelmed, take the first five to ten minutes of the session for some "ceremonial venting." This is a necessary process in which you release those individual or shared feelings that will get in the way of productive work unless you *get them out and deal with them.* You can't change your instructors' styles or expectations, but it's healthy on occasion to GRIPE! So let it out, and then move on. . . .

2. Group size is important. For some endeavors, a partner is sufficient, while a good working group has three to five members, preferably with an odd number (not odd members) so there won't be "tie" votes for procedures and practices.

3. Designate a member to be the "digression monitor." This member calls the group back to task if the conversation slips or leaps into topics irrelevant to the group.

4. Get to know your members, and take advantage of individuals' strengths. There will be better organizers, idea people, writers, and speakers in any group. Any group needs a leader; everyone in the group should be assertive, yet someone will rise to the occasion. If no one exhibits leadership qualities, YOU assume leadership, at least temporarily.

5. Never leave a study group without agreeing on the group's next meeting, or each member's next assignment.

6. Make very sure you know how to find and contact one another.

7. Pick a meeting place that is central and agreeable to all members.

8. Include food and beverages as part of the ritual. Snacking is a necessary component of group work. Planning the cuisine is one of the more pleasurable parts of the routine.

9. Have rules and expectations for membership—those who come ill-prepared, planning to "soak up" a bit of knowledge from the working members, need to be given notice that everyone works and contributes evenly, and slackers are out.

The work you do with others may involve a blend of reading, writing, speaking, listening, and of course, through the entire process, critical thinking.

This chapter presents a representative collaborative strategy for reading, writing, listening, and speaking—each of the four uses of language. Again, consider this chapter to be a sampler of strategies—just a start. The many opportunities for learning with other students are constrained only by the limits of the imagination.

A Group Reading Strategy: Shotgunning

Reading in college is a necessity, and technology affords us multiple ways to receive information without the need for textbooks. No matter what the format, college learning requires a large dose of reading. Collaborating with others on heavy reading loads is just one example of working in the "zone"; it saves time, and alleviates boredom—the great enemy of reading.

"Shotgunning"[4] gets its name from the image of the difference between a single bullet and a *blast* of shotgun pellets that effectively covers a large amount of territory (i.e., material to be learned) in an intense, relatively short period of time. If taken seriously and used well, this strategy can be extremely effective. Shotgunning can be performed with any kind of reading/studying situation. Just follow these steps:

1. Target all the sources of information (notes, texts, handouts, articles) that pertain to the learning task.
2. In a group of two to five, all members preview sources and suggest ways to divide up responsibility for sections. The divisions should be by relationship of topics, not by arbitrary numbers of pages. Some members may have more material to cover, but the sections should still be derived from the key areas of the material to be learned.
3. Decide who will become the "expert" on which part(s) of the material.
4. Agree on time limits for individual work and when and where to reconvene the group.
5. As the group comes back together to share its expertise, members agree on the format for sharing.
   - Will each discuss his part while others ask questions and take notes?
   - Will members photocopy their "expert notes" for group members?
   - What about both formats?
6. The group should then predict the most challenging test questions possible and try a mock exam.

Then what? Brainstorm what other strategies the group or individuals should use for further review.

Remember: responsibility heightens learning. When you teach something to another person, you heighten and deepen your own understanding of the material. (Why is this true?) Now think of ways you and your friends can "shotgun" your way through your classes!

A Group Writing Strategy: "Prove It"

In recent years, more and more instructors have begun to assign "group papers." The hazard, of course, is that some students are better and more willing writers than others. To compound the problem, writing is a very personal and idiosyncratic endeavor. Some students enjoy the "chase" involved in research, while others are technologically impaired or suffer from "library anxiety."

If several people are to produce one "work," how do they reach consensus about the main idea and the details to include? What about organization? What if one member of the group is determined to write the paper and leave everyone else out in the cold? How does everyone feel about getting a shared grade for what may not be a shared experience?

Try the "prove it"[5] technique. Partners find a text or texts to read, then

- **Predict**—important points from a preview of the text. Students may or may not write their predictions. The predictions set purposes for reading.
- **Read**—to confirm, build on, or alter predictions. Students read for the main ideas and to summarize in their own words.
- **Organize**—important ideas are made into a response. A response includes a retelling of text-contingent information and a reaction to that information. Reactions relate the author's ideas to the student's background experiences. Up to this point, each student is working alone. When each is finished, summaries are exchanged.
- **Validate**—partner's ideas are validated and partners are asked to verify— "I don't remember that the author said that; it's misinformation; prove it!"

Compare the summaries to the original text, and discuss. After partners validate and verify to each other's satisfaction, each will:

- **E**dit—her summary, taking cues from her partner and improving both the form and content.

Have partners pick and read different pieces of text, but exchange and evaluate everyone's summary. You may find it interesting to see how the lack of exposure to parts of the text changes responses to partners' summaries. Do you tend to ask for more verification or less when you've not read the passage?

You will eventually see that students can spot concerns in summaries and write good questions for their partners without prior knowledge of partners' texts. You don't have to know the answers to write good questions if you're a good predictor!

When you become comfortable with this activity, you will find summarizing a welcome aid to comprehension. In addition, you will see that edited summaries are more useful for studying than are the original texts, because one's own language is more meaningful than the often inconsiderate language of textbooks.

A Group Speaking Strategy: "Tag-Team Teaching"

Along with the increase in the assignment of group papers, there is a renewed interest among college instructors to plan curriculums with more occasions for students to speak (not including basic communications or public speaking courses, naturally). Though a typical instructor does most of the talking in a particular course, there may be a requirement for individual or group oral presentations. The hazards of such assignments are similar to the group paper traps—agreement on content, assignment of responsibilities, too much or not enough leadership, being at the mercy of others for your grade, and so on. (Chapter 3 contains a thorough discussion of speaking strategies.)

Imagine this strategy to be a bit like professional wrestling. We know that teaching others is the most powerful way of learning information for ourselves, for we learn topics more deeply and broadly by explaining them to others. In professional wrestling, although the moves are fake, there is a worthwhile principle in action. In wrestling, as in teaching, it's best to enter the ring when we have some good, fresh moves to use. The parallel to a group project that involves speaking is humorous, yet useful.

Most oral group presentations fall into a rather predictable pattern, as in this four-member group:

- Speaker #1, who gives the obligatory introduction
- You, Speaker #2 (more stuff)
- Another speaker (sigh!)
- The "clean-up" or wrap-up speaker who winds it up, presumably with some degree of insight.

This is a linear, step-by-step, everyone-for-herself order of speaking.

Wouldn't it be great if a class presentation could be more like authentic conversation? What if you and your group *did* have areas of responsibility to discuss in a planned order, but could also interject into each other's discussions? You could add to and draw upon each other's knowledge, and expand the power of the "separate but (maybe) equal," step-by-step approach to an oral presentation. In so doing, each member would be more knowledgeable about the entire subject! You'd seem more like those well-versed discussants on "Firing Line" or "Meet the Press," or the commentators on CNN.

Now, what exactly is the connection to tag-team wrestling, you may ask? You could arrange a signal between you and your co-presenters. The signal could be a gesture or a word, but among you it means, "Let me interject something at this point . . . " which is very much like the way wrestlers seem to orchestrate their comings and goings at the wrestling ring. With this understanding, your presentation could appear spontaneous, natural, democratic, and highly superior to the usual 1–2–3–4 order that usually lacks spontaneity, enthusiasm, and creativity.

Don't try this tag-team approach without practice. Do you know how hard those steroid-pumped professional wrestlers work to plan their seemingly spontaneous moves, leaps, and gyrations? Theirs is a well-orchestrated act; they have quite a large following of fans. The fans know the whole event is planned, but they love it anyway because it *appears* so genuine, so creative. Your instructors and your peers will no doubt appreciate the planned spontaneity, or they may just think your group is intelligent, versatile, and quick on its feet. (To give you an example of how this conversational flow might proceed, see "interactional scaffolding" on pages 63–64 in Chapter 3.) In what courses that require oral group presentations could you try the "tag-team" approach and "wow" your listeners?

A Group Listening Strategy: "Share the Load"

The good news is that effective group listening work is easy, efficient, and has fewer traps and hazards than do group speeches and papers. Although listening (see Chapter 3 for a detailed discussion of listening and speaking) is an important part of all college-level individual or group learning tasks, there are few, if any, assignments in college that actually require and assign a grade to a pure group *listening* project. Listening is a part but not an end product of college requirements, with the notable exception of the listening components of foreign language or music appreciation classes. There are some collaborative strategies that you can use with classmates—in lecture and in later study—that can really help you in certain classes.

Imagine you are in a biology, physics, or chemistry class. What is likely to be happening simultaneously and at lightning speed? The instructor is explaining a lengthy, complex process. She is talking too fast to follow well enough to get decent notes, and at the same time she is inundating the class with charts, diagrams, equations, and explanations. Smoke may be rising from the overhead projector.

This is information overload, and there's no way that one person can successfully watch, listen, copy the visuals, and duplicate the dialogue all at the same time. The end result may be that you were able to copy the visuals but were unable to record the explanations. The other scenario may be that you get what the instructor said but not the visuals that she was explaining. In either case, you are in trouble because you couldn't get it all.

The remedy is a partner listening strategy, "Share the Load." This is a great practice in science and problem-solving courses. To begin, pick a partner to work with during and after the lecture. Ideally, your partner will agree to work with you through the whole semester. The procedure is as follows and, as always, is subject to modification.

1. Before the lecture begins, agree on each person's responsibility during lecture.
2. One of you will be in charge of accurately and completely copying everything the instructor presents visually. Your task is exact duplication of the visuals.
3. The other partner will be responsible strictly for the spoken explanations. This must be a tight, complete version of the teacher-talk. Sketch *only* if you need a point of reference for the explanations. Remember that your partner will provide the visuals.
4. After lecture, get together as soon as possible to review and put together what each of you has captured. Ask each other questions in order to assure the cre-

ation of a complete drawn and written note set. You will even remember some details that you did not take time to sketch or write, so the collaboration after class should produce a superior set of information—enhanced by your discussion—to what either of you could ever capture on your own.

5. If appropriate, refer to the text to "fine-tune" your pictures and notes.

6. Here's a tip: The person doing the drawing seemingly has an easier job because the task is mere duplication of visuals. On the other hand, while capturing the teacher-talk seems to be a more complicated task, the student who is listening and recording the explanations will likely have the *simpler* task because attention to explanations is a baseline comprehension strategy. With these issues in mind, be wise about which task you pick.

If you frequently need collaboration on notes in a particular course, you and your partner can take turns being the sketcher and the writer.

LEARNING WITH AND FROM PEERS: A SUMMARY

In college settings, a group is any two or more students working together in the name of understanding and learning. Working with others heightens learning; it's a smart, invaluable practice. Group work in high school may have been inauthentic if the teacher formed the groups, told them just what to do, and regarded group projects or presentations as very little more than "playtime." Some, though not all, high school group work may have been really no more than an opportunity for the teacher to sit back and let the students do their own thing for a change.

Get serious! Those days of group work as frivolous play are over! Collaborating with other students to enhance learning is serious, important business. If you're lucky or wise or both, you may be able to establish friendships that blend the academic with the social. In any case, think of those student groups who traditionally and by design have the most at stake academically—law students, medical students, and others enrolled in course-dense, concept-dense, intensely professional programs. No one at that level of schooling would consider doing a whole graduate or professional program by himself—there's too much to learn and far too much riding on the outcome—success or failure, embarrassment or pride in a job well done.

Don't wait four or five years, until you finally graduate and strive for an advanced degree, to tap into the power of learning with and from other students. Many students choose to or are forced to leave college because they have never established any "learning relationships." Your academic and social selves will be nurtured and broadened by the power of learning with and from your peers. Imagine the possibilities. . . .

Journal Reflections

5.1 Brainstorm a list of all the reasons you may prefer to study alone. What were your experiences with collaborative learning in your prior schooling? Was working with other students teacher-directed or self-initiated? Did these collaborations involve mostly reading, writing, speaking, or listening, or some combination of these? In which ways and under what conditions do you or would you prefer to work with other students? Why?

5.2 Review Chapters 1 through 4. List the learning strategies that seem to lend themselves best to group work. Discuss these possibilities for collaboration in your current courses. Turn loose your imagination! Speculate also on collabora-tive possibilities for some of the courses you will have in the future. Imagination and creativity lead to less effort for good grades!

5.3 Doodle a picture—a cartoon or web, perhaps—of what a previous study group experience was like for you. Portray and label the members and depict their dif-ferent behaviors. What is your role in this sketch? How would you change the sketch (or some members portrayed) to show more effective results from these relationships?

Experiences

5.1 GROUP PROBLEM SOLVING

You finally have a firm commitment from three trusty friends who are in a "killer" course with you. No one is failing; no one is pulling an A, either. You're all a bit fed up and have agreed to meet at least twice weekly. You've picked the time and place, so everything looks promising for a good study group. Whoops! The best-laid plans often fall apart. Discuss, with a small group or in writing, how you would respond to the following scenarios and what action (if any) you would take. Be direct, assertive, and creative.

a) One member of the group never shows up. He doesn't call to cancel; he just never keeps his commitment. What should the group do?

b) One of the group is the "taking over" type. She talks too much and won't let anyone else into the conversation. It's as if she needs to let everyone else know how smart she is. The information she provides is accurate; it's just that she doesn't know when to let others in. What should the group do?

c) The group is meeting at the designated time and place and everyone attends. The problem is that it takes about an hour to really get into any kind of produc-tive work because the members bring their materials, but are never sure how to proceed. What should the group do?

d) There have been two exams in the course for which this group meets. There will be two more exams and then a final exam. The problem is that the instruc-tor changes the format of the exams and the number of items on each test, so it's hard to predict what the next exam may be like. What should the group do?

e) The first exam in the course was tricky multiple-choice questions, and the class as a whole did abysmally. The average was 65 percent. Since the instructor was unhappy with the class's overall performance, she announced that the next exam would be primarily essay questions. What should the group do?

5.2 OBSERVE A SUCCESSFUL STUDY GROUP

Ask around among your friends and find two or three who are members of long-term, hardworking, consistent study groups. This inquiry may take some time; enduring, successful study groups are hard to sustain. Everybody has the same dilemma of having a lot to do in not enough time, and falling back on studying alone is really common—out of necessity. Yet, working groups do persist. When you find a group or groups, ask permission to watch a group or two in action, and jot down some observations: How do the members work together? What dynamics of the group contribute to the group's success? Analyze the effective components of this working group.

5.3 WEB ACTIVITY

The Web site *www.tpa.org/geese.htm* offers several facts about geese flying in a flock. It then goes on to derive lessons about teamwork and working in groups from the observed behavior of the flock and individuals in the flock. Does your group agree with the lessons the writer points out? Are there other possible lessons on teamwork that could be found by observing geese? By watching other animals and plants?

5.4 WEB ACTIVITY

In 1983, an outbreak of the deadly Hantavirus occurred in the southwestern United States. The article at *www.bocklabs.wisc.edu/ed/newhant1.html* (part 1 of the article) and *www.bocklabs.wisc.edu/ed/newhanta.html* (part 2 of the article) discusses the effective use of teamwork by scientists in various fields to successfully combat this outbreak. Based on what you've learned in this chapter, describe the strategies used by the scientists. In particular, what made these scientists work together so effectively? What lessons can you learn from this actual case study?

Can You Relate?

Test your knowledge of ways to learn with your peers by drafting answers to one or more of the following questions. After you prepare, plan to write for approximately 30 minutes on each question. You may wish to do a prewriting outline, chart, or other plan for practice in essay organization techniques.

ESSAY 5.1

Discuss the social nature of learning and the benefits of constructive, purposeful studying with others. How can it be true that "all learning is social" when students spend so much time working alone? Describe in detail three distinct ways that students could utilize study groups or other kinds of collaborative learning. Use examples from your own experiences.

ESSAY 5.2

Referring to the above answer, critique different study group experiences that you've had so far in college. What makes group study powerful and effective? What factors such as size, location, and a lack of well-defined goals lead to unproductive study groups that waste your time? Develop a set of rules for the operation of effective study groups, including recommendations for types of members, size of group, choice of location, time constraints, and parameters for operation. You may wish to use an actual course as an illustrative example.

ESSAY 5.3

What are some of the implications for your successful learning from Vygotsky's notion of "the zone of proximal development"? Have you tested this theory in real-life practices? Have you ever experienced a "zone for learning" with others much the same way the "zone" works in sports? What are the characteristics of the "best" kinds of students you should invite to study together—the very brightest, the most popular, the best looking, the most reliable, or those most dedicated to efficiency of learning? Why? In what ways can you find a "zone" with others in your classes?

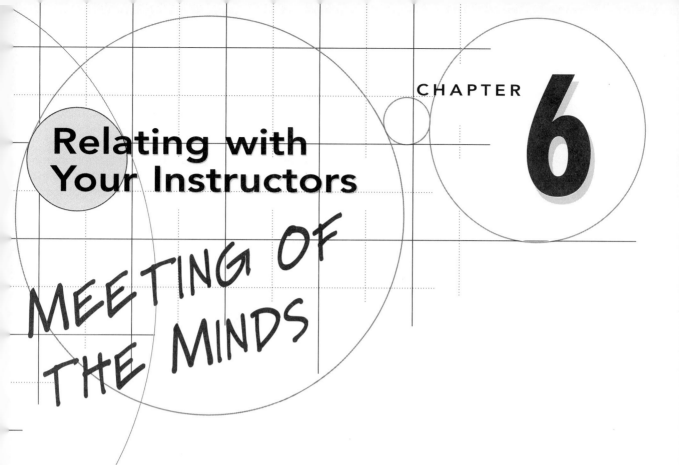

Relating with Your Instructors

CHAPTER 6

MEETING OF THE MINDS

In Chapter 5, you explored the many ways that learning with other students is a natural, necessary, easily achieved, and cheap (i.e., doesn't take much effort) part of your college experience. Working with other students is an opportunity too good to miss, especially if the group has an understanding of ways to be productive without digressing into small talk, gossip, or even less productive ragging about instructors.

Of course, it seems less risky to seek out and connect with your peers and to avoid your instructors for the purpose of studying and learning. Why? College instructors are intimidating, if not downright scary! Studying with other students is an obvious, usually less risky way to enhance your learning. Let's face it—one of the biggest differences between high school and college is that in high school, teachers were by comparison rather conveniently located and easy to talk with.

On the other hand, in college you may be in large classes where the instructors seem distant and somewhat inaccessible. Some instructors, much like actors, have purposefully invented classroom or lecture hall "selves" that range in style from scholarly and serious to casual and down-to-earth. To add to the classroom challenge, if you are from a small town but attend a large university, you could be in classes with more people than live in your hometown! You may feel that the only source of learning from instructors is what they present in the classroom. Wrong! Relating with your instructors apart from what may be minimal classroom interaction is just as important as, if not *more* important than, working with your peers to enhance learning.

The truth is that most college instructors are eager, valuable, and essential resources for your learning and understanding. A history professor at a large Midwestern university once lamented, "I always keep my office hours and no one ever shows up! I'm going to get a cot and catch up on my sleep if this keeps up!" Instructors appreciate students who come to them outside of the classroom environment to learn *with* them. Unfortunately for both instructors and students, instructors are an underutilized natural resource for interaction, advice, and learning.

The larger your school, the more difficult it may seem to connect with your instructors. This chapter will acquaint you with the different types of instructors you may encounter in college and compare and contrast the different ways in which they may be helpful to you. It will suggest different strategies for using instructors' office hours, seeing them by appointment, and using tutors to heighten your learning. You will understand why and how to take advantage of out-of-classroom learning situations and why and how to, in the process of learning with your instructors, take control and find that "right person." She or he could become your long-term **mentor,** perhaps your private "guardian angel" for your college years and beyond.

mentor a person who takes a heavy interest in you, who may be very much like the person you hope to be in the future

INSTRUCTORS, TEACHING ASSISTANTS, AND TUTORS

Instructors

College instructors do have many different titles or designations, depending on their educational status, experience, and their roles on campus. As in every other system, "rank" implies status. Starting with the top, college instructors may hold one of the following titles.

tenure an employment policy for instructors that guarantees continual employment after completing a certain number of years of teaching and publishing scholarly articles

Professor (or Full Professor)
Associate Professor
Assistant Professor
Lecturer
Instructor
Teaching Assistant
Graduate Assistant

Considered faculty; full professors have attained **tenure,** which gives them academic job security. All three levels have doctoral degrees, but "associate" and "assistant" professors may still be working towards tenure.

These designations do not imply or ensure excellent versus poor teaching. Academic titles reflect amount of schooling, time spent in research projects, involvement in committees, longevity at the institution, consulting, and other related academic activities. Any instructor you may have in college is working on his or her own further education and professional advancement. College instructors care about their disciplines, but (let's be honest here) they have varying degrees of enthusiasm for presenting their material, interacting with their students, and valuing their teaching roles.

The Syllabus

Rules, work, advice, schedules, deadlines, more work . . .

One of your challenges—one of your duties—is to get to know your instructors and the reputations of potential future instructors. Every college and university has a wealth of terrific instructors. In fact, in college, the instructor is ultimately a more important consideration than the course itself, and the instructor is certainly more important than the time of day the course meets! (For further discussion on picking instructors, see "Shopping Around," later in this chapter.)

Goals and Attitudes of Your Instructors

Figures 6.1 and 6.2 reveal goals and attitudes of instructors based on survey responses of 33,986 faculty members at 384 colleges and universities, for the years 1995–96.[1] It is interesting to note the gender differences in college teachers' goals and attitudes.

FIGURE 6.1) *Goals of college instructors.*

	PERCENTAGES		
Professional goals noted as essential or very important	All instructors	Men	Women
Engage in research	54.6	57.5	48.7
Engage in outside activity	49.3	45.8	56.3
Provide services to the community	41.9	37.6	50.3
Participate in committee or other administrative work	28.3	24.2	36.6
Be a good colleague	86.6	84.5	90.9
Be a good teacher	99.2	99.1	99.3

Source: *The American College Teacher: National Norms for the 1995–96 H.E.R.I. Faculty Survey.* Published by University of California at Los Angeles Higher Education Research Institute.

FIGURE 6.2) *Attitudes of college instructors.*

	PERCENTAGES		
Professional goals noted as essential or very important	All instructors	Men	Women
Racist/sexist speech should be prohibited on campus	53.1	47.1	65.0
Western civilization and culture should be the foundation of the undergraduate curriculum	53.2	57.7	44.0
College officials have the right to ban persons with extreme views from speaking on campus	32.2	33.0	30.5
The chief benefit of a college education is that it increases one's earning power	26.7	27.2	25.6
Promoting diversity leads to the admission of too many underprepared students	31.0	35.8	21.3
Colleges should be actively involved in solving social problems	62.6	60.1	67.5
Community service should be a requirement for graduation	31.0	25.7	41.6
Tenure is an outmoded concept	38.3	34.6	45.8
Tenure is essential to attract the best minds to academe	54.3	58.8	45.3

Source: *The American College Teacher: National Norms for the 1995–96 H.E.R.I. Faculty Survey.* Published by University of California at Los Angeles Higher Education Research Institute.

What Instructors Do

- Your college instructors may do much more than teach and test; they perform many functions, such as conducting research, writing scholarly articles or books, advising students in their major areas, sitting on any number of campus or departmental committees, holding offices in faculty and professional organizations, and so on.

- Regarding the courses they teach and their relationships with students, your instructors are experts in their fields who plan what is to be taught, how it is to be taught, and how your knowledge is to be assessed and evaluated. Remember that they are resources for your learning.

- College instructors pick or produce their teaching materials, such as the required and suggested texts. More and more instructors are writing their own materials and making them available on the World Wide Web.

- College instructors may or may not take roll, notice if you in particular are in class, or ask you direct questions. It depends on the size of the class. However, nothing can replace your being in class, listening, taking notes, and working to understand the material.

- College instructors prepare course outlines, often called the syllabus (see Chapter 1) to show you the organization of the course content, reading assignments, time lines for quizzes, homework and exams, their grading policies, rules, and expectations, and their office hours.

What Instructors Expect

academic honesty
doing academic work autonomously, and giving proper credit for other's contributions to your work; avoiding academic misconduct

academic freedom
the ability of instructors and students to pursue knowledge without external control or censorship

- Your college instructors expect you to attend and keep up with class, experiment with your learning strategies and your motivation, know the rules and regulations of your school, and manage your time and tasks. They expect you to read and understand their syllabuses, take notes on what they say in class, figure out what to do with your textbooks, and seek help if necessary. (Whew—that's a lot!)

- College instructors expect **academic honesty** (see Chapter 8).

- College instructors expect you to respect their **academic freedom** to say what they believe, as long as human rights, privacy, and/or lives are not jeopardized. They do not, however, expect you to agree with everything they say. Sometimes it is necessary to separate the content of the course from the personal points of view or the personalities of your instructors. (See page 17 later in this chapter.)

Teaching Assistants

Different schools and colleges have different criteria for selecting and using teaching assistants. These assistants are usually graduate students who are working on their own advanced degrees, either a master's or a doctoral degree, and are hired as assistants to faculty instructors. At some schools, teaching assistants may be the autonomous instructors of some courses, such as composition courses, lower level mathematics courses, and so on. Larger schools with higher enrollments are more likely to use teaching assistants in both capacities—to assist faculty instructors as well as to teach certain classes by themselves. Smaller schools use various ranks of instructors in their teaching assignments, depending on the school's budget.

What TAs Do

- If they are teaching autonomously, teaching assistants may perform any or all of the duties of other instructors.

- If the TA is a true *assistant,* she will likely be in charge of the discussion sections that meet to reinforce the lectures. In this situation, the TA and not the head instructor may be the grader for the course. If you have more than one instructor, it's very important to know who will be evaluating your written work and what sorts of grading standards and expectations the grader has.

What TAs Expect

Teaching assistants have the same expectations for your performance that all other instructors have. TAs may be closer to your age, but that does not automatically make them easier or "soft touches." On the other hand, since TAs are also taking classes, they may be more understanding of your situation. Again, getting to know each of your instructors is the only way to be sure of their expectations.

Tutors

Tutors in college play an important role in the learning process. Chapter 8 explores in detail the roles of campus resources and services, including the role of campus learning centers that make tutors available to students. Different kinds of learning resource centers have different budgets for tutorial support for students; some hold small-group help sessions, which are more cost-effective, while some are able to assign individual tutors. Of course, you are also capable of finding tutors (usually for hire) on your own; however, campuses increasingly provide students academic support and supplemental instruction at no cost. There are all kinds of tutors, yet your understanding of how to learn best from your tutors is a key issue in learning in college.

Strategies for Working with Tutors

It is very common for a tutor to re-explain course content and to answer your questions. Tutors also assist with homework. It's very important for you to have a wide variety of ways of interacting with and learning from your tutors. Student-tutor interactions may include all of the following:

- The tutor will answer your questions. Be prepared to guide the session and use the time to your advantage.

- The tutor may reiterate the lecture; it's helpful if he explains concepts in alternate ways from the instructors so you get a slightly different version. Having more than one explanation enhances learning. If the tutor's discussion is too close to the instructor's version, you might ask, "Can you say that another way?"

- The tutor could provide "mock" test questions for you to answer in a testlike environment; i.e., with time limits and without referring to notes. This sort of test rehearsal can help your tutor see what you do and do not understand, while you are "training to the task" of the upcoming test. (See Chapter 4, pages 79–81 for more on test preparation.)

Research Assistants

Research assistants are like teaching assistants in that they are working on their own advanced degrees. Instead of teaching as part of their employment, they work with instructors in performing their research investigations. Though they are not hired to be instructors, many are good sources for learning.

OFFICE HOURS AND APPOINTMENTS

Ordinarily, instructors alert students to the times they will be available in their offices by including this information on the course syllabus, the instructor's plan for the course. (The syllabus is discussed in detail in Chapter 1, pages 5–6.) If instructors are also available by appointment and/or through electronic mail, they usually include these options for interaction on their syllabuses or will issue these invitations early in the course. You always have the right to request time with an instructor. Not all are equally accessible, but you are paying money to learn from these people—give them a chance to get involved in your learning!

BOX 6.1 | EXPLORATION: WHAT DO YOU BELIEVE ABOUT THE "MEETING OF THE MINDS"?

Test your assumptions about using office hours and connecting with your instructors. "Teaching assistants" in this activity refers to those graduate students who help your instructors with their courses.

Rate each item *true* or *false*, then justify your answers in the spaces provided.

1. If you go to an instructor's office hours *prior* to your first big exam, your instructor will assume you are having trouble with the course. Circle T or F and justify.

   ....
   ....
   ....

2. College instructors want students to utilize their office hours but are never available by appointment. Circle T or F and justify.

   ....
   ....
   ....

3. It's always best to go to an instructor with a list of specific questions. Circle T or F and justify.

   ....
   ....
   ....

4. Graduate teaching assistants are more help than the head instructors (who may be professors). Circle T or F and justify.

   ....
   ....
   ....

5. Appealing a grade never works in favor of the student. Circle T or F and justify.

   ....
   ....
   ....

6. Using study guides that are sold along with many textbooks is always the best way to study for those courses, so they make talking to the instructor unnecessary. Circle T or F and justify.

   ....
   ....
   ....

(continued)

BOX 6.1 | Continued.

....

7. If an instructor says her exam will come mostly from her lecture, there is no reason to study from the text or to talk to the instructor outside of class. Circle T or F and justify.

....
....
....

8. A good out-of-class relationship with an instructor ends when the course is completed. Circle T or F and justify.

....
....
....

9. Test reviews are the best times to find out what to study for a particular test and make talking to the instructor unnecessary. Circle T or F and justify.

....
....
....

10. When in doubt, get an instructor's old tests and use them to prepare for the exams; instructors use the same questions over and over on exams. Circle T or F and justify.

....
....
....

11. If you have an foreign-born instructor, you are automatically at a disadvantage. Circle T or F and justify.

....
....
....

12. It is best to wait until you get your first test score before you visit with an instructor. Circle T or F and justify.

....
....
....

13. If you use office hours wisely, instructors will tell you more about how to study and what to study than they have told the class during lecture. Circle T or F and justify.

....
....
....

(continued)

BOX 6.1   Continued.

....

14. If you miss a class, a "good" student's notes will be as helpful to you as a visit with your instructor. Circle T or F and justify.

....

....

....

15. If you take your class notes and textbooks to office hours, you have a solid basis for a good discussion with your instructor. Circle T or F and justify.

....

....

....

    Now compare your answers with those of other students. What do your beliefs about relating with instructors indicate about your willingness to expand your opportunities for learning and understanding in college? Are you willing to try to establish ongoing relationships with your instructors? The above items may raise interesting issues about your views on relating with your instructors. Next is a discussion of strategies for enhancing office hours and other out-of-classroom learning.

STRATEGIES FOR WORKING WITH INSTRUCTORS IN THEIR OFFICES

The following are strategies for meeting and working with your instructors:

Before the First Exam

• There is no reason to wait until after that first big test to connect with instructors. They won't assume you're clueless and desperate if you connect with them earlier! There are legitimate questions they can answer for you early in the course: "How do my notes look?" "How should I use my textbook with my notes?" "In your particular discipline, what are good ways to take notes and organize the content?"

• Remember that, compared to high school, there are a lot fewer quizzes and examinations contributing to your final grade. Therefore, it's very wise to get off to the best start possible in each of your courses.

• Arrange to meet with your instructor; take your class notes, your textbook and other related materials, and your syllabus; and arrive with curiosity and an open mind. If office hours conflict with your schedule or if many other students are taking advantage of the posted times, ask your instructor for a private appointment.

• Make the focus of the conversation your *academic work;* show your initial strategies for organizing and learning the material. You are not there to get your instructor to tell you the test questions! Instructors are impressed when students are willing to display their efforts at learning and understanding.

• Be willing to let your instructor review your system and make suggestions for more effective ways to record lectures, use the texts, and/or predict areas to study for tests.

• Be open to your instructor's suggestions, and feel free to ask additional questions about managing the information or about particular aspects of the material.

• Give your instructor a chance to be helpful; often instructors really open up with great suggestions for success in their courses. If you care enough to come to them, they are likely to give you very helpful extra advice that they would never suggest to the class as a whole.

• If you also have a teaching assistant, find out if he has worked with the head instructor before. Experienced teaching assistants can also be good resources for strategies for managing and learning information; often they will be more eager informants about the course than are the instructors. Sometimes they can demystify the head instructor's teaching style. It's worth the time you take to inquire!

• Understand that this sort of interaction may not be what your instructors are used to; some are accustomed only to answering students' specific questions. Give them time and room to open up to you.

• If you are a differently abled student and need special accommodations, such as extended time on tests, note takers, tests in alternative formats, and so on, you will be working with your campus office for students with disabilities or the campus office designated to help you. However, you will still need to communicate with your instructors about the nature of your disability and your special needs. The Americans with Disabilities Act of 1991 assures you of many kinds of support in overcoming physical barriers or the effects of learning disabilities.

After the First Exam

The purpose and tone of a visit with an instructor may certainly change after the first exam.

• Remember that the goal of reviewing an exam with your instructor is to understand the kinds of adjustments you need to make immediately in your information management systems and study strategies for the next test. Don't wait too long to get feedback on a first exam; your goal is to modify your learning strategies right away, in time to make positive gains on your next test. You need to learn more from your test than just your score.

• If you have been "successful" on the first test, or obviously if you did not receive the score you expected, you may wish to ask to see your exam if you have or have not been able to see it or keep it. For security reasons, not all college instructors return their exams; they only post the grades. Others return your exams so you can see your score and get a quick sense of where you went wrong or did well, but it is rare that you spend much time going over the test during class.

• You always have the right to request to see your exam during office hours.

• Be a willing and open-minded learner, not an adversary, even if it feels like you got "robbed" or "fooled." (Later in the chapter appears advice on dealing with difficult instructors.)

• Although your score alone can give you an indication of the effectiveness of your knowledge and preparation, spending a few minutes reviewing that first test can give you terrific insights into ways to refine your studying for the next exam. As you review your exam for the items you missed, consider the following:

• Did you misread the question?
• Did you run out of time?
• Did you miscalculate a problem?

- Did you not recognize the topic?
- Did you memorize definitions only to discover the questions were not merely about definitions? (That was high school.)
- Did you eliminate all but two answers on a multiple-choice test and consistently pick the incorrect answer?
- What was the instructor's source for the questions and for the wording of the questions?
  - Lecture content?
  - The textbook?
  - A topic covered in lecture, yet in the language of the text, or vice versa?
  - An illustrative example given in lecture that you didn't bother to record?
  - Who knows?
- Were you more or less successful with different kinds of test questions? For example, did you do well on the essay but bomb the matching and T/F items?
- Certainly, if you do not understand the nature of your errors, you can ask the instructor for clarification of the content and clarification of the above issues.

Throughout the Semester or Term

- As the course progresses, you may wish to visit with your instructors on a regular basis. Arrive prepared; use your time with instructors wisely.
- If the course requires papers or projects, you may wish to meet with instructors to clarify writing assignments, brainstorm ideas for content or research sources, or even to borrow a book or two.
- If your instructor shares office space and the topic of the visit is sensitive, you may wish to ask for more privacy.
- Be open to the "unfolding of the instructor's personality." Many instructors have a different "presence" in front of the class than they do when they are meeting with you one-on-one. On the other hand, some instructors are the same (for better or for worse) in and away from the classroom.

After the Course has Ended

- Depending on your level of interaction with the instructor throughout the course, you may wish to stay in touch and consider taking another course from her.
- Also, you may wish to keep in touch because it's important to know instructors who could and would write letters of recommendation for you in the future. It's shocking how many students inevitably wish to apply for jobs or graduate programs, but don't know any instructor well enough to ask for a letter of support!
- Again, depending on the quality of your relationship, you might not stay connected to a particular instructor. You won't appreciate your instructors equally, and that's an important part of learning in college.
- Instructors may develop a genuine interest in you and your academic progress. They may appreciate your thinking of them and dropping by to keep them updated on your accomplishments and activities.

Distinguishing Between the Course Content and an Instructor's Personality

Relating with your instructors in office visits may help you better understand and appreciate your instructors, but if not, remember:

- There is no way that you will like all your college instructors. As in all of your college experiences, you may judge instructors and others by their appearance, personality, sense of humor or lack of one, and by other attributes that have nothing to do with the content of their courses.

- You may not like certain instructors' "politics" or their personal values. You must not let your difference in beliefs block you from learning the knowledge they are offering you.

- It's more important to learn from your instructors than to like them!

- If you feel you have been treated or graded unfairly, every department has an administrator to whom you can take your concerns, but start with the instructor first. When in doubt, consult your academic dean for advice on how to handle your complaint.

OTHER OUT-OF-CLASSROOM LEARNING OPPORTUNITIES

Learning and understanding through relationships with instructors may occur anywhere! On many campuses, instructors are now spending time holding reviews for exams, and on residential campuses, some instructors are spending time in the residence halls, working with students where *they* live. Strategies for productive out-of-classroom learning opportunities include the following:

- If you live in a residence hall, find others in your residential area who have the same courses and instructors that you do.

- Invite the instructor to the residence hall for a test review, or just to discuss the course in a more relaxed setting. It's a good idea to invite the instructor to have a meal with you, even if it's cafeteria food you're offering. (It would be good for them to see what residence hall life and food is really like!)

- Some instructors will enjoy informality; others will prefer a more "formal" academic setting. If you wish to create a more "formal" setting for out-of-classroom learning, advertise a "symposium" or "lecture series" that features different instructors as part of an ongoing residential learning series.

SHOPPING AROUND FOR INSTRUCTORS

You're pretty picky about your close friends, aren't you? And about the person who styles your hair? Well then, you owe it to yourself to investigate the world of instructors on your campus. How? Ask juniors and seniors who've been around. Visit an instructor whose class you are considering, and find out about the course expectations and assigned reading load; ask to see a syllabus. Many campus bookstores post instructors' required book lists. Academic advisors and other staff who have experience with the campus may be good sources for instructor selection. Sit in on classes. Shop around!

If, on the first or second day of class, your instincts are shouting, "No can do!" because the information on the syllabus or teaching style of the instructor will put you at academic risk, be a smart consumer. If others are teaching the course, find a different instructor if possible.

SELECTING A MENTOR (AN ACT OF SERENDIPITY)

Every college student should find a mentor. A mentor is someone on campus who can help make good things happen for you and with you. A mentor is a role model and a guide. You may be lucky and find your "guardian angel" very early in your college career, or you may not find that special person until you get into your major course of study. Mentors may be current or former instructors, tutors, campus employers, student affairs staff members, academic advisors, learning specialists from the campus learning resource center, or even administrators.

There is an old adage that "you'll never find Mr. 'Right' when you're trying too hard to find him!" So it goes with mentors. You'll find a mentor in the midst of your everyday hard work, through a positive presentation of yourself, when the chemistry is right. You and your mentor will admire one another for intellectual, social, personal, and professional reasons. When you discover potential mentors, let them know that you trust, admire, and feel comfortable with them.

Mentors are ready to do any or all of the following.

- Listen to you with both ears and a kind heart
- Challenge you and make you think
- Give you constructive criticism—even disagree with you
- Treat you like an adult instead of a kid
- Assist you with your choice of major and with career decisions
- Help you connect with other campus resources and services
- Share their passion for being part of the campus community
- Promote you and increase your visibility among their peers, other instructors, and potential employers
- Help you when you are in a bureaucratic jam, such as needing to add or drop a course, withdraw from a course, or (in the event of an emergency) withdraw from school
- Assist you if you wish to continue your schooling in a graduate program

Journal Reflections

6.1 Consider your relationships with your instructors. What qualities made your high school instructors easy to talk with? What qualities make college instructors seem more or less approachable? What would be appropriate ways to get to know your college instructors?

6.2 Did you have a mentor in high school? If so, what sort of support did you receive? What qualities do you seek in a mentor in college? What affiliations do you think you should have with a potential mentor? Must this person have a connection to your presumed academic major? Should a mentor be a current or previous instructor? Does rank matter in the selection of a mentor? What other factors matter in the selection of a mentor?

Experiences

6.1 BREAKING THE ICE: AN EARLY MEETING WITH AN INSTRUCTOR

Early in the term, before the first test, pick an instructor (regardless of rank) with whom you'd like to meet in office hours or by appointment. Don't go empty-handed; take the course materials and be prepared to explain your system of study.

You might take a list of questions, but getting the answers should not be the main purpose of your visit. Find out how your instructor prefers to be addressed and make clear the name you prefer for yourself. Take note of any suggestions your instructor offers about how to manage and learn the course material. Be sure to solicit advice on ways to use that expensive textbook to enhance your learning. After the visit is finished, find a quiet place and finish writing down your instructor's suggestions and comments. Suggest that a friend in the same class visit the instructor also, and compare the results of your visits. What did each of you learn? How might you improve the relationship in successive visits?

6.2 INVESTIGATE YOUR INSTRUCTORS

Find students who have taken courses with your current instructors. Interview them about their relationships with those instructors. What else might you learn from their experiences with those instructors?

6.3 INTERACTIONS WITH INSTRUCTORS

Imagine that you have finally gotten up your nerve to seek out an instructor's guidance by appointment. Discuss with a small group or explore in writing how you would respond to the following scenarios and what action (if any) you would take.

- The instructor does not come to the set appointment
- The instructor is obviously preoccupied and is trying to rush the session
- The instructor "talks down" to you, giving the impression that you are handling the course inappropriately
- The instructor diverts the topic of conversation from the content to your personal life
- The instructor asks "Do you have any questions?" and you have none prepared
- The instructor is willing to take time and care with you, no matter how the conversation begins
- The instructor offers to meet with you regularly to supplement the classroom instruction, yet your free time is very limited
- The instructor shows you copies of tests from prior semesters

6.4 PERSONAL INQUIRY

Interview at least four friends about their experiences with meeting their instructors. Start a list of creative positive approaches to relating with your instructors. As you proceed through the term and compare experiences with others, add to your list. (If this list is thorough and helpful, you may be able to market it to your peers for a little pizza $$$!)

6.5 WEB ACTIVITY

Determine which of your instructors have a Web page, and check them out. What are their Web addresses? What information do their pages contain? Do they contain the course syllabuses, lecture notes or outlines, or old exams? Is it possible to email them from their Web pages? Is this information useful to you? How might it be improved?

Can You Relate?

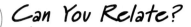

Test your knowledge of ways to relate with your instructors by drafting an answer to one or more of the following essay questions. After planning your essay, expect to write for approximately 30 minutes. You may wish to time yourself to assess your pace in writing the essay and to work on your essay production strategies.

ESSAY 6.1

Compare and contrast the different strategies for working with instructors, teaching assistants, and tutors to enhance your learning and understanding in college. If you can, use real-world examples from your own experiences to illustrate your answer.

ESSAY 6.2

Let your imagination take over and describe your perfect mentor. Then describe your perfect instructor. Compare and contrast the qualities of each. Finally, invent and describe the ways you will find these terrific people. Be very specific; imagination plus desire can work miracles!

ESSAY 6.3

Invent and discuss different creative ways you could develop relationships with your instructors in campus settings other than the classroom and the office. Illustrate with real-world examples, even if they are hypothetical. Feel free to involve other students in this adventure, and be creative!

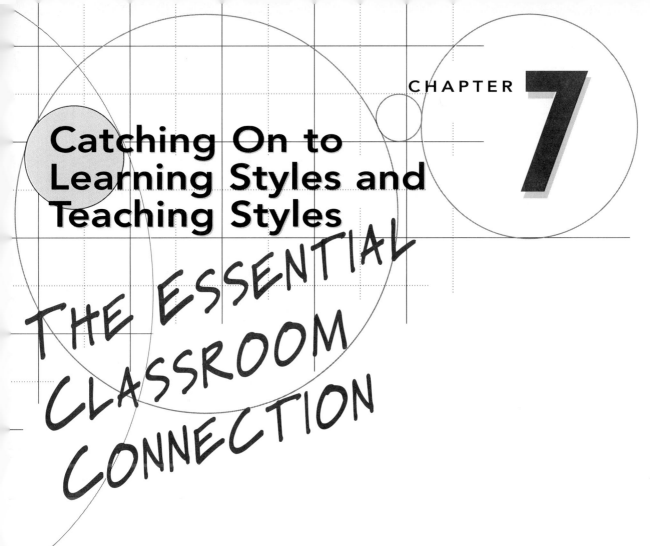

Catching On to Learning Styles and Teaching Styles

THE ESSENTIAL CLASSROOM CONNECTION

H ave you ever sat through a class that made no sense or seemed obscure or unnecessarily difficult? As you look around at your classmates, do they appear to know what's going on better than you do? Has an instructor's presentation style ever confused or eluded you? It may not be your lack of knowledge or a case of inattention. Different people learn in different ways, just as you have a firm preference for right- or left-handedness. You are not solely responsible for educational outcomes, and your instructors have a much more specific responsibility than to merely present material; they should present a variety of materials in a variety of ways.

This chapter focuses on the advantage you gain when you understand your learning styles and your instructors' teaching styles. Ultimately, the goal for you is to increase your awareness of both styles present in your college-level teaching–learning relationships. It is unlikely that you can change your instructors' styles; however, it is very likely that you can use the information in this chapter to minimize the problems inherent when teaching and learning styles are mismatched—or in conflict.

You will enjoy a course more, and likely be more successful, if you see that you can use your strengths as a learner, and that your personal abilities will be tapped and perhaps improved through an understanding of the teaching–learning relationship. Even if your initial motivation for a course is low, you can do well if you can understand ways to use and improve your abilities—if you have strategies for success. Therefore, success in learning is derived first from your own self-awareness of how you take in and process information. This awareness and the success it brings do not happen by accident. Do you know how *you* learn and *your* particular strengths as a learner?

Success in learning also depends on course structures, teaching methods, and instructor attitudes. Have you been able to take time and attention away from the course content to watch and analyze your instructors' teaching styles? It's a fascinating process to watch how instructors convey information

PERSONAL LEARNING STYLES AND PERSONALITY TYPES

Ancient Measures

Just for fun, here's a little bit of history with which you may be familiar. The Greeks, in their ancient and very wise ways, categorized people by personality types, or certain combinations of psychological and behavioral traits. Scholars such as Aristotle (a philosopher and natural scientist) and Hippocrates ("the father of medicine") developed a theory based on *humors,* or excessive amounts of certain substances in the body. In ancient times the four humors were blood, black bile, or yellow bile (produced by the kidneys), and phlegm (from the respiratory tract). According to Greek belief, a "preponderance of blood was said to lead to a *sanguine* or enthusiastic temperament; the sadness of the *melancholic* was attributed to an excess of black bile; an overabundance of yellow bile produced the irritability of the *choleric;* and finally, the slowness and apathy of the *phlegmatic* was due to the influence of phlegm."[1] Does this theory seem credible?

The Greeks also believed that each type had distinguishing facial features and body types. There was a bit of medical truth to the Greeks' theory; today, people are often analyzed medically on the basis of hormones in the body. Yet, while there was some validity to the theory of humors, as the field of psychology matured, researchers began to see that people were more psychologically complex than mutually exclusive "types" governed by body chemistry.

Contemporary Measures of Learning and Personality Styles

There is an endless number of measures of learning and personality styles. Knowing your personality and learning style can help you with improving learning, selecting a career, and understanding others—including your instructors. There is great debate among educators, counselors, and psychometrists (professional test-givers) about which instrument is best, most reliable, and most accurate.

The purpose of this chapter is not to provide or evaluate different inventories to make recommendations to you about their individual merits. Instead, this chapter is designed to give you knowledge of and access to a variety of instruments to help you align your learning with the different methods of teaching you will encounter in college.

Sensory Styles

An easy way to get an idea of your learning style is to determine your dominant sensory style or styles. In other words, do you need to see something to remember it? Is hearing information your preferred mode of learning? Is vocalizing information a powerful way to make sense of it for you? Sensory styles include the following.

1. **Visual:** You need and prefer to see information in order to understand it, believe it, and remember it. (See Chapter 1 for ideas about note taking and Chapter 2 for reading strategies.)

2. **Aural, or auditory:** You need and prefer to hear information to understand it, believe it, and remember it. (See Chapter 3 for listening and speaking strategies.)

3. **Vocal:** You need and prefer to hear yourself talk through information in order to understand it, believe it, and remember it.

4. **Tactile, or "kinesthetic":** You need and prefer to doodle, physically manipulate, or get hands-on experience with information in order to understand it, believe it, and remember it. In college, your preference for "hands-on use" may translate into drawing, writing, or making charts or webs. (See Chapter 1 for ideas on reading, writing, and drawing to learn.)

It is absolutely true that the more senses we can use while we are learning new information, the easier the learning endeavor will be. That's why seeing and hearing in classes are both so important. Unfortunately, the sense most directly connected to the memory is the sense of smell, but really, how much of your college work can be enhanced by using your sense of smell?

Witkin's Embedded Figures Test of Cognitive Styles

As early as 1940, Herman Witkin and his associates examined a number of cognitive styles and modes of perception and their relationships to learning. This research has resulted in a cognitive task that sorts learners into "field sensitive" and "field independent" learners. With the Embedded Figures Test,[2] a subject is shown a simple geometric figure such as a square or a rectangle. Then she is shown a more complex figure with the first, simple figure embedded somewhere within it. The subject then must find the first figure within the more complex geometric second figure. Some people find this task easy; others find it next to impossible.

Those who quickly recognize the simple figure, perhaps because they were not influenced by the surrounding "field" of information, are called "field independent." These learners are "tree learners" who are cognitively drawn to the "trees" of discrete details, analysis, math, and science. Persons who cannot recognize or have difficulty finding the simple figure in the more complex one within a time limit are called "field dependent" or a more neutral term—"field sensitive" learners. By contrast, these are "forest learners" who are cognitively more drawn to the "forests" of connections, interpersonal relationships, and fields such as social science, humanities, or teaching.

There are not two kinds of people in the world—those strictly "field independent" or "field sensitive." However, we can generalize some basic differences between students with the two cognitive styles as shown in Figure 7.1.[3]

Kolb Learning Style Inventory (LSI)

Yet another approach to learning styles comes from David Kolb.[4] His work suggests that to be effective a learner needs four kinds of abilities, each with particular emphasis, as listed in Figure 7.2.

This inventory may be available at your school's career or counseling center. Taking the LSI can help you identify your preferred learning styles, possible majors, and future occupations. The more inventories and tests you take, the more information you will have about yourself as a learner, and the more sense you can make out of specific teaching-learning situations.

Myers-Briggs Type Indicator (MBTI)

Perhaps the most complex assessment of learning styles is the Myers-Briggs Type Indicator (MBTI), originally designed in 1967.[5] Consisting of 94 items, the MBTI assesses cognitive and personality characteristics on four scales that combine into 16 personality types as described in Figure 7.3. The four scales that best determine

FIGURE 7.1 *Field independent vs. field sensitive learners.*

	FIELD INDEPENDENT LEARNERS	FIELD SENSITIVE LEARNERS
1	Are more independently analytic and think less globally	Are more interactive, global thinkers and less analytic
2	Can use discrete details out of context without knowing the "big picture"	Cannot use discrete details without a framework of the overall "big picture"
3	Are more likely to use outlines even if not provided by the instructor	Need outlines provided by the instructor
4	Often prefer to work alone and prefer the lecture format	Often prefer to work with or consult others and prefer discussion classes
5	Select majors that stress problem solving and computation, such as mathematics, engineering, and science	Select majors in which interpersonal relationships are important, such as the social sciences, education, counseling, and sales
6	Refer more to themselves as they talk; use more personal pronouns, such as "I"	Refer more to others as they talk; use more pronouns such as "we" and "you"
7	Are more influenced by self-motivation	Are more influenced by others' reactions or criticisms
8	Have less trouble making decisions and career choices	Have more trouble making decisions and career choices
9	Have better memories for details and data; less for social information and people's faces	Have better memories for information including social content and people's faces
10	Are less likely to meet with instructors	Are more likely to meet with instructors

Source: Claxton & Ralston, Erickson & Strommer

FIGURE 7.2 *Kolb's learning style abilities.*

ABILITY	DESCRIPTION	EMPHASIS
Concrete Experience (CE)	The learner involves herself fully in the new experience.	Feeling
Reflection Observation (RO)	The learner observes and reflects on the experiences from different perspectives.	Watching
Abstract Conceptualization (AC)	The learner creates concepts that integrate his observations into sound theories.	Thinking
Active Experimentation (AE)	The learner uses the theories to solve problems and make decisions.	Doing

Source: Kolb

your learning styles are extraversion–introversion; sensing–intuition; thinking–feeling; and judging–perceiving.

The MBTI is no doubt available to you at your career or counseling center. When you take the MBTI, your results assign you a four-letter code, such as ESTJ or INFP. For your purposes as a college student, the most helpful dimensions for you to consider are extraversion-introversion and sensing-intuition.[6] After taking the MBTI or the Keirsey Temperament Sorter (see below), refer to Figure 7.3 to gain insight into your learning style according to your code.

FIGURE 7.3   *Myers-Briggs types. (These match with Keirsey types.)*

E/I   EXTRAVERSION (E)

- Prefer the "outer world" of people and things to reflection
- Active
- Gain energy from others

- Want to experience things in order to understand them
- Work by trial and error
- Like variety

S/N   SENSING (S)

- Like facts
- Realistic and practical
- Observant about what is actually happening
- Work steadily and step by step

- Enjoy owning things and making them work
- Patient, good with detail

T/F   THINKING (T)

- Fair, firm-minded, skeptical

- Analytical and logical
- Brief and businesslike
- Critical
- Clear and consistent principles

J/P   JUDGING (J)

- Decisive
- Industrious and determined
- Organized and systematic
- Take deadlines seriously

- Like to have things decided and settled

INTROVERSION (I)

- Prefer reflection and the "inner world" of action
- Prefer writing to talking
- May enjoy social contact but need to recover from it
- Want to understand something before trying it
- Persistent
- Like a quiet space to work in

INTUITION (N)

- See possibilities and patterns
- Imaginative, speculative
- Like to see the overall picture

- Work in bursts of energy with quiet periods in between (need inspiration)
- Like variety

- Impatient with routine

FEELING (F)

- Warm, sympathetic, aware of how others feel
- Trusting
- Enjoy pleasing others
- Need harmony
- Clear and consistent values

PERCEIVING (P)

- Curious
- Flexible and tolerant
- Leave things open
- Pull things together well at the last minute
- Sample many more experiences than can be digested or used

Source: Adapted from Bayne

Keirsey Temperament Sorter

Developed by David Keirsey and Marilyn Bates in 1978, the Keirsey separates the 16 Myers-Briggs types into four temperaments.[7] A good reference for understanding results of the Keirsey is *Please Understand Me* by David Keirsey and Marilyn Bates. The temperaments that are the focus of this instrument are included in Figure 7.4. As with the Myers-Briggs types, your results assign you a four-letter code that has implications for your personality and learning styles. Within each code, four combinations of temperaments reveal the most about learning styles.

FIGURE 7.4 *Keirsey temperaments.*

SP
- Excitement and adventure
- Responding to crises
- Flexibility and freedom

SJ
- Being responsible and useful
- Planning in detail
- Stability and security

NT
- Developing new theories/models/ideas/systems
- Analysis, criticism, and understanding
- Competence

NF
- Harmony
- Self-development
- Supporting other people

Source: Adapted from Bayne

In many ways, you are very likely to get similar results from taking the Myers-Briggs and the Keirsey, since the Keirsey draws upon the categories of the Myers-Briggs. An advantage of the Keirsey to you as a student is that it is available on line for easy taking and scoring. (See Experiences 7.1 and 7.2 for Keirsey on the Web. Interpretation information is available on line; you may also get help with interpretation through your career or counseling center.)

Applications of Learning Styles Information

"Types" and "temperaments" indicate radically different ways that people learn and behave, yet it is important not to stereotype people on the basis of one instrument or another. One of the most positive aspects of learning styles research and discussion is not to promote one instrument's superiority or validity over another, but to highlight just how complex a process learning really is. Understanding your personality and learning style can help you in many ways. The box below summarizes the benefits of applying knowledge of your learning style to your schoolwork and life.

BOX 7.1 **BENEFITS OF UNDERSTANDING YOUR LEARNING STYLE**

1. Knowing your learning style can help you make adjustments in your approaches in classes where the instructors' teaching styles are in conflict with your preferred ways of learning.
2. Working with students who have learning styles different from yours can open up new possibilities and approaches to the class that may never have occurred to you.
3. You will be able to make more informed decisions about possible majors and careers.
4. You will be more successful in your future work because your personality and learning style will become your professional working style, and you'll understand how to fit into the system.
5. You will begin to better understand yourself—why you are gifted in some areas and not so gifted in others.

Looking at Teaching Styles

There are different cultures of students and instructors. Instructors' knowledge and awareness of different learning styles should imply instructional alternatives for students. Teaching is more than the transmission of information. However, instructors' teaching styles are very much extensions of their own learning styles. Teaching styles are also partial imitations of the instructor's past instructors. The teaching styles in Figure 7.5 are derived from research utilizing the MBTI types.[8] You may generalize similar trends in teaching by applying the Keirsey temperaments.

Do any of these teaching styles remind you of any particular instructors? Have you had an easier time with some than with others?

FIGURE 7.5   *MBTI type and teaching styles.*

EXTRAVERSION (E)

- Develop student-based classrooms
- Active instruction, full of talk
- Utilize group projects

- Encourage experimental learning

- Allow students choices about what and how they learn

INTROVERSION (I)

- Develop teacher-based classrooms
- Prefer lecture to discussion
- Structure tasks from text and other materials
- Prefer to pre-plan or mentally rehearse classroom presentations

SENSING (S)

- Focus instruction on narrow range of assignment choices
- Prefer to discuss practical applications

- Ask for facts and details
- Tend to keep activities centralized
- Concentrate on factual and concrete questions and subjects

INTUITIVE (N)

- Allow for a wide range of assignment choices
- Emphasize concepts, relationships, and implications of facts on larger problems
- Ask for synthesis and evaluation
- Move around more in the classroom
- Focus on "What if . . . ?" questions and theory

THINKING (T)

- Treat class as a collective group
- Excel at challenging students

- May offer little feedback or make critical/objective comments
- May prefer teaching math, science, or technical subjects

FEELING (F)

- Treat class as individuals
- Attempt to attend to each student's needs

- Motivate through support, praise, and empathy
- May prefer teaching in arts, humanities, or social science areas

JUDGING (J)

- Develop orderly classrooms
- Utilize plans, schedules, and deadlines
- Evaluate students' learning by completion of tasks

PERCEIVING (P)

- Develop spontaneous classrooms
- Utilize movement, open-ended discussion, and flexible schedules

---

Source: From Bayne, adapted from Jensen

RELATING LEARNING STYLES TO TEACHING STYLES

What are some of the benefits of relating your learning styles to different teaching styles? You will gain greater academic success, less frustration, better use of your time, and self-knowledge that can help you in school, work, and life. Whether you can identify particular teaching styles or merely the mismatches between the instructor's style and yours, you always have some control and some choices in how you approach each course to improve your ability to be successful.

Sometimes this process requires that you use different learning strategies to undo the mismatches in your instructors' presentation style and your accustomed approaches to learning. Sometimes this process requires your elimination of counterproductive attitudes toward an instructor or course. Sometimes being more successful in a course requires seeing the course purposes differently from what they originally appeared to be. This change in thinking about a course and the instructor's style can eliminate typical student reactions of "This course is stupid," or "This instructor is impossible to follow," or "There's no way—I might as well drop this one."

Figure 7.6 suggests strategies for aligning your learning style with different instructors' teaching styles. It will help you to refer back to Chapter 6, "Relating with Your Instructors," to get more ideas about enhancing the teaching-learning relationship. Many of the teaching traits listed here are problematic for some students but not for others. You may find that some of the traits are difficult for nearly all learners to deal with, regardless of their personality and learning styles.

FIGURE 7.6   *Aligning teaching and learning styles.*

TEACHING TRAIT	LEARNING STRATEGY
Instructor lectures but presents no visuals whatsoever.	Review the visuals in the text before class; take the book to class, or review the text soon after class. Add pertinent pictures or diagrams to your notes.
Instructor uses so many visuals and explanations that keeping up with note taking is impossible.	Use the strategy, "Share the Load" found in Chapter 5: "Learning with Peers."
Instructor provides no outline of the lecture to follow and is very disorganized in presentation.	Review the accompanying text material and your previous note sets before class. Reorganize and add to your notes as soon as possible after class. Compare your notes with other students.
Instructor begins with a discussion of terms with no context.	Take notes on the terms; as soon as possible after class, review the related chapter and add the context, main ideas, or missing structure to your notes. Compare your notes with other students.
Instructor spends so much time on the overview that she never covers the important details.	Take notes on the overview, including the real-world examples, then use the text or outside readings to supplement the details. Compare your notes with other students.
Instructor writes illegibly on the chalkboard or overhead projector.	Let the instructor know, in a diplomatic and private way, that you can't read what he is writing.
Instructor does not summarize the important points of a lecture.	Draw a line at the end of the note set; re-read the notes, synthesize the information, and add your own summary.
Instructor does not review any material from the previous class.	Meet with others in the class to discuss what has been presented; review your past notes before class.

(continued)

FIGURE 7.6   *Continued*

TEACHING TRAIT	LEARNING STRATEGY
Instructor uses, but does not define, technical terms.	Annotate your notes with discussions of the terms derived from the text. Visit the instructor in office hours for clarification. Compare your notes with other students.
Instructor does not follow the syllabus.	Visit the instructor for clarification of the intended order or choice of topics. In class, ask for the new organization of the material.
Instructor lectures mainly over topics not covered in the textbook.	Use office hours or appointments to ask for suggestions on how to integrate the lecture and text material. Try to find out the instructor's view of how the sources relate. You might show the instructor your notes and ask for tips on how she sees the sources connecting. It may be time for a study group.
Instructor gets "off track" frequently.	Keep taking notes. Don't stop; you may have to reorganize or decide what's important later by consulting with other students in the class.
Instructor's speech, accent, or dialect is unfamiliar to you.	Sit in the front; ask questions to generate more discussion from the instructor to get more accustomed to the dialect. Visit office hours and have a conversation—you'll get more accustomed to the dialect or accent in face-to-face contact.
Instructor offers criticism but rarely helpful comments or suggestions.	Use office hours or appointments to discuss your work; request strategies for improve your performance.
Instructor gives few choices or alternatives for assignments.	Use office hours or appointments to clarify assignments and/or negotiate alternatives. Give the instructor a chance to broaden your choices of topics or formats.
Instructor doesn't know you; the class is huge.	Use email for a "safe" introduction; soon after, start using office hours early in the course and in a variety of ways. (See Chapter 6 for different strategies.)
Instructor prefers "open" discussion to lecture and often calls upon students at random to add to the discussion.	Don't get caught with nothing to say! Go to class prepared with notes from the readings, insights from previous discussions, and other "cue cards" that will help you have impressive observations to contribute to the discussion.
Instructor isn't particularly helpful in office hours. This may be due to a lack of a "desk-side manner" or to her own introverted nature.	You may have better interactions with some instructors via email; they may be more willing or able to connect with you through this means of communication. Additionally, other students and tutors are good resources when the instructor is of little assistance.

Journal Reflections

7.1 Refer back to the information on sensory styles. Though these categories are not mutually exclusive, there is a lot of merit to understanding your dominant sensory styles and strengthening your less dominant styles. Which sorts of sensory learning work best for you? Which work less well for you? What are the implications of your preferred sensory styles for you as a learner? What ideas do you have for developing the power of your sensory styles?

7.2 If you were a Greek citizen during the time of Aristotle, which personality type would you likely have been? Why?

7.3 Refer back to the list of MBTI types and teaching styles in Figure 7.6. Describe your "ideal type" of teacher, according to your preferred teaching style(s). In which sort of teaching environments are you most comfortable and successful? Why do you think this is true?

7.4 Are you more comfortable with analytical, detail-oriented work, or do you consider information in a more global or holistic way? Do you prefer working alone or with others? If you were to take the Embedded Figures Test discussed earlier in the chapter, do you think the results would classify you as a "field independent" or "field sensitive" learner? Why do you think so?

Experiences

7.1 WEB ACTIVITY

The Keirsey Temperament Sorter is a shorter version of the Myers-Briggs Type Indicator. It can be found on the Web at *http://csdept.keene.edu/~deck/cgi-bin /keirsey1.html*. An alternate site is *http://sunsite.unc.edu/jembin/mb.pl*. Find one of these sites and complete the 70-item test. The computer program will automatically score the test for you. According to the results, what is your personality type? Look at several of the links available to learn more about your type. What tendencies do you have as a learner? How can you use this information to become a more effective learner?

7.2 WEB ACTIVITY

Another type of personality instrument is the theory of "multiple intelligences" developed by Howard Gardner. The theory divides how we think into eight categories of intelligence. This instrument can be obtained from the Web site *http://users.mwci.net/~sauer/index.htm*. This site provides both an interactive MI inventory and descriptions of each type and links among them. What are your strongest and weakest types? How can you strengthen your weaker areas? Do you think Gardner's MI theory has merit? Why or why not?

7.3 DOES RACE OR ETHNICITY INFLUENCE ONE'S LEARNING STYLE?

Find two or three other students in your class with learning styles (according to your Keirsey codes, derived from Experience 7.1) different from yours. As a group experiment, read the excerpted article "Teaching to the Distinctive Traits of Minority Students" (Figure 7.7). Each group member should individually read, summarize, and respond in a two- to three-paragraph informal writing. After about 20 minutes, get together and compare your written responses. Did the different learning styles or race/ethnicity of the members impact their different points of view?

7.4 OBSERVE AN INSTRUCTOR'S TEACHING STYLE

Pick a course in which you are currently enrolled—one where your instincts tell you that the teaching style does *not* complement your learning style. Make a deal with another student in the class to provide you with a day's note set so that you can observe the instructor's teaching style for an entire class period and take notes on what you observe.

Soon after, share your observations with a classmate to validate your observations. It may very well be that other students in the class are experiencing the same difficulties. Using the information from Figure 7.6, discuss and invent strategies for aligning your learning style strengths with your instructor's teaching style. In what ways can you improve your abilities to handle the course effectively?

Can You Relate?

ESSAY *7.1*

Write a letter to one or all of your current college professors in which you explain your personality and strengths and your preferences about how you learn in college. Your letter should be written in the first person and organized in a way that makes it easy for the instructor to see what you need to be a successful learner. Include an interpretation of your Keirsey and/or Multiple Intelligences Inventory to help provide as much information for the instructor as possible. Proofread your letter; add details as you revise. Your letter should be a well-organized, 350 to 400-word analysis of yourself as a learner, including recommendations for how the instructor(s) can help you. Be thorough; you just may want to send this letter to one or more instructors you will encounter while in college!

ESSAY *7.2*

Learning styles may be defined as "differences among people in the attitudes, values, and approaches they bring to learning." Much attention has been given to learning style theories, differences among the learning styles of different racial and ethnic groups, and the educational implications of these differences. There has been a great deal of controversy surrounding these issues.

To investigate a particular point of view about learning styles, read the excerpts given on the following page in Figure 7.7 from a 1990 article written by James A. Vasquez.[8] His premise is that different ethnic minority groups learn in different ways. You may wish to mark noteworthy information. Note the language the author uses to refer to different groups. Be a critical reader; find points with which you agree and/or disagree.

After reading and annotating, brainstorm ideas. Then, in a well-constructed essay, review some of the learning style theories discussed in this chapter and cite the differences among learning styles of the various groups mentioned in the excerpted article. Finally, respond to the implications of these theories for you as a learner. Do you agree or disagree with the author's basic premise? Support or refute the notion that different groups tend to have different learning styles. Is this notion true, or is it merely stereotyping? Use examples from the text and your own experiences to support your argument.

FIGURE 7.7) *Excerpts.*

"Teaching to the Distinctive Traits of Minority Students"

. . . It is not uncommon to find that many teachers, both minority and mainstream, are unable to identify distinctive traits among ethnic minority youths. . . . In this article I will identify several traits in each of three minority student groups and will show their distinctiveness when contrasted with traits commonly believed to characterize students from mainstream society. . . .

. . . Many Hispanic students are distinguished by a sense of loyalty to the family. . . . Socialization of this type cannot help but produce in the individual a sense of motivation that is other-directed, one that seeks its impetus . . . from the family. I contrast this to the strong sense of individualism . . . that is found in many mainstream families, where young people are taught that life is in their hands.

. . . Hispanic and mainstream youths also differ significantly along the dimensions of cooperation and competition. . . . We find that mainstream youths are said to learn early on to be competitive . . . that it is okay to achieve at school at someone else's expense.

. . . [Another researcher] wrote that research has found black students, from an early age, to be more significantly person-centered than mainstream children, who are characterized by an object-centered approach to learning. . . . This distinction between black and white children takes on considerable importance when we become aware of the requirement in typical classrooms to focus on objects (mathematics, natural phenomena, letters of the alphabet, rules, etc.), not people, for extended periods of time in order to learn well . . .

. . . [The same researcher] noted that Afro-American children . . . are taught to concentrate on many stimuli at one time . . . although Euro-American children were apparently socialized to "tolerate monotony or unvaried presentation of material . . .

. . . Black children may be more receptive to learning that allows them to use their skills in the oral tradition . . . although mainstream children are thought to have a stronger orientation to the written word as a major source of gathering information . . .

. . . Some Native American students are said to be characterized by a deductive, or holistic, approach to learning . . . Students so characterized are thought to be more responsive to an overview or "big picture" presented at the beginning of a lesson. . . . Many, if not most mainstream students . . . learn better when the details are presented first and the direction of learning is from the particulars of a lesson to more general concepts . . .

. . . Some Native American children have difficulty in coping with the direct type of criticism that failure in the classroom inevitably brings. . . . Researchers reporting this trait suggest that in some Native American communities, learning among youth often takes place as the learner practices the skill to be mastered privately, and only after an acceptable degree of mastery . . . will he or she attempt to publicly demonstrate it.

. . . Yet traditional practice in the public classroom assumes no difference in this area among students, and teachers regularly make failure an inevitable experience in the classroom. . . . The emphasis on keeping one's errors within one's own private experience . . . combined with a relative lack of competitive spirit among Native American students, seems to work to their disadvantage . . .

The basic point in seeking to implement culturally appropriate instructional strategies is to assure that the strengths students bring to the classroom are the factors that give shape to the content, context, and mode of instruction employed by the teacher.

Source: Vasquez

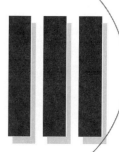

Relating with Your Institution

LEARNING AND DECISION MAKING

CHAPTER 8 Negotiating "the System":
Finding Your Place

CHAPTER 9 Exploring Majors and Careers:
Why, When, and How

CHAPTER 10 Managing Time, Jobs, Money, and Stress:
Keeping It All Together

CHAPTER

8

Negotiating "the System"

FINDING YOUR PLACE

YOUR INSTITUTION

Part I of this book discusses relationships with ideas and information, and Part II describes relationships with instructors and other students to improve your learning in college. Part III examines relationships with your institution—the instructors, the people who keep it running, and the ones who create and enforce the rules, as well as the many different kinds of students who learn and are trained there. No matter whether your school's total enrollment is 300 or 30,000, you need to understand the workings of the system at your institution and find *your* place in it. More people are participating in higher education than ever before, and everyone needs a niche—a place to belong.

Colleges, universities, and their citizens come in all sizes, shapes, designs, and colors. Type and governance, size, graduate vs. undergraduate emphasis, gender balance, race/ethnicity, and resource criteria ($$) characterize each institution. There are key characteristics and unique features of each. Which type of school do you attend? Which is right for you? The "goodness of fit" between you and your school is certainly an important factor in your level of success and satisfaction while in college.

The two broadest categories of postsecondary schools are *colleges* and *universities,* and within these two categories can be found all of the following.

- *Colleges,* with the exception of "community" and "vocational" colleges, are four-year (or five-year) institutions that grant bachelor's degrees. If you obtain such a degree, you are a "college graduate." Colleges and universities are supported by a mixture of state funds (if public), endowments, investments, alumni support, tuition charges, and grants.

- *Universities* are large colleges—schools with a wide array of academic offerings. Universities offer bachelor's degrees; in addition, they offer master's degrees, which require one to two years of study past the bachelor's. About half of all universities offer doctoral degrees (Ph.D., Ed.D., etc.) which require additional hours of credit, time, and work in areas of study beyond the master's. Universities are often organized by schools or colleges, such as the College of Education or College of Liberal Arts; School of Business, Agriculture, Health-Related Professions, Law, or Medicine. Think of a university as a big collection of colleges.

- *Public colleges and universities* often have a high research orientation, a strong emphasis on resources and reputation, higher student-faculty ratios, lower student-faculty interaction, and greater distances in communication between students and the administration.

- *Public four-year colleges* are considered to be "comprehensive colleges and universities."[1] Most of these schools have master's programs, and many have doctoral programs and professional schools, yet their primary mission tends to be undergraduate education, which is very good news for the undergraduates! Four-year colleges are complex, diverse institutions.

- *Private colleges and universities* have smaller student bodies, lower student-faculty ratios and higher student-faculty interaction; therefore, retention rates tend to be higher in these schools.

- *Independent (nonsectarian) colleges* typically have high student satisfaction, with student support services and opportunities to take interdisciplinary courses. They tend to be permissive and liberal and to have a high degree of academic competitiveness.

- *Historically Black colleges* have a high social change and diversity orientation, and attendance at such colleges has been shown to have positive effects on students' GPAs, student-faculty relationships, and overall satisfaction with the college experience.

- *Tribal colleges* emerged in the 1960s as a reaction to an educational void within the dominant society, and by 1992 totaled 24 tribally controlled colleges "scattered from the state of Washington to Michigan and from North Dakota to Arizona. These colleges serve a wide variety of tribes, but all adhere to several basic principles in their mission statements."[2] They operate as two-year schools that combine preservation of Native American cultural heritage with preparation for transfer to a four-year school or successful entry into employment. Other Indian schools, such as Haskell Indian Nations University in Lawrence, Kansas, are four-year schools funded by the Bureau of Indian Affairs.

- *Women's colleges* have a strong emphasis on leadership, academic development, small institutional size, residential life, diversity orientation, and overall academic development.

- *Predominantly men's colleges,* a fading phenomenon, generally rate high satisfaction with the overall quality of instruction, faculty, and individual support services.

- *Protestant colleges* tend to have a strong emphasis on majors in the humanities, a faculty that tends to be conservative, and less emphasis on research orientation than some other colleges and universities.

- *Roman Catholic colleges,* according to Astin,[3] tend to have a low level of permissiveness, a low level of racial conflict, a strong commitment to social activism, and a high percentage of women on the faculty. There tends to be a low level of racial diversity at Roman Catholic colleges.

- *Community colleges and two-year colleges* "were originally founded as relatively small institutions with the primary mission of providing young people of traditional college age with the first two years of a liberal arts education. [Yet] these institutions now serve primarily a different clientele: older, part-time, adult, and vocational or terminal education students."[4] These institutions are diverse, especially by age, and they are often nonresidential. Classes tend to be small and are mainly taught by regular faculty. Attendance at these schools is on the rise.

The beauty of the development and transformation of community colleges and two-year schools is that though the student body is diverse, a powerful sense of community often develops. Adult students with families, outside jobs, and a wealth of life experience can commute, learn, and pursue educational goals in small daily, nightly, or weekend classroom settings.

THE SYSTEM: PEOPLE AND POLICIES

"Both students and institutional environments contribute to what students gain from college."[5] Who's really in charge at your college or university, anyway? Is it the Trustees (or Regents or Curators), the president, chancellor, provost, deans, alumni, or what combination of players? In some ways the title of the chief academic officer does not matter, because a college or university is a hierarchical **bureaucracy.** A good administrator and a good instructor don't have the same qualifications. To serve effectively, administrators and instructors must have different interests and loyalties. The bottom line is how effectively schools can operate and serve students with the constraint of limited resources for operation.

bureaucracy an agency characterized by systematic administration, specialized function, "top-down" governance, often full of layers of procedures and "red tape"

Administrators are interested in productivity. They keep things going and under control; they make sure the budgets get stretched and the bills get paid. They keep the bureaucracy operating through good management and public relations, setting standards, establishing committees and task forces to investigate the need for changes, and by top-down decision making (this often means the people with the highest salaries have the most influence). Jacob Neussner, a former professor at Columbia University, Dartmouth College, Brown University, and other schools, makes an important distinction between bureaucrats and college teachers.

> The mentality of bureaucrats stands at odds with what they administer in schools and colleges. It is one thing to write the book of rules and follow them when one is a captain in the army or a director of a government bureau or the manager of a corporate office. It is quite another to bring those same values into the schools. What makes a good teacher is not the ability to follow a book of rules, but the ability to criticize the rules and ask why they are there. That is not because criticism is what we do. It is because teaching is what we do. And to teach, we must bring to life our students' and our own capacity for response, for thought and reflection—and that means to criticize.[6]

All sorts of administrators, faculty, and support staff, such as secretaries, computer programmers, custodians, food service employees, library staff, coaches, security guards, university police, and academic advisors, run a college or university. Secretaries, as in all bureaucracies, are the first contacts—the gatekeepers for nearly all campus resources and services. Since the students are the main consumers in colleges and universities, the ways students are treated by different members of the hierarchy say a lot about the content and fabric of your campus community. Neussner has a powerful, appropriate vision for the ways colleges and universities should treat students.

> Universities ought to carry out the policy that education happens everywhere and all the time. Hence clear operating routines should express the policy that we are

here to solve the students' problems as best we can, to make them happy, to accommodate their wishes so far as we can. This we do by an appeal to reason and good sense, by a systematic and consistent refusal to say no when there is any possibility of saying yes. The world at large accommodates peoples' whims and allows people in authority—however trivial—to show the world how they feel this morning. We can do very little about the grouchy bus driver who closes the door in our face. We cannot get back at the rude salesperson, the needlessly officious guard or customs inspector, the one who never smiles, the one who never says yes. But in a university we do a great deal to cultivate a friendly spirit, an attitude of solicitous concern for students and all people.[7]

Whether you are 18 or 48, you may end up in the middle of a personal, academic, or financial situation that requires help from one or more offices on your campus. However, what Neussner is trying to say is that the people who work and teach at colleges and universities are interested and concerned about you, although the systems seem large and impersonal at times. If you get to know how the campus system works, for any problem you have there is a solution, and there are good people to help you—you just have to find them.

In Loco Parentis and Matters of Conduct

Rules! It is appropriate and expected for campuses to have both written and unwritten standards of behavior and character among the many parts of their identities. All campuses are communities, and all communities have both written and implicit, well-understood expectations for student behavior. Up until the student "revolution" of the 1960s, administrations of colleges and universities maintained a position of *in loco parentis,* "in place of the parent." Acting in place of the parent had many implications for the degree to which a school could meddle in students' private affairs or make judgments about their welfare. Not surprisingly, the parents of the students appreciated this "parental" institutional position more than did the students! You can no doubt relate. . . .

Thus, for decades the courts backed colleges and universities in their role as "parents," but that legal authority has diminished over time, and institutional policies have been changing along with the law. For example, up until the 1960s, schools could deny admission to students who were married and/or pregnant. Thirty years ago, men's and women's residential halls were separate, but not equal. Women had hours restrictions; they had to be in their rooms by a certain time (slightly later on weekends), and the residence hall staff could go room to room performing "bed checks." Men were either not allowed in women's living quarters at all, or there were strictly enforced rules for their visits. (For instance, believe it or not, a visiting couple had to keep at least one foot each on the floor at all times and the door had to be open.) Administrators actually thought the "one foot" rule would keep couples from doing anything "naughty!" Can you imagine what college life was like back then?

According to David A. Hoekema, the old *in loco parentis* doctrine had four related powers:

1. The authority to direct the behavior of students beyond the rules of other social institutions.
2. The authority to punish rule violations, within limits.
3. The special authority of care for students.
4. The exemption from limits on searches carried out in conjunction with the enforcement of school rules.[8]

However, "the times they are a' changing. . . ." Today, 18-year-old college students, along with older students, are legally able to vote, sign contracts, marry,

apply for credit, or incur debt without parental consent—in some states, even purchase alcohol. If you are 18 or older, you are eligible for medical treatment without
your parents' consent; you can even block your parents from finding out your
grades! Overall, college and university students have *come of age,* and all these
legal changes have diminished the college's role as parent. So what, then, is the
most common, current relationship between postsecondary institutions and you,
their students?

Higher education advocate Ernest Boyer suggests that what is needed now is a
post *in loco parentis* theory of governance—"a set of agreed-upon standards to
guide the conduct of all members of the community and give direction to the institution overall."[9] College handbooks are beginning to reflect the fact that many
institutions' stances have changed to more of an *in loco avunculi* ("in place of the
uncle") relationship, which Hoekema calls a more "directive stance" that is "neither
restrictive or permissive."[10]

Schools that adopt such an approach to conduct and discipline do not seek to
control student behavior directly; they try to influence behavior by means other
than disciplinary rules and sanctions, such as education programs dealing with
alcohol, drug abuse, sexual harassment, and rape. Many schools are integrating diversity awareness and issues of personal and civic responsibility, such
as volunteerism, into the curriculum—the fabric of the institution. Many
schools now rely on example, persuasion, and codes of ethics and values
rather than endless rules and policies to be enforced. At least you don't have
to keep one foot on the floor anymore!

There are many types of campus policies, but no campus is neutral, and
none should be, with regard to issues of conduct and behavior. All campuses
have disciplinary philosophies that are meant to protect both the rights of individuals and the well-being of the campus community. According to Hoekema, there are
three basic, legitimate purposes for student conduct regulation.

1. To prevent or punish exploitation and harm inflicted or suffered by students
2. To prevent or punish behavior that undermines the academic values of free discussion and learning
3. To foster a sense of moral community and mutual responsibility[11]

The above list is a worthwhile general framework for student rules, yet, unfortunately, today's campuses still have difficulty regulating the areas of alcohol and
drug abuse, harmful or unsafe sexual behavior, hate speech, and "anonymous"
hate crimes. To illustrate, a 1990 study by Ernest Boyer found that "two-thirds of
all college presidents rate alcohol abuse a serious problem and at research doctoral institutions it's 82 percent. . . . When [the Boyer group] asked *all* presidents
to name their greatest concern, substance abuse, especially alcohol, was listed
number one."[12]

Such areas of the college experience are difficult to legislate or enforce, but
these issues are very important. The end of *in loco parentis* places more responsibility on you and other students. You are affected daily by your actions regarding
these areas. Students stay in or leave colleges because of good or poor decision
making in these, as well as other, aspects of their collective college experiences.
Staying in college is about much more than grades alone.

One of your responsibilities as a member of any campus community is to
understand and define acceptable codes for your conduct. Because of the changes
in the laws, you need to be aware of the outcomes of your and your friends'
choices of actions. Take time to read your student handbook or the campus policy
book, or whatever it's called at your school. You'll learn a lot about your school's
overall philosophy toward policies and discipline. Misunderstanding campus policies can bring unpleasant consequences, and being informed can help you avoid
bad decisions.

Some student rules by necessity remain in print, and the violation of such policies can have devastating effects. For example, one such enduring, universal area of concern among colleges and universities is the serious problem of plagiarism and/or academic dishonesty.

Plagiarism and Academic Dishonesty

Academic honesty is a mark of *integrity*. While colleges and universities have moved away from *in loco parentis* and have placed more responsibility on students for regulating their own behavior, most of today's campuses still do not leave matters of plagiarism and academic honesty to the sole discretion of students. There have been some student-initiated attempts on some campuses at using codes of honor to deter academic dishonesty. However, there are firm rules in place to govern academic dishonesty, especially at large or small public institutions. *Get to know and fully understand your school's policies regarding academic honesty!*

Academic dishonesty is considered to be a highly serious offense in every academic community. In fact, instructors at most colleges and universities are required to include a formal statement of the serious consequences of academic dishonesty in their syllabuses or course outlines. For example, at Yale University, the rules in the *Undergraduate Regulations* against cheating are meant to include all forms of "misrepresentation in academic work," including

a. the submission of the same paper in more than one course without the explicit authorization of the appropriate instructors;
b. cheating on tests, examination problem sets, or any other exercise;
c. any form of plagiarism, especially failure in an essay to acknowledge ideas or language taken from others, and the submission of work prepared by another person; and
d. submission of a scientific research report that misrepresents in any way the work actually done.[13]

plagiarism the robbing of others' words to use as your own

Plagiarism may be defined as using another's work, words, or ideas without giving credit or "citing" your source(s). Why is plagiarism considered to be such a heinous crime? In the academic world, the most important "currency" or object of exchange is *ideas*. Therefore, the academic *theft* of ideas by lack of not citing, or giving credit for, the borrowing of words and ideas, is one of the biggest, most serious crimes you can commit while in college. Honesty in your academic work is considered to be a sacred trust, and plagiarism results in very serious sanctions against those who attempt it.

The consequences of plagiarism may range from a failing grade to suspension (forced withdrawal for a term or a year) to total expulsion. How can you avoid plagiarism? Again referring to Yale University's *Undergraduate Regulations,* the following are some wise points to follow:

- Take clear notes in which you keep your own thoughts distinct from those you derive from your reading, so that you do not inadvertently submit the words or ideas of others as your own.
- Remember that you should acknowledge unpublished as well as published sources. This includes the work of other students and ideas that you may have derived from lectures and conversations.
- Do not suppose that because your instructor is an expert in the field, he or she needs little or no documentation in your work. An essay must stand on its own and not as a form of conversation with the instructor. In preparing a paper, it will help you to assume a larger audience than your instructor; imagine everyone in your class, for example, reading your paper; this will give you a surer sense of what to document and what to take as common knowledge.

- Mark and identify all quotations; give the source of translations; regularly acknowledge specific ideas; and give the source of facts not commonly known. If you are in doubt as to what may be "commonly known," that is a signal that you should document it, even at the risk of appearing overcautious or simplistic.[14]

What then, constitutes cheating? You probably have a fair idea. Copying from notes or another person's work during an examination; borrowing another student's problem sets, computer programs, or homework assignments and submitting them as your own; getting help of some sort on take-home examinations; and so on— all are considered cheating. The punishments for cheating in college are nearly as stiff as those for plagiarism. Such sanctions may include a failing grade, suspension, which is a required withdrawal, or even expulsion. Some schools mark the "F" on the transcript as resulting from academic dishonesty.

Acts of academic dishonesty, such as plagiarism or cheating, may very well remain on your permanent record. Most schools refuse to remove them. In some cases having committed an act of academic dishonesty could result in not being hired for a job or being denied certification necessary for certain careers such as education and social work. The effects of an intentional or even unintentional act of academic dishonesty can have devastating, long-term consequences. When in doubt about citing sources, ask your instructors for specific guidelines; leave nothing to chance. With regard to cheating, *don't do it; it's not worth it!*

All Students Have Basic Rights

In addition to sanctions against dishonesty, colleges and universities also have means to *protect* their students from potentially harmful situations. You have legal rights concerning your official college records (right to privacy, right to access) stemming from the 1975 Family Educational Rights and Privacy Act. In addition, your customary, procedural rights include the three general rights shown in Figure 8.1.[15] Every college and university has specific procedures and guidelines created for students to protect their rights. It's important to get to know in detail your school's procedures!

Overall, the faculty, staff, and administrators at your college or university want you to have a successful and satisfying experience, and they use important channels and procedures to protect you and to help you learn and grow to your fullest.

GETTING TO KNOW CAMPUS RESOURCES AND STUDENT SERVICES

Getting oriented involves much more than knowing the rules, your rights, your course schedule, and how to find your classes. By now, you've probably become somewhat acquainted with the layout of your campus. However, the larger the campus, the more

---

FIGURE 8.1   *Basic student rights.*

1. Grade appeal. This right permits you to submit a dispute over test or course grade to an arbitrator, such as the course supervisor, department head, or a special student–instructor grievance committee.
2. Adjustment of course requirements for illness or personal emergencies. This right permits you to make up missed examinations, to have extensions of due dates for papers or research projects, or to substitute independent study for class work missed because of unavoidable absences.
3. Proper and professional conduct of instruction in a course. This right permits you, in the unlikely event your instructor is unqualified or unprofessional, to appeal to a course supervisor, department head, or academic dean.

complex this task becomes. Your schedule of classes, the campus telephone directory, your student handbook, and/or the course description catalogue no doubt contain campus maps. Most campuses have maps with "You are here" marked to help orient new students and visitors. Many first-year students tour their campuses a day or two before classes begin, at least to locate their classrooms and the library, so they won't look lost and clueless when classes begin. In fact, many first-years don't like to be seen in public holding their schedules, because *everyone will know they are new students!* It is very important that you get to know all about your school.

Support Services and Facilities: The Places for Assistance

There are many important places on campus that you may never seek out unless you need or want their specific services. Even if your campus is huge, get acquainted with key buildings and offices *before* you may need them; don't wait for a potential crisis! Take a stroll around campus and get to know your "community." Different schools have different numbers and kinds of resources and services, yet many are standard in all colleges and universities. Figure 8.2 lists some of the more common services and opportunities, with spaces provided for you to add location and telephone number for ready reference if and when you need help or want to "get involved." After all, you're going to refer to this fine book for years to come, right?

STAYING IN COLLEGE MEANS GETTING A LIFE

In *Ethics and College Student Life,* Strike and Moss suggest that there are five components to "getting a life" in college: "authenticity, discovering what's worthwhile, finding a place, finding a vocation, and developing a resource base for one's life."[16] Let's examine what each of these components may mean to you.

Authenticity. You're probably tired of hearing that college is a time for "self-discovery." It *is* true. While you're in college, you get to examine who you are and explore who you want to become. These explorations are a sum total of all that you choose to do and learn. If you listen closely to the ideas of others—students, parents, instructors, staff—you will get a world of advice, and that's important. Ultimately, however, you are the master of your own fate. You gain authenticity when you do the hard work over time to determine who you are and to find the purposes for your life. As you become open to new ideas, this journey will help you stay in college and more fully enjoy the rest of your life.

Discovering what's worthwhile. Turn off the TV and video games, and get out and about! Consider the following ways to broaden your horizons:

- Find out, if you don't already know, which activities are suited to you. Might one be music? What kinds do you like, and what kinds have you never experienced? Art and culture—where can you find them? Would you like to perform? Would you prefer to watch others perform? What are your favorite activities? What do you want to try that you've never experienced? The college years afford you nearly unlimited opportunities to indulge in your passions—and to explore and discover new activities to experience and enjoy.
- Attend cultural events; broaden your horizons. Check with your Student Organizations and Activities office and investigate all the clubs and social organizations available to you.
- Colleges and universities have great museums!
- Participate in the extracurricular world. Join an organization just for fun. Attending and joining are about meeting new people and having new experiences.

FIGURE 8.2 | *Campus services and resources.*

ORGANIZATION	LOCATION	TELEPHONE
Academic Support or Learning Center; tutoring services		
Admission and Registration Offices		
Advising Center		
Athletics (intercollegiate or intramural)		
Bookstore		
Campus police		
Campus religious organizations		
Campus-sponsored activities, such as lectures, concerts, films, speakers		
Career Center		
Cashier or Bursar's Office		
Clubs, such as those for chess, engineering, French		
Community churches		
Counseling Center		
Financial Aid/Scholarship Office		
Fraternity/sorority system		
Honor societies and the Honors College		
Library (and other specialty libraries such as Law Library)		
Nontraditional student services		
Political organizations, such as Amnesty International, College Democrats and Republicans, NAACP (National Association for the Advancement of Colored People), NOW (National Organization for Women)		
Residential Life/Housing Office		
Specific interest groups, such as those for African-Americans, Hispanics or Latinos, Native Americans, international students, women, gays and lesbians, other minorities		
Student Center or Commons (gathering place with food and recreation available)		
Student Government Office		
Student Health Clinic		
Student Legal Services		
Student Life Center (where you can find out about campus clubs and organizations)		
Student Recreation Center (gym)		
Study Abroad programs		
Others? You name them!		

Are you interested in becoming a member of a fraternity or sorority? For some students, the Greek system is a great means of academic and social support.

- Spend time with students from other racial, ethnic, or social groups. If you are lucky, you may meet new people who will remain lifelong friends, or you may simply add to your set of acquaintances. There's more to getting involved in college than finding "Ms. Right."

- As discussed in Chapters 5 and 6, academic involvement beyond attending classes is worthwhile and will make a huge difference in your success and satisfaction. Alexander Astin, whose extensive research has examined all aspects of college life, lists involvement as a key component in the undergraduate experience. Student-faculty and student-student involvement are critical, and may include such activities as talking with instructors outside of class, having an instructor critique your work, working on instructors' research projects, participating in campus demonstrations, tutoring, or working in study groups. Obviously, academic involvement (see Chapters 5 and 6) will help you stay in college.

vocation a "calling" or life mission—work that enables you to be true to your abilities and your heart

Finding a place. Attending events, joining organizations, relating to instructors, staff, and other students of all ages, shapes, and colors will help you find out where you belong. Your place may be working in a particular job, working for a particular cause (see pages 150–151 for a discussion of volunteerism), or spending time with friends who hold similar values and interests. All students must have places to grow besides their classrooms and their residences! Finding your *place* will help you stay in college.

Finding a vocation. Finding what you are meant to do is a key part of your college experience. Sometimes finding what you are *meant* to do involves more than picking a major that, if you are successful, will lead you to a satisfying, even high-paying, job. All students must find their way through the mazes of majors and careers. (See Chapter 9 for a discussion of majors and career choices.) You may spend a good deal of time, energy, and perhaps frustration in making and acting on your career decisions and your major course of study. However, a **vocation**, considered to be different from a job, is more than what you do for a livelihood. A vocation is work that you do for reasons more complex than money or pleasure. A vocation is a match with your inner self—with your heart and your spirit. If you are open to the possibilities, your college years may help you find not just a job, but the vocation for which you have energy and passion. Finding your vocation may be a key to the rest of your life.

Developing a resource base for your life. We traditionally think of resources in terms of acquiring marketable skills, getting a job, and having an adequate income. Going to college can also give you the resource of a life perspective—a feeling for who you really want to be and what your values are. Strike and Moss advise:

> We suggest that the real trick to getting the most out of college is to be open to change about the kind of person you want to be, what you think is worthwhile, what you want to do, and where you belong. Indeed, the trick to developing your economic potential is to apply these questions to the marketable skills you seek to acquire, as well as asking, 'how much does it pay?' All students should ask themselves 'How do I wish to be transformed? To what possibilities about myself am I open?' Even (especially) about [my] future occupations?[17]

Multiple Senses of Belonging

Well, where *do* you belong? One astute observer of undergraduate education notes that "except on a limited number of small campuses, most students' sense of belonging will be multiple."[18] The reasons for and ways of getting a life in college require that you play many roles in many different settings. The size and/or hetero-geneity of your school could inhibit you from forming relationships broadly throughout the entire campus. While a campus is a community, remember that communities consist of neighborhoods, fascinating cultures and subcultures, cliques, and an endless number of different groups.

No matter what your age, a personal goal while in college should be to actively develop a "multiple sense of belonging," which comes from exploring campus resources, services, organizations, opportunities, neighborhoods, intersections, nooks and crannies, and the broader community of which your school is a part. With which parts of campus life do you currently identify? Which "neighborhoods" or cultural milieus have you yet to explore? Make the time to find your *places* in college, with people both like you and different from you.

INCLUSION AND DIVERSITY ON CAMPUS

America's growing diversity makes it more important than ever for all of us to understand people who are different, in a variety of ways, from ourselves. Because of the multicultural nature of colleges and universities, campuses have a unique opportunity and a heavy responsibility to address diversity issues. Along with campus policies and rules, attitudes about diversity are evolving on college campuses and throughout the country.

For example, a first-ever collaborative statewide poll on diversity in higher education was conducted from March 6 to March 13, 1997, in the state of Washington.[19] The poll reached 600 registered voters by phone and was supplemented with 100 additional interviews with African-Americans, Asian-Americans, and Hispanics. Excerpts from the Executive Summary include attitudes toward diversity such as those shown in Figure 8.3.

The results of the Washington State poll have important implications. Think back to the notion of "multiple senses of belonging." Your college years afford you the chance to get to know a wide variety of students, instructors, and staff. On your campus you may encounter and get to know a broad array of people, especially other students from many diverse groups.

FIGURE 8.3 *1997 Washington State diversity poll (excerpts).*

- Diversity education was defined as "formal course work and campus activities aimed at teaching differences among people in terms of culture or background. This includes issues of race, ethnic background, social class or gender."
- Nine out of ten respondents thought that in 20 years, they "would be living in neighborhoods that were more diverse . . . than now."
- 73 percent agreed that diversity on campus has a positive effect on the "general atmosphere on campus."
- 77 percent agreed that diverse student bodies have positive effects on the education of students.
- 78 percent agreed that it's just as important for colleges to prepare students to succeed in a diverse world as it is to provide them with technical or academic skills.
- 70 percent agreed that there is a lot of important information about various cultures in the United States that has been overlooked by college faculty in the past.
- 79 percent agreed that the changing characteristics of America's population make diversity education necessary.
- 87 percent agreed that in our multicultural society, the more we know about each other, the better we will get along.

Source: Association of American Colleges and University of Maryland

Colleges and universities, all in their own various ways, are working to dismantle the ignorance which causes oppression based on racism, sexism, ageism, classism, homophobia, and discrimination against the differently-abled individuals. As in the case of student conduct issues, campuses have both official and implicit yet understood policies regarding sensitivity to diversity on campus. The official federal nondiscrimination clause is part of all public colleges' and universities' print policies. Most often it is printed in the following wording:

"[Insert name of school or college] *does not discriminate on the basis of race, color, religion, national origin, ancestry, sex, age, disability, status as a disabled veteran, or veteran of the Vietnam era.*"[20]

Never mind the official "policy" of nondiscrimination. While such policies have both real and symbolic significance, part of your challenge as a college student is to examine your own beliefs and actions and to take some risks and grow intellectually. College life affords you the time and experiences that can enable you to truly become "a citizen of the world" and to become acquainted with all the groups that are currently attending colleges and universities right along with you.

Who Are Currently Attending Colleges and Universities?

The statistics may surprise you. Figures 8.4 through 8.10 list groups and the percentage of total U. S. college enrollment each group represented in 1995–97.[21] Note that you are a member of more than one of these groups, and you will find yourself counted in more than one set of the figures.

- **How many colleges and universities are there nationally?** Figure 8.4 shows the numbers in 1997.
- **What are the backgrounds of students enrolling in colleges and universities?** Figure 8.5 shows educational levels, gender, and racial and ethnic variety among students nationwide.
- **What are the ages of college students today?** Figure 8.6 shows college enrollment by age of students, Fall 1995.
- **What was the college enrollment by racial and ethnic group in 1996?** Figure 8.7 reveals those data.
- **Who were the college first-years in the fall of 1997?** Figure 8.8 shows racial and ethnic backgrounds by gender.
- **Why did the first-year students of Fall 1997 choose the schools they did?** Figure 8.9 gives reasons noted as very important in selecting the college attended, split for comparison by gender.
- **What were the top ten countries of origin of international students in terms of total enrollment in 1996–97?** Figure 8.10 enumerates those countries.

FIGURE 8.4 *Colleges and universities in the U. S., 1997.*

COLLEGES/UNIVERSITIES	NATIONAL TOTAL
Public 4-year institutions	613
Public 2-year institutions	1,088
Private 4-year institutions, non-profit	1,510
Private 4-year institutions, for-profit	144
Private 2-year institutions, non-profit	184
Private 2-year institutions, for-profit	470
Total	4,009

Source: *The Chronicle of Higher Education*

FIGURE 8.5) *Student enrollment in the U. S. focusing on minority enrollment, 1997.*

STUDENT ENROLLMENT	NATIONAL TOTAL
At public 4-year institutions	5,806,036
At public 2-year institutions	5,314,463
At private 4-year institutions	2,998,157
At private 2-year institutions	248,864
Total Enrollment	**14,367,520**
Undergraduate	12,326,948
Graduate	1,742,260
American Indian	137,557
Asian-American	828,166
Black	1,505,565
Hispanic	1,166,108
White	10,263,865
International	466,259

ENROLLMENT HIGHLIGHTS	NATIONAL PERCENTAGE
Women	55.8%
Full-time	57.8%
Culturally Diverse	26.2%
International	3.2%

PROPORTION OF ENROLLMENT MADE UP OF CULTURALLY DIVERSE STUDENTS

At public 4-year institutions	23.8%
At public 2-year institutions	30.9%
At private 4-year institutions	21.6%
At private 2-year institutions	31.8%

Source: *The Chronicle of Higher Education*

FIGURE 8.6) *College enrollment by age of students, Fall, 1995.*

AGE	NATIONAL TOTAL
Less than 18	2.0%
18 and 19	19.6%
20 and 21	18.4%
22 to 24	16.5%
25 to 29	14.8%
30 to 34	9.1%
35 to 39	6.9%
40 to 49	8.7%
50 to 64	2.5%
65 and older	0.6%
Age unknown	1.0%

Source: *The Chronicle of Higher Education*

FIGURE 8.7   *College enrollment by racial and ethnic group, 1996.*

RACIAL/ETHNIC GROUP	NATIONAL TOTAL
American Indian	137,600
Asian-American	828,200
Black	1,505,600
Hispanic	1,166,100
White	10,263,900
International	466,300

Source: *The Chronicle of Higher Education*

FIGURE 8.8   *Racial and ethnic background of first-year students, Fall, 1997.*

RACIAL/ETHNIC GROUP	TOTAL	MEN	WOMEN
American Indian	3.1	3.0	3.2
Black	10.6	9.9	11.1
White	80.7	80.7	80.7
Mexican-American	1.5	1.4	1.6
Puerto Rican	1.1	1.2	1.0
Other Latino	1.6	1.7	1.6
Chinese-American	1.4	1.6	1.2
Filipino-American	0.8	0.8	0.8
Japanese-American	0.4	0.4	0.4
Korean-American	0.7	0.7	0.7
Southeast Asian-American	0.6	0.7	0.6
Other Asian-American	1.4	1.5	1.3
Other	2.9	2.9	2.8

Source: *The Chronicle of Higher Education*

Did any of the above data surprise you or contradict your assumptions about the college population in the United States? It would appear from Figures 8.4 through 8.10 that all ages, gender distribution, races, ethnicities, and countries of origin have been accounted for in the most recent information available from *The Chronicle of Higher Education's 1998 Almanac Issue.* Can you find yourself and your friends among the statistics? This publication is one of the best, most thorough sources for information concerning the state of higher education in the United States. However, there is an "invisible minority" on campuses and throughout the world that does not get included in most displays of statistics such as the ones above.

Whom Do the Educational Statistics Overlook?

Research as old as the groundbreaking Kinsey Reports of 1948 and 1953 established early on that at least *ten percent* of the population is made up of gay, lesbian, or bisexual persons.[22] However, the federal nondiscrimination clause that many schools, cities, and organizations use as a model does not include the phrase "sexual orientation." In academia and in society at large, gays, lesbians, bisexuals, and transgendered persons are usually either ignored, or, quite often, harassed. These omissions and/or abuses deeply hurt a large number of faculty, staff, and students. If you are a gay, lesbian, or bisexual student, you may feel isolated and without support.

Ignorance and intolerance lead to violence and self-hatred; teenagers and young adults can be debilitated by the self-doubt caused by homophobia. A 1989 study conducted by the U. S. Department of Health and Human Services found that gay,

FIGURE 8.9 *Reasons noted as very important in selecting college attended, Fall, 1997.*

REASONS FOR SELECTING COLLEGE	TOTAL	MEN	WOMEN
Relatives' wishes	9.5	8.8	10.1
Teachers' advice	4.3	4.8	4.0
College has a very good academic reputation	53.9	49.7	57.4
College has a good reputation for its social activities	25.5	24.6	26.2
Offered financial assistance	33.8	29.6	37.3
College offers special education programs	21.8	18.0	25.0
Low tuition	30.1	26.8	33.0
Advice of high school counselor	8.2	8.1	8.3
Wanted to live near home	21.1	16.5	25.0
Friend's suggestions	10.1	10.0	10.2
Recruited by college	4.5	5.4	3.7
Recruited by athletic department	6.7	9.9	4.0
Not offered aid by first choice	5.2	4.9	5.5
Graduates gain admission to top graduate/professional schools	31.1	27.7	34.0
Graduates get good jobs	50.3	48.1	52.1
Religious affiliation/orientation of college	6.2	5.3	7.0
Size of college	34.4	27.4	40.3
Not accepted anywhere else	2.9	3.7	2.3
Rankings in national magazines	9.1	9.4	9.0

Source: The UCLA Higher Education Research Institute

FIGURE 8.10 *Top ten countries of origin of international students, 1996–97.*

COUNTRY OR TERRITORY	NUMBER OF STUDENTS
Japan	46,292
China	42,503
Republic of Korea	37,130
India	30,641
Taiwan	30,487
Canada	22,984
Malaysia	14,527
Thailand	13,481
Indonesia	12,461
Hong Kong	10,942

Source: *The Chronicle of Higher Education*

lesbian, and bisexual youth were two to three times more likely to attempt suicide than other young people, and that they may account for up to 30 percent of completed youth suicides.[23] An editorial in the October 17, 1998 issue of the *New York Times* entitled "The Death of Matthew Shepard" (the young gay man murdered in Wyoming in October 1998), quoted FBI statistics showing that "gay men and lesbians are six times as likely to be physically attacked as Jews or Hispanics in America, and twice as likely as African-Americans."[24]

Have you witnessed, experienced, or participated in acts of prejudice or discrimination based on sexual orientation? Are you part of the problem or part of the solution? Instructors and other campus personnel who deal with issues of diversity are often reluctant to discuss sexual orientation because of their fears of students' reactions to the topic: "If I include gays and lesbians in my discussions, will my students assume I am gay and reject me?"

homophobia the fear of people whose affectational orientations are towards others of the same gender

The truth is that discussions of diversity and discrimination on campuses or in the larger social order are incomplete unless **homophobia** and **heterosexism** are addressed and become a part of discussions about sensitivity to diversity and genuine inclusion. To address the omission or fear of these students, instructors, and staff on college and university campuses, there need to be clear understandings about the ways certain terms are used—or misused.

heterosexism the belief that heterosexuality is the only legitimate sexual orientation

"Homophobia refers to the actual fear and active resistance to individuals who are homosexual and to the idea of homosexuality. On the other hand, heterosexism is a common practice of defining everyone as heterosexual—that heterosexuality is the norm, the natural, the *only kind of sexuality.*"[25]

What difference does your level of understanding and appreciation make in the content of your life? If you are interested, there are no doubt groups on your campus whose function is to provide a more complete type of diversity training and multicultural awareness. If you are a gay, lesbian, or bisexual student, there very well may be one or more student organizations for you that will add social and emotional support to your life. We're living in a time when campuses, like society, are growing in their understanding and recognition of the "hidden minority."

RELATING TO THE COMMUNITY THROUGH VOLUNTEERISM AND "SERVICE LEARNING"

A former president of the American College Personnel Association, a powerful group of educators dedicated to improving student learning, has made an important observation: "Off-campus agencies (e.g., community service) and settings (e.g., work, church, museums) offer rich opportunities and students should be systematically encouraged to think about how their studies apply in those settings and vice versa."[26] In that spirit, high schools, community colleges, colleges, and universities are increasingly including volunteerism, community service, and/or "service learning" (community service for college credit) as part of the student learning experience. Service offers opportunities that are available to you in no other way; you learn about different people, their lives, and their ideas. Service to your campus or the community helps you understand and feel that you live not just on a campus, but as a member of a community and the world.

Going to college can make you feel isolated and disconnected from the rest of life around you. We all need to feel that we are part of something greater than ourselves. Therefore, do not resist the opportunity to give back to the campus or community. Many, many campus groups are involved in community service. Some college courses now include a service component, and there are programs that offer college credit for service, especially when the work is connected to your major or career goals. Check around—there are endless opportunities to work on projects that will add special meaning to your life.

Examples of types of volunteering include fundraising (The American Heart Association and similar organizations) or disaster relief (such as the cleaning up after a tornado) through the American Red Cross. There are plenty of service activities with kids, such as Big Brothers and Big Sisters or working with children in the public schools. You can work for needy people in soup kitchens or build homes for Habitat for Humanity. The list also includes church service projects, charity organization projects (the local United Way would be a good source of such projects) or work on election campaigns. You could work with elderly people or retirees, pitch in on environmental projects such as river and stream cleanup and recycling, do hospital or hospice service, work for The American Cancer Society, or work with people with AIDS.

If you cannot find a group involved with service to the campus or community, start one. It's easy to be lonely, but it's much better to be connected. Many students report that their volunteering increases their sense of responsibility, relieves stress, heightens their self-esteem, and helps them think through their career goals. In one report from Kent State University's Office of Service Learning, "about 90 percent of student volunteers [said] service-learning experience was as valuable or more valuable to them than their classroom work.[27]

Negotiating your way through your campus "system" and finding your "places" while you are in college is some of the most important work (and it is work, make no mistake) that you will do while in college. The future is in the hands of you, your peers, and all those who are doing the hard work now to prepare for a safer, saner, more humane and just tomorrow. Is that a possible "mission" you may choose to accept?

Journal Reflections

8.1 Find out about campus opportunities for volunteering within the community. Are there courses at your school that require community service? Would you be interested in such courses? Whether or not volunteerism is part of your school's curriculum, would you be interested in volunteer work? In what sort of service or agency would you like to get involved? Why?

8.2 Sometimes "questioning authority" is a worthwhile practice, and student voices can be a powerful means toward change. Does your school have a policy or policies with which you disagree? What is the policy, and why do you disagree? To whom on your campus would you (should you) take your concern? Do other students share your concern? Why or why not? What are the procedures for "questioning authority" at your college or university?

8.3 Look again at the Washington State Diversity Poll on page 145. What do the levels of agreement on each item seem to suggest about people's attitudes toward diversity issues? If you were to poll your student body about these issues, how do you think your campus's attitudes would support or differ from the Washington State results?

8.4 Review the discussion of the "hidden minority" on pages 148–150. What are your honest reactions to the discussion on heterosexism and homophobia? How do you react to this group? What is your campus climate toward gay men, lesbians, and bisexual students? How do the instructors and administrators on your campus react to this group? What recommendations do you have for recognizing and including this group of instructors, staff, and students?

Experiences

8.1 POLICY MANUAL INQUIRY

In pairs or small groups, investigate and discuss your school's student policy manual. After reviewing the policies, create lists of areas of conduct that have explicit rules, such as grading, academic honesty, drinking and drug use, smoking, and privacy of student records. What *are* the rules? Compare these with the policies that rely on codes of behavior for the community, such as tolerance and respect, free speech, personal space, and sexual behavior. What do you conclude about your school's overall philosophy regarding campus rules? What are the boundaries for your legal relationship with your school?

8.2 IMPORTANT POLICIES ON YOUR CAMPUS

After reviewing the policies, create lists of areas of conduct that have explicit rules. Refer back in your text to Hoekema's three purposes for student conduct regulation on page 139. Pick three to five different campus policies that you feel are most important to the safety and well-being of the campus community. Determine what purpose or purposes these regulations serve. Then write a justification for each policy to which other students and instructors would relate and agree.

8.3 CAMPUS POLICY IMPROVEMENTS

Review campus policies from the perspective of a disabled student, a commuter student, an "adult" or nontraditional student with job and family, and/or a part-time student. Which campus policies do and do not pertain to these lives in the campus community? Are the needs and concerns of "nontrads" appropriately met on your campus? (For example, is day care available on your campus?) What areas of policy might your campus need to address to meet *all* students' needs?

8.4 GET TO KNOW YOUR CAMPUS

Take a deep breath, round up a couple of friends, and get to know your campus! Find a detailed campus map and telephone directory, and make your goal to *locate* and get familiar with all the resources and services listed in Figure 8.2. You may wish to mark your map for future reference. This journey may not be as fun as a traditional scavenger hunt, but a resource and service "hunt" will pay you back for your efforts when you or one of your friends needs help!

8.5 HOW "DIVERSE" IS YOUR SCHOOL?

Examine Figures 8.4–8.10. In pairs or small groups, summarize the national statistics regarding the makeup of the undergraduate student body in the United States. Next, consult your campus registrar (or whoever can give you your campus enrollment statistics) and compare and contrast the national picture of those attending colleges and universities with your school's enrollment. Is your school more or less "diverse" than the national averages?

8.6 WEB ACTIVITY

Most community colleges, colleges, and universities now have their own Web sites. Determine whether your institution has one. If so, what is the Web address? What information is available on the site? Be very thorough. Consider all the following: administration, admissions, registration, course information, campus organizations, faculty and student information and directories, campus crime statistics, athletic events and schedules, campus employment opportunities, financial aid and scholarship availability, and library information. Which of this information is useful to you, and what else did you find of use? What would make this Web site easier to use?

Can You Relate?

ESSAY 8.1

Reflect on your progress in "negotiating the system and finding your place" in college so far by doodling a chart, web, or other visual representation (see Chapter 2) that illustrates your relationships with students, instructors, campus resources, and services. Use your sketch as an outline for the following essay. After planning, expect to write for 30–40 minutes; use real-life examples from your experiences to illustrate your essay.

Refer back in your text to Weingartner's notion of "multiple senses of belonging." Think of all the many ways you do or wish to belong on your campus. How far-reaching have your relationships on and with the campus become?

Characterize your current roles and "places" on campus. Be specific. Then speculate about your future—do you see your sense of belonging growing (perhaps in new directions) over time? In what areas? Look six months into the future, and then two years into the future, and contrast those future times to your present life. Describe your evolution as you continue to negotiate the system and your place(s) in it.

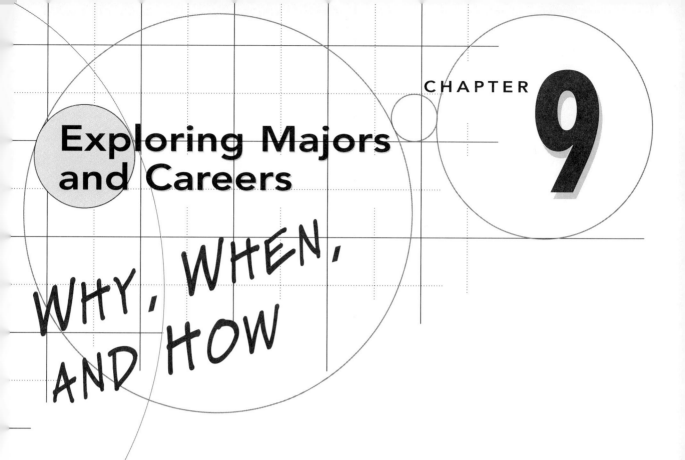

Exploring Majors and Careers

WHY, WHEN, AND HOW

Majors and Careers: Two Sides of the Coin?

"So what's your major, anyway?" If someone asks you that question, do you feel obligated to have an answer? Majors and careers—careers and majors—what's a student to do? How are you supposed to know what you want to do in college if you've never been in college before—or even if you have? This chapter suggests strategies for investigating majors and careers. Your college major ultimately will be the area in which you will take one-third to one-half of all your course work. The reason for having majors or "areas of concentration" has increasingly become to prepare students to enter the world of work. At least that's what most students, instructors, advisors, and department chairs think. Always keep in mind that working toward a major should be a somewhat pleasurable experience!

However, there's a widespread belief that if you major in *blank,* when you graduate you will become a *blank.* Actually, majors and careers are not precisely two sides of the same coin. Employers hire people, not their majors. More importantly, finding a major and a career is only one of many, many purposes of a college education. It's healthy and smart not to think of your choice of major merely as the key to big bucks. . . .

As you make your way through college, you will no doubt be required to take course work that seems irrelevant to your majoring in *blank* so you can become a *blank.* Why is that? Your college or university undoubtedly has "general education" requirements.

GENERAL EDUCATION REQUIREMENTS: HOW DO THESE RELATE?

"Core" Courses: Why?

"I'm going to be a biochemical engineer! Why do I have to take literature courses?" "I am a journalism major. I am a good writer, but I hate math. How will I ever pass statistics?" "I want to teach math in high school; do I really need to take a course in geography? What for?" "I'm terrible in [that subject], and a low grade will ruin my GPA!" Can you relate to these sentiments?

Depending on what you want to do when you get out of school, why must you enroll in a wide variety of introductory courses, many of which don't interest you? Why do most schools have a menu of "general education" courses that cover a broad spectrum of subjects? Why should a computer science major have to take history and literature?

In his important book, *College: The Undergraduate Experience in America,* Ernest Boyer has aptly observed:

> The foundation for a successful undergraduate experience is proficiency in the written and spoken word. Students need language to grasp and express effectively feelings and ideas. To succeed in college, undergraduates should be able to write and speak with clarity, and to read and listen with comprehension. Language and thought are inextricably connected and as undergraduates develop their linguistic skills, they hone the quality of their thinking and become intellectually and socially empowered.[1]

Language, then, is the key to learning—Boyer's message is one of the main themes interwoven into this book. General education courses in college afford language skills and information in a variety of areas. These courses help you see connections among disciplines and broaden your world perspective. As early as 1987, 95 percent of all four-year colleges were offering some form of general education.[2] General education courses include studies in such areas as English composition, mathematics, science, social and behavioral sciences, foreign language, the arts, literature, history, and computer skills.

Boyer's investigations have revealed that 75 percent of undergraduate students surveyed felt as though the general education program at their school "add(s) to the enrichment of other courses [they] have taken," and "help(s) prepare [them] for lifelong learning."[3] Yet there remains a natural tension between students' wanting to be well-rounded learners and to be specifically trained for jobs. Ordinarily, at a four-year school, your last two years of study will focus on your major area of study.

"Enriched Majors"

Ernest Boyer also has a vision for an "enriched major" as the "centerpiece of the undergraduate curriculum . . . This program of study encourages students not only to explore a field in depth, but also to help them put their field of study in perspective." For a major to be truly meaningful, then, Boyer says it must provide answers to the following questions:

- What is the history and tradition of the field of study to be examined?
- What are the social and economic implications to be understood?
- What are the ethical and moral issues to be confronted?[4]

These are excellent questions to explore. They help you understand the relationship between your plans for the future and the history and values of your chosen area of study.

How would an "enriched major" translate directly into your college experience? Ideally, your field of study should contain more than the acquisition of skills. If you are a biology major, you might study the history of biology and the lives and work of those who made groundbreaking biological discoveries—Leeuwenhoek (who?), Pasteur, Salk, Madame Curie, Watson and Crick (the double helix men). You may take a course in biomedical ethics to examine the social and ethical implications of biomedical research. If you are an engineering student, you may have course work that explores the effects of technology on the environment. If you are an aspiring journalist, you will no doubt study the ethics of reporting and the parameters of the First Amendment and the meaning of "freedom of the press." Mathematics majors usually study some history of mathematics and early mathematicians such as Pythagoras and Euclid.

If your four- or five-year plan of course work does not require courses in the history or ethics of your chosen field, you may wish to create your own "enriched major." You might use any elective hours to get more of a world view or "big picture" about your chosen field of study and its place in the broader society. The more you understand the history of your chosen profession, its relationship to you as a practitioner, and the larger social and ethical implications of your work, the more the field will have deep meaning for you, both while you're in college and as you enter the professional world.

Study Abroad Opportunities Enrich Your Major and Your Life

An old Armenian proverb says: "It is not he who has lived the longest, but he who has traveled the farthest, who knows the most." Does your school have a study abroad program? Study abroad programs are one of the fastest growing and most exciting opportunities available at many colleges and universities. These programs offer international educational opportunities for a summer, a semester, or a full year. An international experience will make you a better scholar, a more conscientious student, and a more effective professional. The challenge of living in a culture other than your own, learning to work with many different people, and overcoming difficulties experienced in another country can change your life.

Between campus-sponsored programs and partnerships with other international agencies such as the American Institute for Foreign Study (AIFS), students can now study everything from art history at the Louvre in Paris to rain forest ecology in Ghana. Other countries that provide educational opportunities for students include Australia, Costa Rica, Denmark, Germany, Ireland, Italy, Japan, Korea, Mexico, the Netherlands, Spain, Taiwan, Thailand, and the United Kingdom (including Scotland). The course offerings include intensive study of language and culture, science, nursing, engineering, business, and general courses applicable to most majors.

Currently, many students who study abroad do so during their sophomore year. Of course, if you wish to take advantage of this special experience, you have to investigate opportunities and plan early in order to balance your school's general education requirements and necessary study-abroad courses. Be sure to determine if the experience will add extra time to your college career, but know that the additional time is worth it! Many institutions have a goal of sending 10 percent of their students to study abroad by the year 2001.

Additionally, study-abroad programs and scholar programs, such as the Fulbright Program, may be exchange programs; therefore, you could also have the opportunity to host an international student and have that sort of cross-cultural experience. The Fulbright Program, in its 51st year, supports 900 international students at the master's and doctoral levels. If your school has an International Center, contact such an office for information on hosting and other opportunities for connecting with international students.

UNDECIDED, MAJOR-CHANGING, AND DECIDED STUDENTS

It's a universal quandary—a topic of ongoing debates among colleges over *what* and *how* they should teach you in order to help you define and achieve your goals for life during, and especially after, your college experience. One of your challenges as a college student is to find relevance in your general education requirements to your possible major and career goals.

Of course, choosing your major is also a big decision in and of itself. Many students enter college without a choice of major. Unfortunately, most colleges start asking you about your major the moment you express an interest in attending. It may not be easy, but you are not "at-risk" by being undeclared.

College admission forms always ask you to designate your choice of major, whether you have very firm goals or not a clue. Your institution asks you up front about your major and career aspirations in an effort to place you—to sort you into the "right" division. Having firm ideas about your major is a positive step, but you may be sure and definite or tentative, unsure, conflicted, or clueless. It's not bad to be an undecided student. Don't think that your college wants you to hurry up and pick a major. Choice is risky and scary. Try to remain comfortable during the process and time you need to find the right major!

The overwhelming conclusion of a study by nationally-known advising expert Virginia Gordon is that there are no real differences between students who have decided on a vocation and those who have not.[5] Other studies cite some differences in personality traits and demographic variables among decided, tentatively decided, and undecided students. All the same, it's all right to be undecided, a major-switcher, or a firmly decided student!

"Undecideds"

Most first-year students are undecided about majors and careers. New student orientation is a good time to begin to think about majors and careers. It is comforting to parents who attend new student orientation to see that there are often information sessions available that offer academic major and career information to students early on. However, one study has estimated that "over 20 percent of all students change majors between admissions and the start of classes."[6] Often, if you are undecided, you are undereducated about your options, and above all, you need strategies for decision making. You have a goal as much as the student seated next to you who *has* chosen a major. Your goal is *self-discovery!* Explore the answers to the five categories of questions in Figure 9.1 to help you in the process of finding a major that is right for you.

"Major-Changers"

It's not bad to be a major changer, either. Estimates reveal that 75 percent of college students are major changers.[7] Virginia Gordon describes five types of major-changers.[8] Do you recognize yourself or any of you friends among these "types"?

"The Drifters"

If you are a drifter, you may have entered college with a tentative plan for a major, but, sensing that your initial choice is wrong for you, you float around among your classes, avoiding making a decision until your school forces you to do so. You may have an excessively long undergraduate career. Don't you need some advice?

FIGURE 9.1 *Questions for undecideds.*

1. Interests
   - What did you like to do when you were younger? What kinds of games did you play?
   - What courses and activities did you like most in high school or in prior college work? In which courses did you receive the highest grades?
   - Why are you in college?
   - Which areas of study interest you now that you are in college? Which do not?

2. Skills
   - What do the results of your college entrance exams reveal about your areas of academic strengths and talents?
   - What useful skills have you developed throughout your life? In prior schooling or work experiences? What are you good at?
   - What skills would you like to cultivate to become the person you want to be?
   - What is the relationship between your skills and talents?

3. Aptitudes
   - For what sorts of activities do you possess some natural talent?
   - For what sorts of activities do you seem to lack natural talent?
   - Are you more of a math/science or humanities/social studies type?
   - What does having an "aptitude" really mean about you?

4. Personality
   - Are you more of an introvert or extrovert?
   - What qualities do your friends and family most appreciate about you?
   - Based on your investigation of your personality and learning styles in Chapter 7, for what areas of study and work might you be most suited?
   - What areas of study and work will enable you to be the person you want to be?

5. Life Goals and Work Values
   - In what sort of work environment do you see yourself five years from now?
   - Who has influenced your thinking about life goals and work values? In what ways? To what degree?
   - What sorts of occupations are you considering, and what aspects of these occupations do you find most appealing?
   - What is the relationship between your personal values and your work values?

"The Closet Changers"

If you are a closet changer, you have privately made a change in your plans, but you don't tell anyone, least of all your academic adviser, who may become confused at your odd choice of courses. Maybe you wish to avoid disappointing a family member or friend by confessing your change in career goals, or maybe you're just too proud to ask for help. You need some advice!

"The Externals"

If you are an external, you have no problem confessing your frequent major-switching. You'll listen to anyone and everyone for ideas about your major and career goals. Your disorganization in decision making entitles you to membership in the "Major-of-the-Month Club." This route of indecision may be intriguing, but you've got to do some soul-searching, seek advice, and get a plan that makes sense to you.

"The Up-Tighters"

If you are an up-tighter, you may have entered college with only one choice for your major and career. You may discover that this plan will not work, perhaps because the course of study does not match your abilities or interests, but you are reluctant to let go of your initial, and only, plan. Being an "up-tighter" can be a really miserable experience. You need some advice!

"The Experts"

If you are an expert, you are sure you know everything about your choice of major and career. You are not likely to ask anyone for help, and you are likely to have unrealistic goals to which you may steadfastly cling. You may enroll in courses you probably shouldn't be taking because they are too advanced or not really suited to your interests. Your stubbornness will get you into trouble. There are people who can help you. . . .

"Decideds"

Feel relieved, but don't feel superior because you think you are decided on a major and/or career. There's not always a direct connection between a major and a career. If you enter a college or university as a student who has firmly "decided" on a major, you are a bit of a risk-taker. You must possess some clear vision of your vocational goals, and you must have an understanding of which courses of study will best align with those vocational goals. You may be firm on your decision as you enter college, but use the first few semesters to test the "goodness of fit" between you and your chosen major. Taking classes required for your potential major and talking to more advanced students and professionals in your chosen field can serve as a reality check for you. You can also test your choice of major by sampling from elective courses that can show you other options and other possibilities.

How, with Whom, and When to Choose a Major

There are many ways to narrow the field and eventually decide on a major. Sometimes you enter college with a plan that falls apart in only one semester or term, or maybe you have no plan at all, and wonder exactly why you *are* in college.

Who Can Help? Working with Academic and Faculty Advisors

Many campuses have advising centers that are usually staffed full-time by professional advisors. Working with well-trained professional advisors who know about a variety of academic areas can be very helpful to undecided students. Since some students do not like to admit that they are undecided, advising centers offer a sense of privacy. Some colleges and universities now offer academic advising in the residence halls. This advising system may be carried out by professional advisors, instructors, or peer advisors.

The oldest, traditional means of advising is through the instructor or faculty advising system that occurs in instructors' offices. Instructor/advisors can provide specific information about the requirements for majors within their areas of expertise, and they are very helpful with long-term degree program planning. They will also know to whom to refer you if you wish to explore requirements for another major. Student-instructor contact is very important in establishing a good relation-ship (see Chapter 6) that is essential to college success.

Even though traditionally advisors and students spend limited time together, you and your advisor are a team. You must work together to develop a relationship in which your advisor is your teacher, perhaps your guide, but not your decision maker. Whether your advisor is a full-time staff advisor or an instructor, academic advising is about more than which classes you should take in a given term. A good advisor will help you explore career options, plan a course of study, provide infor-mation about degree requirements, *and* help you pick your classes. Unfortunately, some advising experiences focus only on "what you should take," but you have a responsibility to get "the big picture." Ask questions; take care of yourself; find out what you need to know!

Now that you are in college, pursue your interests, abilities, and talents hon-estly—the stakes are higher when you're actually in college and trying to decide what you want to be when you grow up! The survey in Figure 9.2[9] is a useful instru-ment to use to evaluate your situation as a new student and to begin planning strategies for deciding on major and occupation possibilities. While it may help you see your own situation more clearly, an excellent use of it would be to fill it out and take it with you to your next session with your academic advisor.

This information can help get a meaningful conversation started concerning your interests and the best ways an advisor can help you construct at least a tenta-tive course of study. Providing your academic adviser with this information will give you an advantage over students who don't know what to say or ask in their early advising sessions.

Interest Inventories Can Help

Your campus Career Center will have interest inventories available to you; some are on line. Interest inventories are widely used to help you organize what you like to do and what you enjoy. These inventories help answer the question, "Who Am I?" Some of the most widely used are:[10]

- The Strong Interest Inventory (SII)
- Ohio Vocational Interest Survey (OVIS)
- Kuder Occupational Interest Survey—Form DD
- Jackson Vocational Interest Survey (JVIS)

Though these instruments are not foolproof, they have been used successfully for over thirty years, and certain patterns emerge that are good predictors of satis-faction in certain careers.

You may have been given one or more interest inventories in high school, and you may have dismissed the results or at least not taken them seriously.

If you set your mind to use such surveys as recreation, you can answer them in a way that will "rig" the outcome. Some high school students have fun with these inventories, and the results are bogus. For example, one lighthearted senior decided that on the Kuder survey, he wanted to rig the results to indicate that he should be a fireman, just to irk his parents, both of whom were physicians and hoped he'd follow in their footsteps.

Electronic Information Sources

Visit your Career Center and discover which computerized career informa-tion systems are available to you. Each system is updated every year, so you will get the most current information available. Electronic sources include the following.[11]

FIGURE 9.2   *First-year orientation survey.*

1. ☐ Male   ☐ Female

2. Age: ☐ 17–19   ☐ 20–22   ☐ 23–25   ☐ Over 25

3. ☐ Married   ☐ Not married   ☐ Children

4. In which quartile (25%) of your high school class were you?
   ☐ Top quartile   ☐ Second quartile   ☐ Third quartile   ☐ Not sure

5. ☐ First-time freshman   ☐ Transfer

6. I will be living:
   ☐ in a residence hall
   ☐ at home with parents or relatives
   ☐ in own apartment or home

7. Why are you attending the university? (*Check one.*)
   ☐ a. To prepare for an occupation
   ☐ b. To become an educated person
   ☐ c. Because my parents expect it
   ☐ d. Because of the social opportunities
   ☐ e. Because my friends are
   ☐ f. To find myself
   ☐ g. Other (*Please specify.*)

8. How undecided are you about a major? (*Check one.*)
   ☐ a. I am completely decided on an academic major.
   ☐ b. I have an idea of what I wish to major in but am not ready to commit myself.
   ☐ c. I have several ideas but cannot decide on one.
   ☐ d. I am completely undecided about an academic major.

9. How undecided are you about an occupation? (*Check one.*)
   ☐ a. I am completely decided about an occupation.
   ☐ b. I have an idea about an occupation I may wish to work in but am not ready to commit myself.
   ☐ c. I have several ideas but cannot decide on one.
   ☐ d. I am completely undecided about an occupation.

10. What kind of help would benefit you most in deciding on a major or occupation? (*Check one.*)
   ☐ a. Information sessions with faculty about various majors
   ☐ b. Information sessions with workers in various careers
   ☐ c. Career-planning classes to help me explore various options
   ☐ d. Tests to help me find out what I'm interested in
   ☐ e. Information sessions on employment opportunities
   ☐ f. Talking with a career counselor
   ☐ g. Actual field experience in a career area
   ☐ h. Other (*Please specify.*)   (continued)

FIGURE 9.2 *Continued.*

11. For what career would you like specific information? (*Do not check more than three.*)

   ☐ a. Business
   ☐ b. Health-Related Professions
   ☐ c. Social Service
   ☐ d. Education
   ☐ e. Science
   ☐ f. Math
   ☐ g. Computer Science
   ☐ h. Art
   ☐ i. Government
   ☐ j. Law
   ☐ k. Law Enforcement and Criminology
   ☐ l. Agriculture
   ☐ m. Engineering
   ☐ n. Environmental/Natural Resources
   ☐ o. Writing
   ☐ p. Other (*Please specify.*)

Source: Gordon

- SIGI-PLUS is a micro-computer system that examines your work-related values by incorporating your personal interests and skills. SIGI-PLUS creates a list of occupations you may wish to consider and will provide career information about these or other occupations.
- DISCOVER is a career guidance system that presents you with a list of action steps to take upon completion of the program. SIGI-PLUS and DISCOVER are the two most widely recognized electronic career information systems.
- CHOICES asks you to assess your career-related needs, then compiles a personalized list of occupations based on your assessments. CHOICES also offers a comprehensive database of colleges, both undergraduate and graduate, and financial aid information.
- THE SELF-DIRECTED SEARCH helps you examine career interests in a systematic, self-guided way. The inventory focuses on five areas:
  1. Occupational Daydreams
  2. Activities
  3. Competencies
  4. Occupations
  5. Self-Estimates

The search results in a summary of your interests, called a Holland Code. The Holland Code is used to look at occupations that might best reinforce your specific interests.

An additional way to get information about careers is to inquire at your career center if there are ways to seek out information on summer **internships.** These career-oriented summer work experiences can be very helpful in determining possible future occupations. Some may be performed for college credit; some offer

internships
a work or study experience for which students may receive college credit or a salary enabling them to explore careers and work

salaries. One thing is for sure, however: if you don't enjoy a summer internship in an area you are considering to be a future job, you may be barking up the wrong major!

Undecided? Interview Some Instructors

A very helpful way to confirm or discard your ideas about majors and careers is to interview various instructors in the fields that interest you. Instructors can tell you about the courses you'll need for a major in their fields, and they may have interesting stories to tell about how they began in college and the journeys they've traveled in order to find their careers. Many instructors have interesting anecdotes to tell about their work experiences outside of academia; some instructors will confess that they never planned to end up as college teachers!

A conversation with an instructor may convince you that your choice of major is exactly right for you. On the other hand, many students report that their instructor interviews were the most important determinant in their knowing *for sure* which majors and careers to avoid! Another unexpected, yet helpful outcome of interviewing an instructor in your potential major field is that he or she may offer to become your academic adviser. It's a terrific feeling to have an instructor take that kind of interest in you.

WILL EMPLOYMENT PROJECTIONS AFFECT CHANGES IN MAJOR-SEEKING TRENDS?

While considering your interests, skills, aptitudes, personality, life goals, and work values, it doesn't hurt to look into the future of the world of work. The world of work is changing at an alarming pace. Due to rapid advances in science and technology, former "top occupations" will soon be in less demand, though they will not fade into obscurity.

We know that new professions related to technology are evolving all the time. There are no doubt fascinating careers on the horizon that we cannot yet imagine, and these new possibilities make it an especially important and exciting time to be in college. Meanwhile, the need for established professions, such as health care workers, continues to be sharply on the rise. A good background and skills in technology will help you keep on the "cutting edge" in these fields as well. Current information from the United States Bureau of Labor Statistics may surprise you. The BLS employment projections for 1996 to 2006 report the following 10 occupations will have the fastest employment growth, cited in order of percentage of expected growth:[12]

1. Database administrators, computer support specialists, all other computer scientists
2. Computer engineers
3. Systems analysts
4. Personal and home care aides
5. Physical and corrective therapy assistants and aides
6. Home health aides
7. Medical assistants
8. Desktop publishing specialists
9. Physical therapists
10. Occupational therapy assistants and aides

Do these data surprise you or confirm your assumptions about the changing nature of jobs, occupations, and vocations? (For more projections of future employment trends, see Chapter 11.)

Wait! Before you panic that your career goals may become dated, stop a minute and reflect. The invitation for you to recognize the changing world of work is not meant to dissuade you from following your heart and your head when deciding on a major and a career. You may have many different careers in your lifetime. Our world will continue to need historians, poets, sociologists, artists, teachers, landscape designers, theologians, and scientists. You may become one of those among us who makes the world a better place for contributing beauty, wisdom, new ideas, and hope. Global change always begins with committed individuals working at a local level, on projects important to them. Therein lies your challenge—construct a plan for your education that will enable you to engage in projects important to you.

Journal Reflections

9.1 Look back at Gordon's five types of major changers on page 158. Perhaps you have clear goals for your major and career, but if you do not, do any of these types sound like you? What would be some wise steps for you to take in order to get on the right track toward an appropriate and satisfying choice of major and an understanding of the major's relationship to a possible career?

9.2 Refer back to the questions for undecideds. Pick five or six questions that intrigue you, perhaps because they are the most difficult to answer. Let your imagination loose and write freely and unselfconsciously about yourself, your interests, aptitudes, and values. This is an exercise in uncensored self-exploration!

9.3 Review the Bureau of Labor Statistics' projected "top ten" jobs of the future, page 164. What strikes you about the list? What patterns of occupations emerge from the list? What do these projections about occupational growth areas seem to suggest about the social, economic, and political changes we are likely to experience in the next 10 years?

Experiences

9.1 FIND THE RIGHT ADVISOR

Take the time to find an advisor who is right for you! Unless your campus is extremely small, there are many different people who serve as academic advisors. Typically, you may initially be assigned to an advisor according to your expressed interest in a particular major or because you have declared yourself to be "undecided." You may be randomly assigned to an advisor by virtue of your student ID number or by some other electronic, impersonal means. There is no law in college that says that you must stick it out with an advisor whom you do not find helpful. Find out the procedures for changing advisors at your school, and if you need to change, do not feel embarrassed to do so. It's your well-informed decisions that will enable you to graduate with the credentials you want, so find the best possible informant.

9.2 CHANGING DIVISIONS/MAJORS

In the same spirit of exploration, form a small "investigation group" of two or three friends enrolled in different divisions to find out the procedures at your school for changing divisions or changing majors. Inevitably, there will be deadlines and forms to fill out to make changes in your degree program. These procedures are in place to help students find the majors, degree programs, and the best prospective occupations. Do not feel embarrassed, ashamed, or remiss for changing your academic plans. Nearly all students change their academic plans at least once; in some schools the average is three to five times!

9.3 WEB ACTIVITY

Pick a major or career that interests you and a classmate. Working together and using one or more of the search engines available with your Web browser, locate several sites that are related to your major/career. Determine what types of degrees are available. What types of jobs are available? How is the job market for your field? Where is the job market the strongest? What are the typical salary ranges in your field? What are the prospects for future promotion with or without additional schooling?

9.4 WEB ACTIVITY

For more information about the changing world of work, go on line to peruse excerpts from the most recent edition of *The Occupation Outlook Handbook,* a U. S. government publication that includes the latest information from the Bureau of Labor Statistics. You can find this source at this address: http://stats.bls.gov/ocohome.htm.

Can You Relate?

ESSAY 9.1

In a newspaper column written to his freshman daughter Angela, Washington, D. C. columnist William Raspberry suggests that "majors just don't matter that much" and that freshmen should "major in getting an education." In a book written to high school seniors and college freshmen, Prentice Hall author and consultant Carol Carter discusses the notion of *Majoring in the Rest of Your Life.*[13] In a thoughtful essay, explain your philosophy of the purpose of a college education: Are you majoring in getting an education, or are you majoring in the rest of your life? Both? Neither? Why?

Use information from this chapter, class discussion, and your own experiences in college thus far to help formulate your point of view about your purposes for being in college and the strategies you are using for accomplishing your goals for your college years.

ESSAY 9.2

Test your awareness of ways to investigate possible majors and careers and ways to pick a course of study that suits you. To begin, even if you are reasonably sure of your major and career plans, answer the questions for undecideds (Figure 9.1). Next, design a two-week plan that will allow you time to visit your Career Center to explore interest inventories and other electronic sources that can help you understand your interests, skills, aptitudes, personality, life goals, and work values. Be sure to retain the results or take notes on what you learn at the Career Center.

Using the above information as your "research data," construct an essay that compiles and synthesizes the information you have gathered. As you think and write, step outside yourself and imagine that you are analyzing someone else: What do these findings objectively indicate about the "person" you have researched? This essay should be three to five pages long, and end with a set of recommendations for how "this student" should proceed in working with an adviser to construct a degree program and an appropriate course of study. If your "findings" on this student suggests changes in her plans, what do you suggest?

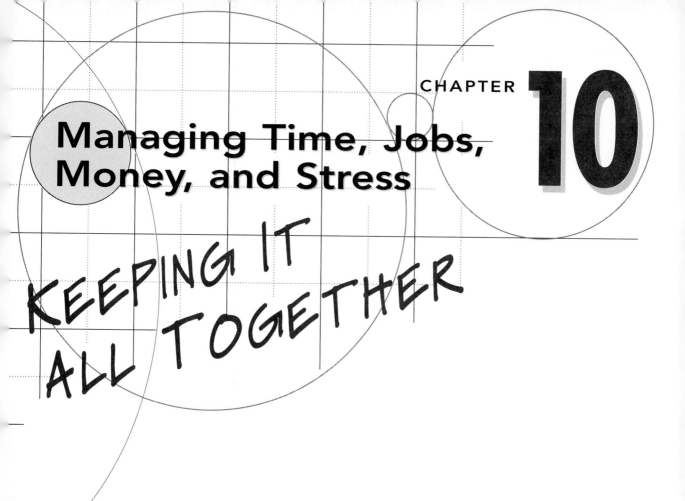

10

Managing Time, Jobs, Money, and Stress

KEEPING IT ALL TOGETHER

Part I of this book gives you a broad foundation to begin your college success—ways to acquire, organize, relate to, and learn the contents of your courses. Part II discusses learning with and from others at school. Part III focuses on "finding your place" and decision making. Having sound study strategies and forming study groups will not fully maximize your learning potential if you are misusing your time and if stress or money or family worries are distracting you.

Are you trying to keep up through late-night cram sessions, Sunday "guilt study" sessions (intended to get you *caught up* all in one night) during football or basketball games on TV, *The Simpsons,* and reruns of *The X-Files?* Did you wait too long to get serious about your first round of tests? Are you ignoring your stress rather than managing it? Is your financial situation preoccupying your thoughts? These are the kinds of concerns new college students experience—what *you* may be experiencing—during the first few terms, until they learn the absolute importance of managing time along with tasks, responsibilities, and stress level. Therefore, Chapter 10 suggests ways to manage your time and responsibilities.

You don't have to begin college with an ineffective or nonexistent system to manage the many parts to your life! High stress and lack of money can often leave you "frozen"—too preoccupied to be the best you can be academically. If you have children and/or a partner, your family has to understand and value your choice to attend college. You won't be very successful if you feel constant guilt about that choice.

Learning in college requires a knowledge of good practices and an understanding of the best ways to balance (it may feel like juggling) educational and social responsibilities with techniques to give yourself space to mellow out, reflect, and unwind. Don't fool around through your first sets of exams and then be sadder but wiser. If you establish good time, life, and stress management right along with good learning strategies, you will have accomplished several fundamental, important, and inseparable parts of a successful and satisfying college life.

All the "life issues" covered in this chapter are interrelated, and each may have a profound impact on your college success. Chapter 10 offers you an opportunity to stop, breathe, and assess the big picture—and to rethink how well you are managing all the aspects of your college life.

MYTHS AND TRUTHS ABOUT TIME/TASK MANAGEMENT

Perhaps more than any other topic related to college success, time management instruction tends to miss its mark. Most books will show you how to fill a daily or weekly schedule and how to stick to it, as though flexibility is a sin. There are many arithmetic formulas for how many hours to work ("For every hour of class spend three outside hours a week" and so on). However, part of your responsibility as an efficient student is to determine, class by class, the amount of time and the best time of each day to devote to particular classes. Creating big blocks of time in the evening or on weekends is not the best way to manage your time!

As is the case with other learning strategies, there is no one right system for all students. The most important issues in time management are

1. The time (when and how much) needed for learning
2. The time (when and how much) actually spent on learning
3. Your well-thought, strategic choices about when to do what sort of tasks

The key to making your system work is knowing how to form appropriate relationships among these three components. Figure 10.1 is a blank weekly planner sheet that you may photocopy and experiment with over time.

MANAGING YOUR TIME

In the discussion of time management strategies, it is necessary to address both what practices to adopt and the best times in which to perform these academic and self-care tasks. Consider the characteristics of the most effective study practices. Generally, effective study is

- Short (30–90 minutes)
- Planned in conjunction with classes and done regularly during the day
- Frequent (a naturally occurring act)
- Regular (as in every day, including *weekends*)
- Purposeful (intended to achieve a reasonable goal)
- Ends with a self-quiz or self-assessment (see page 3).

review study of material directly following, or soon after, a class

preview study of material as a mental "refresher" soon before a class meets

It's not just that you *spend* time; the crucial part is what you accomplish in that time. Try this approach with the daily/weekly schedule in Figure 10.1.

- Fill in your "have to's." These are classes and work hours only.
- Make decisions about how to use the time in between. Ask yourself, "What should I do now?" Experiment with **review** versus **preview** sessions. These strategic times before and after class are often the very best times to work with

new material, while it is still in your short-term memory as well as in your notes and books. This kind of study takes less effort than trying to learn the material days or even hours later.

For longer reading or homework sessions, schedule the time at which you will begin your work. Here is a way to set a beginning and a goal: "I will start my math problems at 7 P.M. and work until I can do three of them without referring to the book." When possible, your ending time should be when you have accomplished your goal, not a preset time such as just an hour later! (See the discussion of "process versus product" study on page 174.) Avoid clock watching!

• Formulate your goals for a study session sensibly. In order to do this, you must become aware of how long it takes you to complete certain kinds of studying. For example, reviewing a biology note set may require an hour, while completing your calculus homework may necessitate more than one hour; you may need a couple of sessions with a break in between for calculus.

• No matter what sort of study task you have selected, teach yourself to get your attention off the clock and on the work. If you have only one free hour, complete the biology and tackle the calculus at a more appropriate time. If you are constantly checking the time to see when you get to quit studying, you are not concentrating on the information. This clock-watching phenomenon is the cause of what many students call *poor concentration.*

• If you need to have a particular end time to your studying, set an alarm clock to ring when you must stop your work. Then turn the clock around so you won't be checking the time instead of concentrating on your course work.

• The most successful students find ways to check on their progress without waiting for and relying on infrequent test grades. Try to never end a study session without proof that you have accomplished a study goal and learned something new. What sorts of self-assessments are appropriate and easy to do? Chapters 1 through 4 are full of ideas for quick self-tests. Go back and get some self-quiz ideas.

This blank weekly schedule (Figure 10.1) is for you to photocopy and use as you experiment with ways to allocate your time. Through a bit of trial and error, you can maximize your time.

Figure 10.2 illustrates a well-constructed plan for the week. Notice how this student has maximized her "in-between" times to include regular review and preview study, church, TV, sleep, "down time," and even Uncle Rufus. She has saved her "product" work such as papers and longer reading sessions for evenings, apart from the times adjacent to her classes. A strong point in her schedule is that she allows herself "down time" and time for her favorite TV shows.

One of the best plans she has to maximize her time is that she intends to shut down her work and get to sleep at a reasonable hour each night, thereby using the most healing hours for sleeping. Of course, getting to sleep early in a busy residence hall is a major accomplishment. She must have an understanding roommate and/or live in a fairly quiet residence hall or apartment!

There is no one perfect way to manage your time and responsibilities. This is that inevitable process of trial and error, and you will probably experiment with your system throughout each term. Additionally, each term will be different and require a different schedule. The challenge to students is to continually assess their scheduling systems, to be flexible, and to trade times for study and other responsibilities. In other words, when you have to rearrange your plans (and you will, on occasion) don't steal your study time; trade it for some down time. This way, you are more likely to stay caught up with all that you have and want to do.

FIGURE 10.1 | *Blank weekly planner.*

TIME MANAGEMENT SCHEDULE

	MON	TUE	WED	THU	FRI	SAT	SUN
7 A.M.							
8 A.M.							
9 A.M.							
10 A.M.							
11 A.M.							
Noon							
1 P.M.							
2 P.M.							
3 P.M.							
4 P.M.							
5 P.M.							
6 P.M.							
7 P.M.							
8 P.M.							
9 P.M.							
10 P.M.							
11 P.M.							
Midnight							
1 A.M.							

FIGURE 10.2   *Sample weekly planner.*

TIME MANAGEMENT SCHEDULE

	MON	TUE	WED	THU	FRI	SAT	SUN
7 A.M.	Sleep	Sleep	Sleep	Sleep	Sleep	Sleep	Sleep
8 A.M.	Preview psych	Nothing	Eng 101	Library	Eng 101		Church
9 A.M.	Break		Break		Break	Visit Uncle Rufus	
10 A.M.	Psy 100	Chem 100	Psy 100	Chem 100	Psy 100	↓	
11 A.M.	Soc 101		Soc 101		Soc 101		
Noon	Lunch	Lunch	Lunch	Lunch	Lunch	Lunch	Lunch
1 P.M.	Gym class	Library	Gym class		Chem lab		Laundry
2 P.M.	Meet w/ Rob	Study chem	Study soc	Study chem	Chem lab	Study, shop	Study
3 P.M.	Flexible	↓	↓	↓	↓	whatever	↓
4 P.M.	Relax	↓	↓	↓	↓	↓	↓
5 P.M.	Dinner	Dinner	Dinner	Dinner	Dinner		Dinner
6 P.M.	Study soc	Study	Preview chem	Write English	English		Relax
7 P.M.	↓	↓	↓	↓	↓	↓	↓
8 P.M.	Study chem	Study	Meeting at church	TV: ER	English	DATE for dinner and	TV: The X-Files
9 P.M.	TV	Read English	TV	Study chem	Work on paper	a movie	Study
10 P.M.	TV	↓	Study	↓		↓	↓
11 P.M.	Sleep	Sleep	Sleep	Sleep	Sleep	Sleep	Sleep
Midnight							
1 A.M.							

COLLEGE RESPONSIBILITIES: DIFFERENT APPROACHES TO UNIQUE SITUATIONS

All students have unique features and challenges in their lives in college and in the years to follow. The following discussions highlight some common situations that can make managing your time and tasks more difficult, and they suggest some strategies for managing potential problems that may interfere with your learning in college.

Enforced Study Halls

Many student groups, including fraternities and sororities, programs for student athletes, and some academic clubs and organizations, use the concept of "enforced study halls" or "mandatory study hours" as a well-intentioned way to ensure that their members are keeping regular study hours. Enforced study halls are a mixed blessing; taken to an extreme, they may be hazardous to your college success. Why would that be?

The best times to study, when possible, are right before and right after each class. This is the "review" and "preview" work mentioned earlier in this chapter. If you are obligated to spend a certain number of hours per day or week in an enforced study hall situation, it would be very easy to fritter away your time throughout the day. After all, you "have to study" at certain designated times as part of your obligation to an organization. This "I'll save it for study hall" mentality can hurt your grades. In order to get the most out of your daily study and maximize the study hall hours, try this approach.

process study on-going, day-by-day learning and building on information from lectures and books, using strategic times before and after class

- Review and preview whenever possible, in between classes, throughout the day. Forget about your obligation to "do the time" later. This way, you'll stay caught up with new material at the easiest time to learn it. This is maintaining **process study** for ongoing learning.

product-based study study and work aimed at producing a "product" such as a paper, speech, or project

- Save papers, projects, and long "keeping up" reading sessions for study halls. Papers and projects, unlike regular review and preview, are **product-based study.** In other words, a paper is something you complete and turn in; you have no long-term memory responsibility toward the content. While learning in between classes is memory maintenance, a paper or project can be successfully completed in longer sessions, away from the prime time, ongoing business of your classes. Since most students have trouble keeping up with their reading loads, study halls are a good time to stay caught up, especially if you use writing to learn strategies described in Chapter 1 and reading strategies suggested in Chapter 2.

- Above all, resist the urge to save all your work for study hall. It's not just "doing the time" that will get you the grades!

Employed While Taking Classes? A Job: To Have or Have Not

Student employment, by necessity, is increasing nationally every year. Many students who receive financial aid must also work in order to meet rising college expenses. Studies on the success patterns of college students reveal these important points about working while in college:

1. Utilizing available financial aid helps students graduate from college.

2. Working off campus negatively affects students' academic work more than working at an on-campus job does. If you must work, try to find on-campus work.

3. Students who work full time have a much greater probability of *not* finishing college. For example, according to the U. S. Department of Education, "31 percent

of students who worked full time while enrolled attained a degree or were still enrolled compared to 79 percent of students who worked 1–15 hours per week and 65 percent of those who worked 15–33 hours per week."[1] Therefore, if you must work, try to limit your hours.

4. A large majority of undergraduate students are working many hours per week. The following list shows the national trends in hours per week that students who began working in college in 1989–90 were working in 1994:

- Students who did not work: 10.9 percent of all students
- Students who worked fewer than 15 hours per week: 31.2 percent
- Students who worked 15–33 hours per week: 43.4 percent
- Students who worked more than 34 hours per week: 14.5 percent[2]

(Not surprisingly, the 42 percent of students who did not work or worked fewer than 15 hours a week were more successful at staying in and graduating from college.)

5. The 1994 graduation or continued enrollment rates of the students who began college in 1989–90 are shown in the adjacent box:[3]

The above figures support the well-researched, surprising phenomenon that to a limit of around 15 hours per week, especially in on-campus jobs, part-time work can actually enhance students' performance while in college. There are two main reasons for this phenomenon. First, part-time work is a good break or change from academics, and it can help get you away from the stress of studying. Second, there is a tendency among many students that the more they have to do, the more they tend to do! Having a job makes you responsible to or for someone else. We are often more reliable and consistent when others are depending on us. Sometimes when we need only answer to ourselves, we are apt to lose our drive or level of industriousness. Yes, having part-time work can improve your chances of graduating from college!

EMPLOYMENT HOURS PER WEEK	OBTAINED A DEGREE OR STILL ENROLLED
Did not work	51.8%
Less than 15	78.8%
15–33	65.3%
34 or more	30.7%

Commuters and Time Management: Sing Your Homework?

In Chapter 3, in the section "To Tape or Not To Tape," you were advised to use tape recorders strategically, to listen to tapes immediately, and not to save up bunches of taped lectures. This is good advice, unless you are a commuting student. In your case, there are different guidelines for using audio tapes if you spend any time traveling to and from school. Whether your travel time to campus is 30 minutes or three hours, you have "down time" in your car or on the bus or whatever. Most cars are equipped with cassette players, and simple hand-held tape recorders, like pocket calculators, don't cost very much anymore. In other words, if you have travel time in your life, you can use that time to an advantage in your learning. Yes, it would be bliss to just crank up the music and get away from academics for a while. Sometimes music is just what you need to set you free for a break in your day.

Once in a while, however, using your commute to reinforce the reviewing and learning of a taped lecture or listen to your own "homemade" tapes of notes, readings, and so on is a terrific idea. Try recording earlier and then reviewing your own discussions when you are talking to yourself to figure out a concept. Listen to yourself in the car or replay a tape of a study group discussion where a group is wrestling with ideas or problems to solve. This commuting time could be a terrific time that you spend in the name of learning. Why not maximize a usually overlooked opportunity? What else have you got to do en route?

Understanding is always heightened when you can use more than one of your senses. If you are listening to taped ideas, you can also visualize some sort of web map or chart to give the ideas a visual frame in your mind. Sometimes students have wonderful "AHA!" experiences in their travels to and from school. Unless someone else is driving, *don't try to read while you are listening and thinking.* Let your wonderful brain create the visuals for you, and keep your eyes on the road. The great part of this strategy is that no matter how involved you get with your listening, thinking, talking, and visualizing, this learning session is yours and yours alone, private, and there's no limit to how far you go with the material. No one can hear you! If it helps, load your brain with ideas and then sing them!

Children, Family, and College Responsibilities

The average age of the college student today is 26; therefore, it would be shortsighted, even negligent, not to recognize children and families as important parts of the lives of many students attending college today. One way to think of the combination of school and family is that going to college is work, hard work, but the work doesn't stop at 5 P.M. as in traditional jobs. Family responsibilities are obviously not 9 to 5 jobs. However, there need not be all-out war between school and family. Peter Senge, author of the best-selling *The Fifth Discipline, the Art and Practice of the Learning Organization,* says there should be natural connections between your educational life and all other aspects of your life.[4] Your choice to go to college is very important to everyone in your household; you do not need to apologize for your choice to further your education.

Senge offers simple yet powerful advice for balancing work (in this case, school) with family. His principles are honest, direct, and fair:

- Identify what is truly important to you
- Make a choice (commitment)
- Be truthful with those around you regarding your choice
- Do not try to manipulate [your partner or children] into agreement or superficial support[5]

Following are some suggestions for keeping home life consistent and fair to all members without sacrificing your schoolwork.

1. If your young child or children are asleep and you can't go out, remember that you don't have to be face-to-face with a study partner to have a terrific study session. You can always study with others on the telephone.

2. If you are a semi-professional chauffeur and have to get children to activities, don't forget the power of using audio tapes to study in the car. Plug in your Walkman at soccer games; the other parents will think you're listening to something hip—they don't have to know it's a tape of the components of the executive, legislative, and judicial systems.

3. If you are a single parent, it is absolutely essential that you get support by finding and getting to know other students with children of similar ages. You can get together, each do your own studying, and your children will soon be happy to amuse one another. Another idea is trading children, so once in a while your friend can keep the kids while you go to the library and vice versa.

4. If there are preschoolers in your home, find time to read and write with them. The importance of reading, writing, and learning is one of the best lessons you can teach your children, so help them learn to value their reading and writing and yours. (See Chapter 11 for a discussion of working with children.) Your own schoolwork may be best tackled after their bedtime, and, of course, throughout your day on campus.

5. If you have a child or children in school, do your "homework" together. Value their work and they will value yours. Maybe your son or daughter can help you with your math.

6. Purposefully schedule times and events that are fun for partners and children and forget school for a while. Create occasions to look forward to. All work and no play make an unhappy family.

7. If your school responsibilities are wearing on you, your family will feel your tension. Reassure them that it's school, and not they who are adding to your stresses. Don't let your loved ones think they are the cause of your discomfort if they are not. The older your children, the more they will be able to relate to your situation. Once in school themselves, children understand that school can get you down now and then, and they will better understand your needs as a student–parent.

Managing Money

Now you're really on your own, and nothing feels worse than being broke. You may have many sources of money that, combined, monitored, and managed, are enough to keep you going. You've probably never had to be this self-conscious about spending and saving. You have to be aware of your sources of income and turn your spending habits into sound spending practices. You must also be aware of all the financial traps lurking around colleges, waiting to get students into big-time trouble.

Identify Your $ Habits

Spending money is a choice. Do you choose to spend your money on *needs* or *wants?* A *need* is literally something you cannot live without. *Wants* are everything else for which you shell out money. As a way of examining your money habits, photocopy multiple copies of the weekly planner shown in Figure 10.1. Then use these sheets to record your expenses (when, what, how much) day by day for several weeks. Just as you need to study how you use your time, you need to study how you use your money.

Beware of Credit Cards and Your School's "EZ" Charge Systems

By some estimates, 64 percent of all college students have at least one credit card, while over 20 percent have four or more credit cards. Credit card companies love students! The companies have clever ways to keep you endlessly in debt. If you have $1,000 in debt on a credit card with an interest rate of 18 percent, and if you pay the *minimum* required each month of $20, it will take you *eight years* to pay off that $1,000 (if you don't increase your debt in the meantime). You will also lose $700–$800 in paying off the interest.

Having credit makes it really easy to overspend. This process of spending money you haven't yet *earned* can become an addictive process: Buy now, pay later. The credit card companies count on this! There is an increase nationally in the number of college students who fail or drop out of school because of overspending, endless debt, and/or working far too many hours at one or more jobs to attempt to lessen their indebtedness. The ability to do well in college is sacrificed for the need to spend.

Many colleges and universities now have "EZ Charge" systems that make your spending on campus much easier. While they are intended to make students' lives easier, these systems, which allow you to charge purchases with your student ID, can also be a trap. On some campuses, you can even get a soda out of a machine with your student ID card. You can charge food, books, clothing, concert tickets, and anything else your college or university has for sale. While this arrangement is certainly handy to students who have very little cash on hand, it is easy to lose track of what you buy "on credit" with your student charge system.

Remember, at the end of the term, someone has to foot the bill! Did you know that, at many colleges and universities, you cannot enroll for a new term if your account balance isn't zero?

Borrowing Money

According to the Consumer Credit Counseling Service of Greater Kansas City, Inc.,[6] there are good and bad reasons to borrow money. Remember, using credit cards is *borrowing money!*

Solutions to Credit Problems

- If you have multiple credit cards, keep one or two for emergencies. Close the other accounts and cut up the credit cards. Closing an account is as easy as locating the company's toll-free number somewhere on the credit card, calling them, and telling them you want to close the account. If they don't respond, put your request to close the account in writing.

- Pay off the entire credit card each month. Figure what you are able to spend toward the card, and do not let monthly expenses exceed what you can pay off entirely. In this way, you won't be losing hundreds of dollars a year to interest charges.

- Shop around for no-cost credit cards (those with no tacked-on annual fees) with the lowest interest rates available.

- Borrow (or charge) money only for worthwhile purposes and only when absolutely necessary.

- Examine the ways you are paying for your college education and expenses, and take advantage of low-risk ways to pay for college.

Borrowing Money

GOOD REASONS TO BORROW
- Financing a home, home improvements
- Education
- Investing in real estate
- Financial emergencies/crises

NOT-SO-GOOD REASONS
- Buying a car
- Starting a business

REALLY BAD REASONS
- Most credit card debt
- Everything else

Low-Risk Ways to Pay for College*

In a perfect world, your parents, grandparents, other relatives, guardians or a kind friend pays your college costs out of pocket, or you have a trust fund set aside to pay for college expenses. Failing those, here are your other options.

Federal Aid, State Loans, and Other Grants

- File the *Free Application for Federal Student Aid* (FAFSA) annually to be considered for state, federal, and institutional funds. Some colleges have a priority deadline, which must be met to receive the maximum amount of aid. The school will determine if you are eligible for grants, federal work-study, or loans once the FAFSA is received.

- Contact the financial aid office at your school to see if the college has any low-interest loans available.

*Source: Brenda Noblitt, Assistant Director, Student Financial Aid, University of Missouri–Columbia. Brenda is a former teacher of a first-year orientation course.

- Your parents or guardians may want to check with their employer(s) regarding tuition assistance or low-interest loans that may be available to help cover college costs.
- Parents or guardians may be eligible to borrow a *Parent Loan for Undergraduate Students* to help pay for college expenses. Contact the financial aid office at your school for more information.
- A relative or friend may be able to loan you the money at a no- or low-interest rate.
- Parents or guardians may be able to obtain a home equity loan to help pay your college expenses.
- Alternative loans: some private lenders have loan programs to aid students in meeting college costs. Contact your financial aid office for information regarding these loans.

Scholarships, Etc.

- Contact the financial aid office and your school or college for scholarship applications and deadlines. Apply annually to be considered each year.
- Free scholarship search services can be located on the World Wide Web at *www.finaid.org.*
- Your parents or guardians may want to check with their employer(s) to see what scholarship opportunities are available.
- ROTC scholarships are available in return for participation in your college's ROTC program.
- Contact your financial aid office for your state's grant, scholarship, and loan programs.

Employment

- You *can* help meet your college expenses by working. If you have to work, you have to work. That's reality—college costs! Some students prefer to work during the summer and breaks to save money, while others prefer to work through the academic term. As mentioned earlier, part-time, on-campus work is the least intrusive on your academic and social lives.
- Some companies will help pay your college expenses. For example, a company that works with people with developmental disabilities will pay twenty percent toward tuition and provide a two-bedroom apartment for students whom they employ.
- Some companies will pay all or some college expenses for their full-time employees. This is beneficial to those students who want to attend college part time.
- You may be able to obtain a position as a Community Assistant or Resident Assistant or another position in your college's residence halls to help meet your expenses.

Other

- Purchase used books from other students or from your college bookstore.
- Sell your used books to other students instead of to the bookstore.
- Buy your books on the Internet; for instance, try *www.bkstore.com* (Barnes & Noble College Bookstores) www.amazon.com.
- Sell your car! (OUCH!) Many students do not need a car while attending college.
- Ask your relatives to give you money in lieu of graduation, holiday, and birthday gifts.

- Students with physical and/or mental disabilities constituting a substantial impediment to employment should consider Vocational Rehabilitation financial assistance.

Taxpayers Relief Act of 1997

The TRA 97 was signed into law in August 1997 and provides the following tax breaks for college expenses. If your parents or guardians still claim you on their tax returns, tell them about the TRA 97. If you prepare your own taxes, you may need to seek assistance to learn how to take advantage of these new guidelines.

Hope Credit

- Up to $1,500 per student for qualified tuition and fees (T&F)
- 100 percent credit on the first $1,000 of qualified T&F and 50 percent on the next $1,000 of qualified T&F
- Available during the first two years of a student's postsecondary education
- Available for qualified T&F expenses paid after December 31, 1997
- Phased out for taxpayers with incomes greater than $40,000 ($80,000 if filing jointly)

Lifetime Learning Credit

- Equal to 20 percent of qualified T&F paid during the taxable year on behalf of the taxpayer, taxpayer's spouse, or dependent
- Student must be enrolled in an eligible institution taking undergraduate or graduate classes to acquire or improve job skills
- Up to $5,000 of qualified T&F paid before January 1, 2003 per taxpayer ($1,000 maximum credit per taxpayer return). Up to $10,000 for qualified T&F paid after December 31, 2002 ($2,000 maximum credit per taxpayer return).
- Same income limitations as Hope Credit
- Credit is available for qualified T&F paid after June 30, 1998

Education IRAs

- Allow taxpayers to establish education IRAs for the purpose of paying qualified higher education expenses of a named beneficiary
- Annual contributions limited to $500 per beneficiary
- Contributions cannot be made after beneficiary reaches age 18
- Contribution is phased out for certain high-income contributors
- Apply to taxable years beginning after December 31, 1997, for expenses paid after that date.

Managing Stress*

Stress is one of the leading contributors to misery in college. There are many approaches to managing stress; one approach uses **self-care** as the centerpiece of stress reduction. Learning to take care of yourself is an important requirement for the best chance at college success. This means learning new information and skills to meet your physical, emotional, and social needs to perform at your best. By

*The discussion on stress management was contributed by Patrick Kane, LCSW, counselor and Assistant Professor of Social Work, University of Missouri–Columbia. Patrick did extensive work and research with the flood victims in mid-America after the devastating flood of 1993. Patrick is a former teacher of a first-year orientation course.

learning and practicing self-care skills, you can cope with the demands of college life on a day-to-day basis, and you will also be prepared when a new, unexpected challenge appears that may threaten the completion of your course work.

stress a sometimes debilitating condition characterized by a physical and mental sensation of being overwhelmed; the body's natural response is "fight or flight"

self-care redirection of and protection from stress and illness that requires physical, emotional, and spiritual work

Physical Self-Care

- *Breathing* with your diaphragm, a sheetlike muscle that stretches across your chest, can both relax and energize you. You can use your breathing skills daily, and particularly focus on them before exams or presentations. The action is so subtle that your classmates will not know you are working on stress reduction right in front of them! More oxygen in your lungs means that your brain will function more effectively. Try this: Place one hand on your abdomen and push your abdomen and your hand out as you breathe in. As you exhale, your abdomen will fall. Slow your breathing and simultaneously deepen it. When you practice this skill for 5 to 10 minutes, you can become very relaxed.

- Daily *aerobic exercise* can alleviate stress, elevate your mood, and make it easier to study and focus on your class work. This activity might be twenty minutes of jogging, 45 minutes of walking, or a good aerobic workout at a gym. Whether you choose these activities or swimming, biking, basketball, tennis, or another sort of workout, what is important is that you *move your body daily*. It's very trendy to walk around with a towel over your sweaty neck and to brag about your workout.

- Many kinds of exercise can be performed while studying. Much of today's exercise equipment comes with racks that will hold reading material, or you can study while listening to audio tapes in a Walkman (see pages 175 and 176 for strategies for using audio tapes).

- *Drink* 8 to 10 glasses of water daily. Drinking H_2O is good! This is not only good for your body but for your brain. It is currently very "hip" to carry around one of those bottles of spring water, then to refill it and keep it with you so your friends think you're really into being healthy and are willing to actually purchase H_2O to do so. Some fashionable activity is also practical!

- Not all *sleep* is equally beneficial. The sleep you get between 10:00 P.M. and 2:00 A.M. helps give you energy for the next day and benefits your immune response system. Ensuring sleep during these hours or four hours close to this time, if at all possible, will keep you healthier and less stressed. Ironically, perhaps sadly, these are very common hours for college students to be awake. Try to close down your days in order to take advantage of the healing properties of sleep at this time.

- REM (rapid eye movement) sleep is when dreaming occurs and the brain is most active. Paradoxically, this is the stage of sleep that is most beneficial to humans and animals because REM aids in consolidating memory.[7] Deprivation of REM sleep causes people to have trouble remembering complex information. Young adults spend 24 percent of their night in REM sleep,[8] so a good night's sleep is a necessity in order to replenish your memory power and alleviate stress. Luckily, the content of the dreams does replace what the sleeper remembers, so you may be dreaming some surreal dream while you are learning your French!

- *Things to avoid:* By not consuming too much sugar, caffeine, and alcohol, you will keep your blood sugar and your nervous system functioning more effectively. Did you know that alcohol and other sugars can cause insomnia?

Emotional Self-Care

- *Feelings.* Begin to identify when you are sad, mad, glad, or scared. When you know how you feel and you share your feelings in writing or with a person you can trust, perhaps a friend or instructor, you will release tension and reduce stress. Friends are good for studying, partying, and *venting*.

• One of the best ways to begin identifying feelings is to write a few minutes every day in a *journal*. Writing helps clarify thinking and feeling. Write about the important events in your day and how you felt about them, e.g., sad, mad, glad, or scared—the four basic emotions. People who keep journals prove to have reduced stress and better health. No wonder this book suggests you keep a journal!

Social Self-Care

The skill of talking to "safe" friends is essential in college. Spending time with people who listen to you without judging—safe people—reduces stress. Find a friend who is willing to hear you tell her or him anything that has triggered sad, mad, glad, or scared feelings in you. This sharing will help you cope with the ups and downs of daily living. Developing friendships makes sense for college success and for the rest of life. As addressed in Chapter 5, learning is social; coping is also a social skill.

Taking care of your stress level is neither time consuming nor expensive. So what possible reason could there be not to work on stress reduction?

Journal Reflections

10.1 Take a good hard look at your monthly income and how you use it, and determine if you have a system for managing it wisely. What are your sources of income versus your system of "outgo"? Does your system of managing money need attention and work? After honest reflection, discuss ways in which you could be more wise with your money. List some steps you can begin to use immediately to get your money situation in balance so that your finances won't be a constant worry.

10.2 What has surprised you the most about your college experience so far? Discuss both academic and social experiences and concerns. You may wish to separate your page into halves by drawing a line down the center and writing "positive surprises" on one side and "negative surprises" on the other. Now, how can you keep the good stuff going while working to eliminate the troubling aspects of your college life?

10.3 Using a blank weekly planning sheet (Figure 10.1), keep a record of how you spend your time (all of it!) for an entire week. Reflect on your choices and consider ways you could reallocate your time for a more productive, less stressful schedule.

Experiences

10.1 STRESS REDUCTION PLAN

Devise a personal stress reduction plan. Use the blank weekly time management form on page 172 and purposefully add occasions for stress reduction work at the times most beneficial to you, according to the rhythm of your weeks. Be mindful of tests, interviews, presentations and other high-stress events, but build in stress reduction as part of your everyday routine.

10.2 COLLEGE EMPLOYMENT INQUIRY

Interview a variety of students who are working while they are going to school. Find a mix of students who work on campus versus off, less than 15 hours per week versus more than 15 hours, students whose work relates to their majors versus students whose jobs have no relevance to their envisioned careers. Find out how they found and relate to their jobs. What conclusions can you draw from your investigation about jobs in college?

10.3 CHECK OUT TYPES OF PLANNERS

Go to a bookstore and investigate a variety of kinds of planners, date books, Day Runners, and other time management equipment. Compare the benefits and limitations of each, including ease of use, amount of space available for notations, and cost. Check to see what sorts of items your friends are using. Jot down pros and cons of each to clarify what sort of planner is best for you.

10.4 WEB ACTIVITY

Conduct a search on the Internet for possible sources of income to supplement your college funds. Find out if your campus financial aid office has a list of recommended Web addresses.

10.5 CURRENT TAX LAW AND COLLEGE

Show your parents or guardians the information about tax credits and IRAs for attending college. These laws and guidelines are new and ever-changing, and they may be good news to those who are helping to finance your schooling! (Every little bit helps, right?)

10.6 WEB ACTIVITY

Review the time management tips offered in this chapter, then compare them to the tips offered at *www-scl.uga.berkeley.edu/CalREN/WhenToStudy.html*. What one activity could you do that would greatly enhance your time management? How can you accomplish this?

10.7 STRESS ON THE WEB

Overstress is very common among college students. The Web site *wellness.uwsp. edu/Health_Service/services/stress/sources.html* offers a stress test, stress management tips, and links to other sites for treating stress. Take the exams to find your levels of stress, the sources of your stress, distress symptoms, and stress balancing strategies. Where did you score? What tips from the text and from this Web site can you use to manage and reduce your own stress?

Writing Experiences

Test your knowledge of the essentials of a good time/task management system by drafting answers to the following short-answer questions. Be sure to incorporate information from the text, class discussions, and your own experiences. Plan to spend approximately five minutes on each answer.

10.1

Why does it seem that you can successfully do certain kinds of schoolwork "at the last minute," while other sorts of preparation require constant attention? What are the differences between "product work" and "process study"?

10.2

How can you accomplish all your academic and social goals if you work several hours a week?

10.3

If you belong to a fraternity, sorority, or other organization that requires "study halls" at set times during each week, how will you handle your study load?

10.4

What if circumstances prevent you from following your time/task management plans? What if these circumstances persist until you are totally off your schedule?

10.5

Why is concentrating on the learning *task* more important than your attention to the clock? Given that all students have limited time, how can you keep your attention away from the time in order to focus on your chosen learning task?

Can You Relate?

ESSAY 10.1

Most high school students come to community colleges, colleges, or universities with underdeveloped time/task management systems or none at all. This is normal; in your educational past, you studied at night or on weekends. One of the main themes of this chapter is to convince you to use your days and nights in strategic ways to enhance your learning. Using information from your text, class discussion, and your own experiences, explain the key characteristics of a sound time/task management system. Be sure to elaborate on how each feature adds to the effectiveness of this approach. Then move from the general to the specific and explain your system, using part of your planner as a point of focus. Brainstorm before you write; plan to complete the essay in 30 minutes. Your reader must understand how you decide when and what to do to keep up with studying and other college responsibilities.

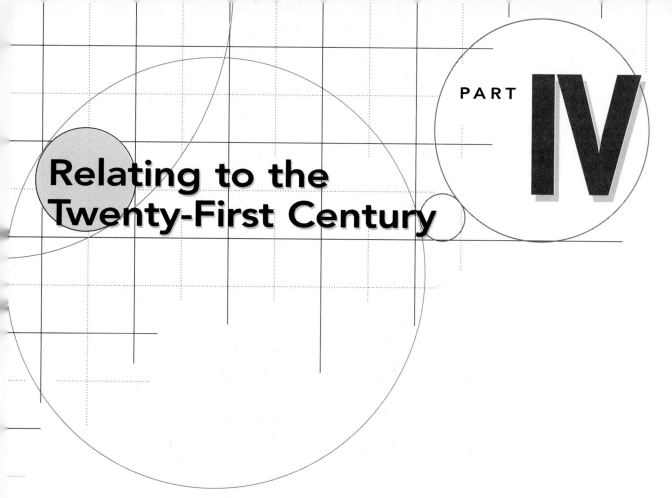

PART IV

Relating to the Twenty-First Century

CHAPTER 11 Making Meaning in the Twenty-First Century: *The Future Is Yours*

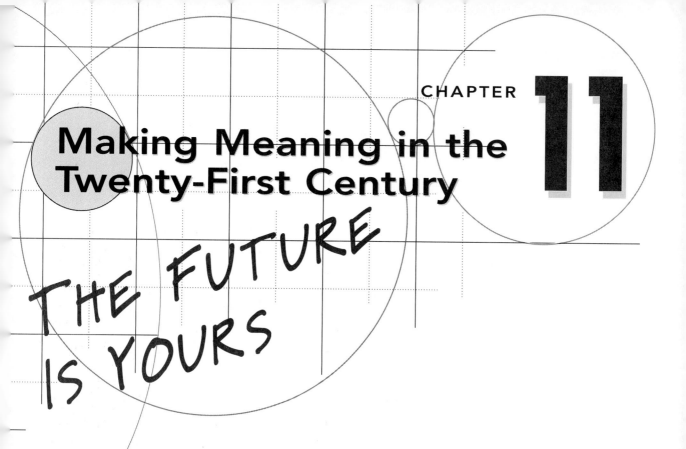

CHAPTER

11

Making Meaning in the Twenty-First Century

THE FUTURE IS YOURS

ON TO A FOUR-YEAR SCHOOL, GRADUATE SCHOOL, OR WHAT?

Have you ever asked yourself what in the world you are doing in college anyway? How often do you wonder if all your efforts will be worth it in the end? This chapter helps to reinforce the fact that you are investing heavily, both figuratively and literally, in your future. According to education specialist Ernest Boyer, each successive year of schooling beyond the high school level becomes more necessary for personal and economic success and citizenship.

> As we move toward the year 2000, almost everyone will need some form of post–high school education if he or she is to remain personally empowered, economically productive, and civically prepared. The twin mandates—quality and equality—remain the unfinished agenda for higher education. . . .If the undergraduate college has succeeded, students, after they are handed their diplomas, will be well equipped to put their work in context and move with success from one intellectual challenge to another. More than that, they should be able to see their jobs in larger perspective. Only then can they be truly creative and fulfilled as individuals.[1]

If you are attending a two-year school and working toward an associate's degree, there are several "hot" occupations for which you might work toward certification. (Chapter 8 discusses community and two-year colleges.) Based on the Bureau of Labor Statistics' projections for employment in the period 1996 to 2006 (if you believe government statistics), here are the top five occupations for which the required education/training level will be an associate's degree[2]:

1. Paralegals
2. Medical records technicians
3. Dental hygienists
4. Respiratory therapists
5. Cardiology technologists

If you are working toward a bachelor's degree, according to the Bureau of Labor Statistics' projections for 1996 to 2006, the top ten growth areas in occupations for which the typical education/training level is a bachelor's degree are[3]:

1. Database administrators, computer support specialists, and all other computer scientists
2. Computer engineers
3. Systems analysts
4. Physical therapists
5. Occupational therapist
6. All other therapists
7. Special education teachers
8. Physician assistants
9. Resident counselors
10. Securities and financial services sales workers

What Do Master's Degrees Provide?

The master's degree is a professional degree that has evolved in the United States to give an extra boost to the professional nature of many fields. Most master's degrees emphasize training in additional skills for practitioners in their fields in order to develop their particular talents in their professions. They are not ordinarily research degrees or degrees aimed at a greater understanding of theories; instead, they are degrees in practice that utilize and combine experiences such as internships, fieldwork, and seminars.

The master's degree usually culminates in some sort of assessment of growth and achievement. Master's candidates are required to write a **master's thesis,** a professional article appropriate for submission to a professional journal, and may be required to pass a comprehensive written examination.

master's thesis a culminating written work that is part of the requirements for a master's degree

Depending on your career goals, a master's degree may or may not enhance your employment opportunities. It is important for you, even as a first- or second-year student, to understand the relevance and relationship of advanced degrees to your undergraduate work. For example, if you are going to become an elementary school teacher, you will be ready (perhaps eager) for your first classroom experience upon completion of a bachelor's of science in education or its equivalent. Teaching is a career that truly requires some time in the field, in a real classroom with real kids, before you need to think about advanced training. However, if you graduate with a bachelor's degree in social work or counseling, you may wish to get more training before you begin working. (See Chapter 9 for a thorough discussion of strategies for making major and career decisions.)

If you aspire toward schooling and training beyond a bachelor's degree, the Bureau of Labor Statistics projects the following occupations to be the biggest growth areas in total employment with a master's degree in the period 1996 to 2006[4]:

1. Speech-language pathologists and audiologists
2. Counselors
3. All other teachers and instructors
4. Curators, archivists, museum technicians, and restorers
5. Psychologists
6. Operations research analysts
7. All other social scientists
8. Professional librarians
9. Urban and regional planners

Don't wait until your senior year to begin to consider whether you should add to your years of schooling in order to accomplish your career goals. Choosing certain major and career paths may add time to your years in college, but extra time in college may be right for what you ultimately wish to accomplish professionally.

IT'S A NEW MILLENNIUM

Good grief—there certainly was a lot of discussion about the coming of the new millennium! All agencies and companies heavily dependent on computer technology were scurrying around, making programming adjustments so that when 1999 rolled over to 2000, the technological world wouldn't accidentally roll back to 1900. Discussions on the news highlighted the grave concern that all our military defense networks could go awry, rendering us unable to attack or intimidate any perceived global enemies. The coming of the year 2000, for some groups, heralded some sort of end of the world. A huge comet might have hurled into Earth from outer space and destroyed the planet; aliens might have invaded. (No doubt they would have been green and slimy, with acid for blood.) Movies and television have had a field day with this millennium theme.

However, here you are today, not only at the beginning of your college career and a new century but on the threshold of what our civilization designates the third millennium of the common era. You have the opportunity to make the most of your life choices during the millennium changeover. You're going to have plenty of time to leave your mark, make your contributions, change careers, and grow older and wiser—all before the fat alien sings.

You will indeed need to be prepared for the 21st century, and this final chapter serves as food for thought about the relationships between the accumulation of all your college experiences—learning (including with the help of this book), understanding relationships, growing—and your future. Perhaps this investigation of the future will help you make greater meaning of your present life.

READING, WRITING, SPEAKING, AND LISTENING AFTER COLLEGE: ALWAYS A LEARNER

The *American Heritage Dictionary of the English Language* defines *millennium* as "a span of a thousand years" but also as "a hoped-for period of joy, serenity, prosperity, and justice." Now, that is a definition with some potential and promise! Until we as a species master telepathy, we will continue to rely on reading, writing, speaking, and listening in one or more languages to communicate, to understand one another, and to understand ourselves. (Chapters 1 through 4 provide an in-depth array of strategies to improve your language and thinking skills.) Reading, writing, speaking, and listening are indeed means of achieving joy, serenity, prosperity, and justice—the ultimate goals of many of us, especially after college when we have some room and time to reflect on all we've been through. Where would we be without the endless possibilities for written and spoken language?

Each of us continues to develop language, both oral and written, over our whole lives, as we encounter new experiences and new needs. Every new interest creates a need for new language. We continue to learn new language every time we experience a new hobby: knitting, bowling, computers; a new class or curriculum: biology, algebra, medicine; a new place: climate, people, traditions.

What's wonderful about our human ability to invent language, individually and socially, is that it never ends. Some people have argued that there's a short, critical period early in human life when language is learned with remarkable ease, after which the learning is much harder. To reach this conclusion, they compare the remarkable speed of early language development with the relative slowness adults show in learning second languages. But what accounts for that difference is simply that most adults shy away from the risks involved in trying out their inventions as they move toward language conventions.[5]

Imagine a world without books. Even with the advent of technological innovations, we will still need to write and read books. In Ray Bradbury's grim futuristic novel *Fahrenheit 451,* written in 1953, the rulers of a rather bleak "advanced" society have decided that books are evil because they make people think. Unsympathetic fire brigades patrol communities to find and burn all the books. (451 degrees Fahrenheit is the temperature at which paper spontaneously bursts into flames.) It's a very bad time for literacy! Fortunately, as in all good tales of a tainted future, there is a group of rebels who defy the government. Each rebel picks her or his favorite book and *becomes* that book by memorizing it, wandering about the countryside and reciting the text verbatim. Unfortunately for the rebels, in preserving the spirits of wonderful books, they have time for little else.

Now imagine being *finished with college!* Go ahead . . . imagine a world in which you get to have more freedom in what you read, write, listen to, and say. Imagine a time in the future wherein there are no syllabuses, reading lists, paper deadlines, homework assignments, or megastressful examinations. Does the notion of being through with college appeal to you? Even if you never attend another school, if you get a job, move to an exotic foreign land, win the lottery, or join a witness protection program with a new identity, you will continue to be enriched, amused, informed, and transformed by the relationship between thought and language. Reading, writing, speaking, and listening are ways of using language to connect with knowledge; they are acts and means of learning. They are also social events: as learning is a social event, they are acts and means of connecting with others.

Learning is a special, never-ending part of the human condition. If you learn to learn in college, you'll have lots of choices after college. Your awareness of the relationship between your learning styles and the teaching styles of your instructors (Chapter 7) will help you learn to learn more efficiently and successfully, and this understanding may help you discover your personality and passions.

Shut your eyes; visualize yourself finished with college and happy in your first job, even if you have no idea right now what it will be. Hold tight to that vision—it will help you keep going. When you leave college, you will be trained in a variety of skills. You will have a lot to be very proud of. You'll probably go through the writing and sending of resumes, endure the stress of job interviews, and maybe even take a series of tests. There will be choices to be made, challenges to accept, people to come to know, procedures to learn, and endless doses of change in your life. Maybe you won't command a huge salary, but there's plenty of time for advancement. Imagine a time when you get to use your education and training to do something or some things that you love. No matter where you begin in the world of work, you will continue to be a learner, a seeker of knowledge, and a sharer of knowledge. Hold tight to that vision.

Literacy and Competencies in the Workplace

In 1990, in anticipation of the advent of a new century, the Secretary of Labor and members of the Secretary's Commission on Achieving Necessary Skills (SCANS) convened representatives from U. S. schools, businesses, unions, and government. Their 12-month mission, named "AMERICA 2000," was to interview business owners, managers, and employees from every facet of the changing workplace, as well as students, to determine "what work requires of schools."[6]

Interestingly, the students interviewed in focus groups believed that whether they were bound for college or for work, the "real training" for work is learned "on the job . . . through extracurricular activities, or by osmosis. In other words, they believe[d] that the skills needed in the real world are, in the words of one student, just 'picked up.'"[7] This attitude sounds as though "schoolwork" is just busywork. Oh, no, it's not! Why else would you be here? When you are in college, the most important work you do is *learning to learn.*

The SCANS report produced some powerful, relevant findings, still valid after more than 10 years. The research identified a three-part foundation of intellectual skills and personal qualities that schools, especially institutions of higher education, can and must bring out—those skills and attributes that you as a student should strive for to be competent in the 21st century workplace.[8]

- *Basic skills:* Reading, writing, mathematics, listening, and speaking
- *Thinking skills:* Creative thinking, making decisions, solving problems, seeing things in the mind's eye, knowing how to learn, and reasoning
- *Personal qualities:* Individual responsibility, as well as self-esteem, sociability, self-management, and integrity

These skills and qualities are not just "something you pick up"; they are what you will derive and enhance throughout your college education. Additionally, the SCANS Report identified five related competencies[9] that are increasingly necessary for high-quality job performance. A good college education will give you ample opportunities to develop these competencies. Both industrial and occupational employers want effective workers for the new millennium who can productively use the following skills.

- *Resources:* Allocating time, money, materials, space, and staff
- *Interpersonal skills:* Working on teams, teaching others, serving customers, leading, negotiating, and working well with people from culturally diverse backgrounds
- *Information:* Acquiring and evaluating data, organizing and maintaining files, interpreting and communicating, and using computers to process information
- *Systems:* Understanding social, organizational, and technological systems, monitoring and correcting performance, and designing or improving systems
- *Technology:* Selecting equipment and tools, applying technology to specific tasks, and maintaining and troubleshooting technology

When you begin to review and analyze the skills and attributes that employers want in their employees, you may begin to appreciate the importance of some of those courses you really did not or do not want to take while in college. (Chapter 9 explains the rationale for general education requirements.) Maybe you didn't want to take that introductory computer course; you already know how to use email! Seeing the inevitable changes in the workplace, you may very well learn to appreciate the concept of the "enriched major" (Chapter 9). It will sustain you in rough times to know that you are getting the kind of well-rounded education that will enable you to be ready for work in the 21st century, after all.

It's easy to see from the SCANS Report that your future employers will appreciate and admire your ability to manage your many responsibilities, such as your time, money, stress, and work and family responsibilities. (Chapter 10 discusses ways to manage these key elements in your life.)

Diversity in the Workplace

While you are attending college, you're learning to see your campus—and by extension, the world—as a highly diverse global village, and this will be helpful as you enter the workplace. Along with proficiency in literacy and oracy, the chance to experience and the ability to appreciate diversity is becoming a part of lifelong learning. (Chapter 8 describes the diverse nature of colleges and universities.) Employment projections provided by the Bureau of Labor Statistics,[10] as shown in Figure 11.1, indicate that the demographic nature of the labor force, *both industrial and occupational,* will change because the population itself is changing, and participation in work is also changing. What will these projections mean for you?

A New Kind of Immigrant

Unlike the immigration phenomenon of the early 1900s, when unskilled workers came to America to get jobs and have better lives, the trend now is for international professionals to seek employment and advancement in American companies. This trend, along with the ever-changing face of the U. S. job force, will almost ensure that even if you do not work abroad, you will meet and work with international professionals, from whom you may learn a lot about your own profession.

Teamwork: From College into the Workplace

There may be a relationship between the traditional model of the late-20th century workplace and 20th century schooling because both are in transition. Historically, in the United States both school and work have stressed mass production, a fragmentation of tasks to be performed by individuals on their own (remember worksheets?), and authority was given to supervisors or teachers at the top.

The traditional world of work has been very hierarchical and has tended to devalue the individual. Even many highly trained professionals have eventually felt isolated in their work. We hear stories all the time of successful lawyers retiring to become soccer coaches, high-level military leaders becoming school superinten-

FIGURE 11.1 *Changes in the labor force.*

- Professional specialty occupations are projected to increase the fastest and add the most jobs—4.8 million. This is very good news for those of you in college who are working toward credentials in particular fields.
- The black labor force is expected to grow by 14 percent, faster than the 9 percent growth rate projected for the white labor force.
- The Hispanic labor force and the work force comprised of Asian and other culturally diverse employees are expected to increase faster than other groups, 36 percent and 41 percent, respectively, due to high immigration and higher than average family size among these populations.
- The women's labor force will grow more rapidly than men's, increasing from 46 to 47 percent.
- By 2006, the black and Hispanic labor forces will be nearly equal in size, as more Hispanics than blacks enter the labor force during the 1996–2006 period.

Source: Bureau of Labor Statistics

dents, or top CEOs stepping down to do work in the community. Ultimately, it's the need to be connected to and with other people that makes well-paid professionals walk away from the "high-roller" world.

Sometimes you probably get the same kind of feeling in college, that of being isolated, disconnected, and just another student number among the masses. Take heart—the future depends on a different kind of organizational structure in the areas of schooling and work. There will be ever-increasing stress on college-trained employees, with you among them, who can and will enjoy working effectively as a team. It will be to your benefit to consider your instructors, teaching assistants, and tutors as members of your "team" as you proceed through college. (See Chapter 6 for a thorough discussion of forming good relationships with your instructors.)

Have you in the past or do you now dislike course assignments that include group work? Do you groan when you are "forced" to work with other students? The workplaces of the future will succeed through cooperative problem solving by people like you who have learned to think and analyze for themselves, but who understand the strengths of combining their resources and talents. There are important implications in this change even now, in college instruction and for you as a college student. This trend probably explains the increased emphasis in colleges and universities on group work—research projects, writing groups, group presentations, study groups, and so on. (See Chapter 5 for a discussion of the power of learning with and from your student peers.) It is a very positive step that many college classrooms are becoming more like "the real world," in which people work together toward common goals.

JOY AND SERENITY: WORKING AND LEARNING WITH CHILDREN AND ELDERLY PEOPLE

One of the ways college work can become more like real work and the real world is through intergenerational experiences. Whether you formally train to work with children or not, some informal "literacy work" is likely to become part of your experience while in college. Your future will include some kinds of experiences with children, whether professional, personal, or both. In fact, it's very likely that you may work with children or elderly people through some sort of volunteering or service learning project (see Chapter 8 for a discussion of the power of volunteering and service learning) while in college. This kind of work is "giving back"—a rewarding local solution to a global problem.

Adults are children's first literacy-learning partners. You may have friends with children whom you like to "borrow" and play with; you may have young relatives; you may already be or may become a parent some day. The odds that you will be interacting with children are very high. Kids are hard to resist.

Supportive Experiences: Sharing How Print Works

Children love stories, picture books, and being read to by a caring adult. Very young children know that reading is something they want to know how to do, and it's amazing how much information about books they pick up as they listen to the stories read to them. When you add these "book experience" skills along with the fun of a story, you give them a foundation for a love of reading even before they begin school. Australian teacher Ann Pulvertaft[11] recommends that you help children learn certain things about books and reading.

- Stories have names (titles).
- Books have covers and pages.

- You read left-hand pages before right-hand pages if you are reading English, French, and so on.
- You usually start to read each page at the top left.
- The black squiggles (print), not the pictures, carry the actual message, though "a picture is worth a thousand words."
- You read along the line from left to right, and then go back to the start of the next line. (You could show children how to do this as you go along, but they usually notice it anyway.)
- Unlike conversation, the printed story comes out *exactly the same* each time. (This fascinates young children—they love it when you read and reread a favorite story! You know what happens if you try to skip a bit!)

Points to Keep in Mind when Working with Children

The information in Figures 11.2 and 11.3 is borrowed with admiration from Debra Jacobson,[12] a parent and elementary school teacher in Tucson, Arizona. Her ideas have been adapted to include both parents and non-parents—loving "others" such as college students and friends—who may serve as "literacy partners" with children.

FIGURE 11.2   *Points on working with children.*

- Children need a lot of support; we need to help them see themselves as capable learners.
- Since we want to help children become independent learners, it is best to ask an open-ended question, such as "What do you think?," rather than to give them the answer.
- Learning to read and write like adults takes time and a lot of experimenting. It is easier to read things in context than out of context. It is not a good idea for children to read word lists.
- Children become fluent readers and writers at different times. Be patient with them.
- Children learn a lot about reading and writing from everyday experiences; they don't need special kits to get them into literacy.
- Children like to try to do the things they see adults do. When you read, encourage the children around you to read.
- Talking is important for children. It helps them to feel good about themselves and promotes academic as well as personal success.
- Parents can contact their child's teacher with any concern about their child's progress or attitude.
- Educational research has shown that sometimes when children make progress in one area, they might regress in others. Be patient.

Source: Jacobson

Ideas for Working with Junior High and High School Students

Opportunities for working and learning with children don't end as the kids get older. In fact, some of the most important work (volunteer or personal and private) can be done with upper elementary through high school aged children, especially those "turned off," reluctant readers and writers. Following are some ideas.

• Talk to teenagers about the roles that writing, reading, and other "school subjects" play in your personal life, school, and/or job. Let them see you reading and writing. It's "cool" to carry around a book to read. Share with teenagers powerful, exciting language that you have read or written.

• Find out what the teenager(s) you are involved with are reading; ask if you can read their choice of materials, and see if you can get into discussions about the topics and issues that they value. This strategy is not about censorship as much as it

FIGURE 11.3   *Activities for working with children.*

• Set aside 15 minutes or more each day to read to children.
• Invite children to "read" to you.
• Encourage them to take an active part in your reading time. They can hold the book, turn the pages, read along with you, talk about the story, pretend to read the book to you, predict what will happen next at different parts of the story, and talk about how this story relates to their lives. Share your favorite books and stories.
• Talk to children about the environmental print they see every day: e.g., street signs, posters, cereal boxes, movie and TV schedules, letters, bills, notes, grocery lists, and recipes.
• Provide materials for children to explore and experiment with writing; for example, bank slips, applications, and mail order catalogs.
• Read the newspaper with your children. Check the ads, clip coupons, and read interesting headlines, photo captions, stories, and comics together.
• Leave notes around the house for your children. Encourage them to write notes to you.
• Enter contests that require filling out entry forms and addressing envelopes.
• Post a "Helpers' Chart" for your children to refer to when it's time to do chores at home.
• Share the cooking with children. Plan and write out menus, read and follow cookbook directions, and measure the ingredients together.
• Encourage children to explore their interests, and help them find books and other materials on those subjects.
• Teach children how to use the telephone book. Help them to look up the names and numbers of friends they want to call, and show them how to use the yellow pages.
• If you are able, teach children about computers.
• Provide quiet times for homework, reading, and writing away from the television, computer games, and Web surfing.
• Write labels on the things that children use each day.
• Encourage children to label and write their names on their possessions.
• Leave toys and food in original containers that have pictures and print on them. Encourage children to find groceries, unwrap household items, and make choices based on the print or pictures.
• Place books, paper, and a variety of writing implements on the children's level for easy and *continuous* access.
• Even if you're no Picasso, draw with children.
• Write down children's stories and observations so that later you can read, illustrate, and share them together.
• Make books about important events in your or others' children's lives.
• Share the mail with your children; read cards and letters to them and give them the catalogs and magazines to explore and play with.

Source: Jacobson

is about forming a trusting relationship. Most teenagers would rather talk to other teenagers than they would to adults, yet young people crave adults' sincere interest.

- Help young people develop interests in current affairs through watching and discussing news programs and documentaries.

- Open up the world to young people by sharing Internet adventures. Help them see and appreciate the "information highway" available to them online. On the other hand, you may very well have a teenager show *you* a thing or two about the Web! The interactive nature of using the Internet (appropriately, with supervision) can be a tempting means to make teenagers want to explore and learn, or to become the expert, the "teacher" of a technophobic adult.

Working and Learning with Senior Citizens

You are likely to have elderly relatives and friends; you may choose to volunteer to work with senior citizens while you are in college. Senior citizens are wonderful natural resources. We must not ignore the wealth of experiences older people possess. They can be partners in literacy, and especially oracy. Chief Dan George has said: "If the very old will talk, the very young will listen." Oral histories can be rich and important. Historians and students in Mozambique, East Africa, interviewed their elders to uncover the stories about their country's past that colonialists had suppressed. The theme of their project was "Our old people are our libraries." You can work and learn with senior citizens in many ways.

- Read to those with failing eyesight. Help them arrange to get books on tape, or help them find out about "books for the blind" services. Audiobooks are widely available in bookstores and libraries, including best-sellers and every genre imaginable.

- Listen to, record, and transcribe the rich stories of elderly people. Preserving "oral histories" is a fascinating way to capture and preserve the past. The book and film *Fried Green Tomatoes* and the 1998 film *Titanic* are good examples of wonderful stories told by elders.

- Your older informant is likely to have a collection of old photographs; pictures are great "story starters."

- Volunteer at a senior center; get to know some of the regulars and join them in their projects.

- Help connect the older generation with the younger generation. You could transport a senior citizen to a school where he or she could become a "literacy grandparent" to younger children—they can read together, share stories, and enjoy each other.

A WORD ABOUT TECHNOLOGIES AND TECHNOLOGY EDUCATION

Referring back to the mention of technophobic adults, it's time for a word about technologies. Education critic Neil Postman observed that "Technology has remade the world and continues to remake it."[13] The word *technology* has its origins in the Greek words *teksna,* "craft of weaving or fabricating," *tekhnikos,* "of art," and from *tekhne,* "art, craft, or skill." It's interesting that *technology* used to mean an art or craft. My, how meanings change. Please remember the wonderful arts and crafts— reading, writing, and speaking— skills that you have, will always have, and will continue to develop.

Now we tend to limit our thinking of technology to electronics, the "information explosion," and computers. Our concept of "progress" has changed to whether a task can be accomplished online. Training for our modern technology, or gaining computer literacy, is a necessity rather than a convenience. It can and will increase your proficiency in mathematics, composition, and a variety of academic disciplines, and it will stimulate your interests in many, many subjects. Technology training enables you to be a better researcher, consumer, worker, and citizen. "To be against technology makes no more sense than to be against food. We can't live without either."[14]

Postman sees "technology education" to be different from technology training and skill proficiency. Technology education is a way for all of us to understand what technologies (including television, radio, speech and writing via voice recognition software, telephones, clocks, and photographs, as well as computers) enable us to do and *prevent* us from doing. According to Postman, if technology education were a core subject in schools, it would be part of the humanities rather than technical education. Students at all levels, especially those in college, would study the history of *all* technology, not just computers, in order to understand the following 10 principles concerning the story of technology:

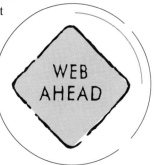

WEB AHEAD

1. All technological change is a **Faustian** bargain. For every advantage a new technology offers, there is always a corresponding disadvantage.
2. The advantages and disadvantages of new technologies are never distributed evenly among the population. This means that every new technology benefits some and harms others.
3. Embedded in every technology there is a powerful idea, sometimes two or three powerful ideas. Like language itself, a technology predisposes us to favor and value certain perspectives and accomplishments and to subordinate others. Every technology has a philosophy that is given expression in how a technology makes people use their minds, in what it makes us do with our bodies, in how it codifies the world, in which of our senses it amplifies and which of our emotional and intellectual tendencies it disregards.
4. A new technology usually wages war against an older technology. Both compete for time, attention, money, prestige, and a "world view."
5. Technological change is not additive; it is ecological. A new technology does not merely add something; it changes everything.
6. Because of the symbolic forms in which information is encoded, different technologies have different *intellectual* and *emotional* biases.
7. Because of the accessibility and speed of their information, different technologies have different *political* biases.
8. Because of their physical form, different technologies have different *sensory* biases.
9. Because of the conditions in which we attend to them, different technologies have different *social* biases.
10. Because of their technical and economic structure, different technologies have different *content* biases.[15]

Faustian in literature, Dr. Faustus made an unwise deal with the devil to get what he thought he wanted; it turned out badly

Yes, these principles are rather deep and complex, yet they need to be considered as we pass into the new millennium. What technologies that we do not yet possess will emerge and change our lives? Will we be ready?

Journal Reflections

11.1 Oh no! Ray Bradbury was right, and the government has decided to burn all books! No, let's honor stories and not be depressed by the predictions of excellent science fiction. For the purpose of this writing, forget about the government. Knowing a book or story by heart was once part of pre-writing cultures and of some literate cultures that viewed some stories as too sacred and powerful to be recorded in writing. What book would you "become" to preserve its truth and magic for the world? Why? What must it take to know a book "by heart"? What other "book people" would likely be your friends?

11.2 Look back to the employment projections from the Bureau of Labor Statistics. How do you think this agency arrives at its conclusions about the changing work force? Do these projections seem realistic to you? Why or why not? According to your observations and predictions about the coming new century, what important "top" professions seem to be missing from the lists?

11.3 Imagine yourself graduated and situated in your dream career. Where will you be, what will you be doing, and how will you be using reading, writing, speaking, and listening for professional purposes? For social purposes? Even if you are out of school, how will you continue to be a lifelong learner?

Experiences

11.1   WHAT TYPE OF TEAM MEMBER ARE YOU?

What experiences have you had in college so far that have taught you about the nature of teamwork? What concessions did you have to make? Were you a natural leader, a follower, or a collaborator? What steps do you take if a team project does not work out well? How might teamwork be a natural part of the work you will do in the future?

11.2 ASSESS YOUR ACADEMIC PREPARATION FOR THE FUTURE

How seriously should we take the projections for the future requirements of the workplace? To consider this question, form a group with two or three other students. Together, reread the skills, personal qualities, and competencies listed in the SCANS Report as necessary for work in the 21st century. Each group member should make a list in column form of all the courses he or she has taken in college, including those in the current term. This is a way of "taking inventory" of your education to this point in your college experience.

Next, work together and use the categories included in the SCANS Report to categorize and label the kinds of preparation for "the real world" that different courses afford you. Some courses may be difficult to analyze and categorize, but overall patterns of skills and competencies will emerge. For example, computer, writing, and mathematics courses naturally fit into the SCANS requirements, whereas "beginning horticulture" may not. Finally, the group should discuss the ways in which their courses of study are or are not providing them with the intellectual, personal, and technical know-how needed for the new century. You may want to extend the discussion if you discover that your combinations of course work are not in line with the SCANS information. Aren't some courses just "good for the heart and soul"? The tricky part is to fit such classes into your general education or foundation areas of study. There is room in your program for such "mellow" courses, and you need them, too!

11.3 WORKING WITH CHILDREN

Children *are* our future! With your own child, one borrowed from a friend, or with a child you have come to know through a volunteering experience, spend some time drawing, reading, and writing together. Pick two or three ideas from this chapter's section on "Working and Learning with Children" to use with your "literacy partner." Afterward, write down some reflections on the ways working and learning with children benefits you academically, socially, and spiritually. You may wish to share and discuss your impressions with other college students who have or work with children. Any parents and education majors in the group may have much to contribute to the dialogue!

11.4 EFFECTS OF TECHNOLOGY ON OUR LIVES

Refer back to Postman's ten principles concerning technology. With a partner, pick two or three principles to discuss. For each, decide what Postman's point is about the effects of technology on your lives as students and on our society as a whole. You may wish to share and compare your interpretations with the rest of the class.

Can You Relate?

ESSAY 11.1

This "final examination question" is borrowed from Neil Postman's thought-provoking book, *The End of Education*. It should be used as a take-home writing assignment, enabling you to take time to think deeply and write well. It has two parts:

> **Part I:** Choose one pre-20th century technology—for example, the alphabet, the printing press, the telegraph, the factory—and indicate what were the main intellectual, social, political, and economic advantages of the technology and why. Then indicate what were the main intellectual, social, political, and economic disadvantages of the technology and why.

> **Part II:** Indicate, first, what you believe are or will be the main advantages of computer technology and why; second, what are or will be the main disadvantages of computer technology and why.

According to Postman, "Any student who can pass this examination will, I believe, know something worthwhile. He or she will also have a sense of how the world was made and how it is being remade, and may even have some ideas on how it *should* be remade."[16]

The writing of this essay should begin with some class discussion and incorporate a bit of research and exploration. It requires creative thinking. There is no one right answer and no particular word length requirement or time limit. Have fun . . . Good luck! How's this for ending a chapter on the new millennium with a note of ambiguity, uncertainty, and challenge? It just seems appropriate somehow.

Endnotes

CHAPTER 1

1. Charles Suhor, "A Study in Media in Relation to English." (Unpublished doctoral dissertation, Florida State University, 1981), 55–59.
2. P. A. Nye, "Student Variables in Relation to Notetaking during a Lecture." *Programmed Learning and Educational Technology* 15 (1978), 196–200.
3. Walter Pauk, *How to Study in College,* 6th ed. (Boston: Houghton Mifflin, 1997), 239–250.
4. Charles Sanders Pierce, Vol. 6 of *The Collected Papers of Charles Sanders Pierce,* ed. Charles Hartshorne and Paul Weiss (Cambridge: The Belnap Press of Harvard University Press, 1932), 90.
5. Charles Suhor, "Semiotics." *Fact Sheet* (Urbana, IL: ERIC Clearinghouse on Reading and Communication Skills, 1982).

CHAPTER 2

1. Frank Smith, *Essays Into Literacy* (London: Heinemann Educational Books, 1983), vii–ix.
2. Frank Smith, *Understanding Reading* (New York: Holt, Rinehart and Winston, 1978), 97.
3. Martha Maxwell, *Improving Student Learning Skills,* rev. ed. (Clearwater, FL: H & H Publishing, 1997), 214.
4. Francis P. Robinson, *Effective Study* (New York: Harper and Row, 1970), 15–42.

5. Kenneth Goodman, *On Reading* (Portsmouth, NH: Heinemann Educational Books, 1996), 43.

6. Ibid., 43.

7. Yetta Goodman, Dorothy Watson, and Carolyn Burke, *Reading Strategies Focus on Comprehension.* 2nd ed. (Katonah, NY: Richard C. Owen Publishers, 1996), 4. The original versions of this model were introduced in *Reading Strategies: Focus on Comprehension* by Yetta Goodman and Carolyn Burke with Barry Sherman (New York: Holt, Rinehart and Winston, 1980), 4–8.

8. S. L. Nist, "Teaching Students to Annotate and Underline Text Effectively: Guidelines and Procedures." *Georgia Journal of Reading,* 12(2), 16–22.

9. Ibid.

10. Ibid.

11. Tirza Kroeker and Margaret Henrichs, *Reaching Adult Learners with Whole Language Strategies* (Katonah, NY: Richard C. Owen Publishers, 1993), 163.

12. Louise Rosenblatt, "What Facts Does This Poem Teach You?" *Language Arts* 57, no. 4 (April 1980), 386–394.

13. Ibid.

14. Ibid.

15. Yetta Goodman, Dorothy Watson, and Carolyn Burke, *Reading Strategies Focus on Comprehension.* 2nd ed. (Katonah, NY: Richard C. Owen Publishers, 1996), 4. The original versions of this model were introduced in *Reading Strategies: Focus on Comprehension* by Yetta Goodman and Carolyn Burke with Barry Sherman (New York: Holt, Rinehart and Winston, 1980), 24.

16. Owen Barfield, *Poetic Diction* (Middletown, PA: Wesleyan University Press, 1984), as reprinted in Ann E. Berthoff, ed., *Reclaiming the Imagination* (Portsmouth, NH: Boynton Cook, 1984), 130–131.

17. Contributed by Doug Clark, University of Missouri–Columbia Learning Center.

18. Henry H. Bauer, "The So-called Scientific Method." *Science and its Ways of Knowing,* edited by John Hatton and Paul B. Plouffe (Upper Saddle River, NJ: Prentice Hall, 1997), 30–31.

19. Jacob Bronowski, *Science and Human Values* (Cambridge: Harvard University Press, 1956).

20. Contributed by Sabrina Friedman, journalism student, University of Missouri–Columbia.

21. A. D. Baddeley, "Working Memory." *Science,* 255, 556–559.

22. Ibid.

23. Ibid.

24. Smith, *Understanding Reading* (New York: Holt, Rinehart and Winston, 1978), 45.

25. Ibid., 49.

26. Ibid., 52.

27. Smith, *Essays Into Literacy* (London: Heinemann Educational Books, 1983), 71.

28. Ibid.

29. Ibid., 118–119.

CHAPTER 3

1. Andrew Wilkinson as cited in Gay Su Pinnell and Angela M. Jagger, "Oral Language: Speaking and Listening in the Classroom." *Handbook of Research on Teaching the English Language Arts,* edited by James Flood, Julie M. Jensen, Diane Lapp and James R. Squire (New York: Macmillan, 1991), 693.

2. Smith, *Essays into Literacy* (London: Heinemann Educational Books, 1983), 45–46.

3. Malcolm Knowles, *The Adult Learner: A Neglected Species* (Houston: Gulf Publishing, 1973), 83.

4. Paulo Freire, *Pedagogy of the Oppressed* (New York: Continuum, 1984), 76, 123.

5. Barbara S. Wood, "Oral Communication in the Elementary Classroom." *Speaking and Writing K–12,* edited by Christopher Thaiss and Charles Suhor (Urbana, FL: National Council of Teachers of English, 1984), 105.

6. Thomas H. Hurt, Michael D. Scott, and James C. McCroskey, *Communication in the Classroom* (Reading, MA: Addison Wesley, 1978), 148.

7. Ibid., 151–152.

8. Ibid.

9. Adapted from Milton Rokeach, *The Open and Closed Mind* (New York: Basic Books, 1960), as reprinted in S. I. Hayakawa, *Language in Thought and Action,* 4th ed. (New York: Harcourt Brace Jovanovich, 1978), 232–234.

10. Ibid.

11. Ibid.

12. Ibid.

13. Donald L. Rubin and Kenneth Kantor, "Talking and Writing: Building Communication Competence." *Speaking and Writing K–12,* edited by Christopher Thaiss and Charles Suhor (Urbana, IL: National Council of Teachers of English, 1984), 42.

14. Stephen Cahir and Ceil Lucas, "Exploring Functional Language." *Speaking and Writing K–12,* edited by Christopher Thaiss and Charles Suhor (Urbana, IL: National Council of Teachers of English, 1984), 156. Washington D.C. Center for Applied Linguistics, 1981.

15. Jana Staton, "Thinking Together: Interaction in Children's Reasoning." *Speaking and Writing K–12,* edited by Christopher Thaiss and Charles Sukor (Urbana, IL: National Council of Teachers of English, 1984), p.158.

16. Hurt, Scott, and McCroskey, *Communication in the Classroom* (Reading, MA: Addison Wesley, 1978), 69.

17. Ibid., 76.

18. Ibid., 100.

19. Rubin and Kantor, "Talking and Writing: Building Communication Competence," in *Speaking and Writing K–12,* edited by Christopher Thaiss and Charles Suhor (Urbana, FL: National Council of Teachers of English, 1984), 69.

20. Hurt, Scott, and McCroskey, *Communication in the Classroom* (Reading, MA: Addison Wesley, 1978), a personal report of communication apprehension—adult version, 155–156.

CHAPTER 4

1. C. Paul and J. Rosenkoetter, "Relations Between Completion Time and Test Score." *Southern Journal of Educational Research* 12(2), 151–157.

2. L. McLain, "Behavior During Examinations: A Comparison of A, C and F Students." *Teaching of Psychology* 10(2), April 1983, 69–71.

3. Quiz contributed by Doug Clark of the University of Missouri–Columbia Learning Center.

4. G. Cirino-Grena, "Strategies in Answering Essay Tests." *Teaching of Psychology,* 8(1), February 1981, 53–54.

5. Irwin G. Sarason, "Experimental Approaches to Test Anxiety: Attention and the Uses of Information," in *Anxiety: Current Trends in Theory and Research,* Vol. 2, edited by Charles B. Spielberger (New York: Academic Press, 1972).

6. David M. Wark and Michael J. Bennett, "The Measurement of Test Anxiety in a Reading Class." *Reading World,* March 1981, 215–222.

7. The discussion of the ACT is taken from Thomas H. Martinson and Juliana Fazzone, *Super Course for the ACT,* 2nd ed. (New York: Prentice-Hall, 1991), 27–30.

8. Gregor Hartman, *How to Prepare for the S.P.L.A.T. (Student Potential Life Achievement Test* (New York: Quill, 1983), 66.

CHAPTER 5

1. L. S. Vygotsky, *Thought and Language* (Cambridge: The M. I. T. Press, 1962), 12.

2. L. S. Vygotsky, *Mind and Society* (Cambridge: Harvard University Press, 1978).

3. Ann Ruggles Gere, *Writing Groups: History, Theory and Implications* (Carbondale, IL: Southern Illinois University Press, 1987), 4.

4. This strategy originally appeared in Carol Gilles, Mary Bixby, Paul Crowley, et al., *Whole Language Strategies for Secondary Students* (New York: Richard C. Owen Publishers, 1988), 53.

5. Ibid., 50.

CHAPTER 6

1. "The American College Teacher: National Norms for the 1995–96 H.E.R.I. Faculty Survey" (University of California at Los Angeles Higher Education Research Institute, 1999), as shown in *The Chronicle of Higher Education* (45,1), 32.

CHAPTER 7

1. Alan Miller, *Personality Types: A Modern Synthesis* (Calgary, Alberta, Canada: University of Calgary Press, 1991), 11.

2. Charles S. Claxton and Yvonne Ralston, *Learning Styles: Their Impact on Teaching and Administration* (Washington, D. C.: The American Association for Higher Education, Research Report #10, 1978), 10–12.

3. Synthesized from Claxton and Ralston (Ibid.) and from Bette LaSere Erickson and Diane Weltner Strommer, *Teaching College Freshmen* (San Francisco: Jossey-Bass, 1991), 55–57.

4. Claxton and Ralston, *Learning Styles: Their Impact on Teaching and Administration* (Washington, D. C.: The American Association for Higher Education, Research Report #10, 1978), 28.

5. Rowan Bayne, *The Myers-Briggs Type Indicator* (London: Chapman and Hall, 1995), 27–39.

6. Bette LaSere Erickson and Diane Weltner Strommer, *Teaching College Freshmen* (San Francisco: Jossey-Bass, 1991), 60.

7. Bayne, *The Myers-Briggs Type Indicator* (London: Chapman and Hall, 1995), 58.

8. G. H. Jensen, *Applications of the Myers-Briggs Type Indicator in Higher Education,* edited by J. Provost and S. Anchors (Palo Alto, CA: Consulting Psychologists Press, 1987).

9. James Vasquez, "Teaching to the Distinctive Traits of Minority Students." *The Clearing House,* Volume 63 (March 1990), 299–304.

CHAPTER 8

1. Alexander W. Astin, *What Matters in College? Four Critical Years Revisited* (San Francisco: Jossey-Bass Publishers, 1993), 319.

2. Wayne J. Stein, "Tribal Colleges: A Success Story." in *New Directions for Community Colleges* 80 (Winter 1992), from *First-Generation Students: Confronting the Cultural Issues* (San Francisco: Jossey-Bass, 1992), 89.

3. Astin, *What Matters in College? Four Critical Years Revisited* (San Francisco: Jossey-Bass Publishers, 1993), 61.

4. Ibid., 416.

5. Charles Schroeder, "The Student Learning Imperative." *American College Personnel Association Publications,* created from the Student Learning Project, 1995, 1.

6. Jacob Neussner, *How to Grade Your Professors* (Boston: Beacon Press, 1984), 116.

7. Ibid., 125.

8. David A. Hoekema, *Rules and Moral Community* (Lanham, MD: Rowman and Littlefield Publishers, 1994), 27.

9. Ernest Boyer, *In Search of Community.* (American Council on Education, Washington, D. C., 1990), 2.

10. David A. Hoekema, *Rules and Moral Community* (Lanham, MD: Rowman and Littlefield Publishers, 1994), 141.

11. Ibid., 134.

12. Ernest Boyer, *In Search of Community.* (American Council on Education, Washington, D. C., 1990), 10.

13. Yale University "Undergraduate Regulations." David A. Hoekema, *Rules and Moral Community* (Lanham, MD: Rowman and Littlefield Publishers, 1994), 204.

14. Ibid., 206–207.

15. Gene R. Hawes, *Going to College While Working: Strategies for Success* (New York: College Board Publications, 1985), 119–120.

16. Kenneth Strike and Pamela A. Moss, *Ethics and College Student Life* (Needham Heights, MA: Allyn and Bacon, 1997), 165–168.

17. Ibid., 168.

18. Rudolph H. Weingartner, *Undergraduate Education: Goals and Means* (New York: Macmillan, 1992), 160.

19. *pollrelease.html* at *www.inform.umd.edu*–Poll developed by Association of American Colleges and Universities and the University of Maryland, in cooperation with Diversity Connections *(diversity-web@umail.umd.edu).*

20. *The Chronicle of Higher Education* Almanac Issue, August 28, 1998, in which their own sources are cited.

21. Ibid., 5.

22. Alfred C. Kinsey, Wardell B. Pomeroy and Clyde E. Martin, *Sexual Behavior in the Human Male* (Philadelphia: W. B. Saunders, 1948).

23. Paul Gibson, "Gay Male and Lesbian Youth Suicide." In *Report of the Secretary's Task Force on Youth Suicide,* Publication No. ADM-89-1623 Volume 3 (Washington, D. C.: U. S. Department of Health and Human Services, 1989), 10, as quoted in the pamphlet "The University of Missouri's Non-Discrimination Clause" (Columbia, MO: Gay, Lesbian, Bisexual Resource Center, 1998).

24. Editorial, *New York Times,* 17 October 1998.

25. Diversity Digest on the Web at *www.inform.umd.edu/diversityweb/digest/w98/identify.html*

26. Charles Schroeder, "The Student Learning Imperative." In *American College Personnel Association Publications,* created from the Student Learning Project, 1995, 3.

27. Ernest L. Boyer, *College: The Undergraduate Experience in America* (New York: Harper and Row, 1987), 216.

CHAPTER 9

1. Boyer, *College: The Undergraduate Experience in America* (New York: Harper and Row, 1987), 73.

2. Ibid., 87.

3. Ibid., 85.

4. Ibid., 110.

5. Virginia N. Gordon, *The Undecided College Student* (Springfield, IL: Charles C Thomas, 1995), 11.

6. Ibid., 54.

7. Ibid., 63.

8. Ibid., 65–67.

9. Ibid., 61–62.

10. B. C. Anderson, D. G. Creamer, and L. H. Cross, "Undecided, Multiple Change, and Decided Students: How Different Are They?" *NACDA Journal 9* (1), Spring 1989, 46–50, in Susan H. Frost, *Academic Advising for Student Success: A System of Shared*

Responsibility. ASHE-ERIC Higher Education Report No. 3 (Washington, D. C.: The George Washington University, School of Education and Human Development, 1991), 49.

11. The University of Missouri Career Center, *http://www.missouri.edu/~cppcwww/self.shtml*

12. U.S. Bureau of Labor Statistics, *http://stats.bls.gov/news.release/ecopro.table6.htm,* 12/24/98.

13. Carol Carter, *Majoring in the Rest of Your Life.* New York: Farrar, Straus & Giroux, 1999.

CHAPTER 10

1. Thomas M. Smith, Beth Aronstamm Young, Yupin Bae, Susan P. Choy, and Nabeel Alsalam, *The Condition of Education 1997,* NCES-97-338 (Washington, D. C.: U. S. Government Printing Office, 1997), p. 72.

2. Ibid.

3. Ibid.

4. Peter M. Senge, *The Fifth Discipline: The Art & Practice of the Learning Organization* (New York: Doubleday, 1994), 307.

5. Ibid., 310

6. Consumer Credit Counseling Service of Greater Kansas City, Inc., *Credit College* pamphlet.

7. Moffit, Kramer, and Hoffman, in R. Kim Guenther, *Human Cognition* (Upper Saddle River, NJ: Prentice Hall, 1998), p. 41.

8. Ibid.

CHAPTER 11

1. Boyer, *College: The Undergraduate Experience in America* (New York: Harper and Row, 1987), 276.

2. U.S. Bureau of Labor Statistics, *http://stats.bls.gov/news.release/ecopro.table6.htm,* 12/24/98.

3. Ibid.

4. Ibid.

5. Goodman, *On Reading* (Portsmouth, NH: Heinemann Educational Books, 1996), 125.

6. The Secretary's Commission on Achieving Necessary Skills, *What Work Requires of Schools: A SCANS Report for America 2000* (U.S. Department of Labor, 1991).

7. Ibid., 5.

8. Ibid., vii.

9. Ibid., 12.

10. U.S. Bureau of Labor Statistics, *http://stats.bls.gov/news.release/ecopro.table6.htm,* 12/24/98.

11. Ann Pulvertaft, "A Collection of Letters About Books, Children and the Joys of Sharing." As excerpted in *The Whole Language Catalog,* ed. Ken Goodman, Lois Bird and Yetta Goodman (Santa Rosa, CA: American School Publishers, 1991), 357.

12. Debra Jacobson, "Information for Parents About Whole Language Teaching and Learning." *The Whole Language Catalog,* ed. Ken Goodman, Lois Bird, and Yetta Goodman (Santa Rosa, CA: American School Publishers, 1991), 365.

13. Neil Postman, *The End of Education: Redefining the Value of School* (New York: Random House, 1995), 190.

14. Ibid., 191.

15. Ibid., 192.

16. Ibid., 193.

Bibliography

Anderson, B. C., D. G. Creamer and L. H. Cross. "Undecided, Multiple Change, and Decided Students: How Different Are They?" *NACDA Journal* 9 (1), Spring 1989, in Susan H. Frost, *Academic Advising for Student Success: A System of Shared Responsibility.* ASHE-ERIC Higher Education Report No. 3. Washington, D. C.: The George Washington University, School of Education and Human Development, 1991.

Astin, Alexander W. *What Matters in College: Four Critical Years Revisited.* San Francisco: Jossey-Bass Publishers, 1975.

Baddeley, A. D. "Working Memory," *Science,* 255. Published in R. Kim Guenther, *Human Cognition,* Upper Saddle River, NJ: Prentice Hall, 1998.

Bauer, Henry H. "The So-called Scientific Method." In *Science and its Ways of Knowing,* edited by John Hatton and Paul B. Plouffe. Upper Saddle River, NJ: Prentice Hall, 1997. First published in Henry H. Bauer, *Scientific Literacy and the Myth of the Scientific Method,* University of Illinois Press, 1992.

Bayne, Rowan. *The Myers-Briggs Type Indicator.* London: Chapman and Hall, 1995.

Berthoff, Ann E., ed. *Reclaiming the Imagination: Philosophical Perspectives for Writers and Teachers of Writing.* Portsmouth, NH: Heinemann Educational Books, 1984.

Boyer, Ernest. "In Search of Community." American Council on Education. Washington, D. C., January 18, 1990.

_____ *College: The Undergraduate Experience in America.* New York: Harper and Row, 1987.

Bronowski, Jacob. *Science and Human Values.* Cambridge: Harvard University Press, 1956.

Cahir, Stephen and Ceil Lucas. "Exploring Functional Language." In *Speaking and Writing K–12,* edited by Christopher Thaiss and Charles Suhor. Urbana, IL: National Council of Teachers of English, 1984.

Carter, Carol. *Majoring in the Rest of Your Life.* New York: Farrar, Straus and Giroux, 1999.

Cirino-Grena, G. "Strategies in Answering Essay Tests." In *Teaching of Psychology* 8(1), February 1991.

Claxton, Charles S. and Yvonne Ralston. *Learning Styles: Their Impact on Teaching and Administration.* Washington D. C.: The American Association for Higher Education, 1978.

Erickson, Betty LaSere and Diane Weltner Strommer. *Teaching College Freshmen.* San Francisco: Jossey-Bass, 1991.

Flippo, Rona F., and David C. Caverly, eds. *Teaching Reading & Study Strategies at the College Level.* Newark, DE: International Reading Association, 1991.

Freire, Paolo. *Pedagogy of the Oppressed.* New York: Continuum, 1984.

Gere, Ann Ruggles. *Writing Groups: History, Theory and Implications.* Carbondale, IL: Southern Illinois University Press, 1987.

Gibson, Paul. "Gay Male and Lesbian Youth Suicide." In *Report of the Secretary's Task Force on Youth Suicide,* Publication No. ADM 89-1623 Volume 3. Washington, D. C.: U. S. Department of Health and Human Services, 1989. As quoted in the pamphlet "The University of Missouri's Non-Discrimination Clause." Columbia, MO: Gay, Lesbian, Bisexual Resource Center, 1998.

Gilles, Carol, Mary Bixby, Paul Crowley, Shirley R. Crenshaw, Margaret Henrichs, Frances E. Reynolds and Donelle Pyle. *Whole Language Strategies for Secondary Students.* New York: Richard C. Owen Publishers, 1988.

Goodman, Ken. *What's Whole in Whole Language?* Portsmouth, NH: Heinemann Educational Books, 1986.

___. *On Reading.* Portsmouth, NH: Heinemann Educational Books, 1996.

Goodman, Yetta, Dorothy J. Watson, and Carolyn L. Burke. *Reading Strategies: Focus on Comprehension.* 2nd ed. Katonah, NY: Richard C. Owen Publishers, 1996.

Gordon, Virginia N. *The Undecided College Student.* Springfield, IL: Charles C Thomas, 1995.

Guenther, R. Kim. *Human Cognition.* Upper Saddle River, NJ: Prentice Hall, 1998.

Hartman, Gregor. *How to Prepare for the S.P.L.A.T. (Student Potential Life Achievement Test.)* New York: Quill, 1983.

Hawes, Gene R. *Going to College While Working: Strategies for Success.* New York: College Board Publications, 1985.

Hayakawa, S. I. *Language in Thought and Action.* New York: Harcourt Brace Jovanovich, 1978.

Hoekema, David A. *Campus Rules and Moral Community: In Place of "In Loco Parentis."* Lanham, MD: Rowman and Littlefield Publishers, 1994.

Hurt, Thomas H., Michael D. Scott and James C. McCroskey. *Communication in the Classroom.* Reading, MA: Addison Wesley Publishers, 1978.

Jacobson, Debra. "Information for Parents About Whole Language Teaching and Learning." In *The Whole Language Catalog,* edited by Ken Goodman, Lois Bird and Yetta Goodman. Santa Rosa, CA: American School Publishers, 1991.

Jensen, G. H. *Applications of the Myers-Briggs Type Indicator in Higher Education,* edited by J. Provost and S. Anchors. Palo Alto, CA: Consulting Psychologists Press, 1987.

Keirsey, David and Marilyn Bates. *Please Understand Me.* Del Mar, CA: Prometheus Nemesis, 1978.

Kinsey, Alfred C., Wardell B. Pomeroy and Clyde S. Martin. *Sexual Behavior in the Human Male.* Philadelphia: W. B. Saunders, 1948.

Kinsey, Alfred C. *Sexual Behavior in the Human Female.* Philadelphia: W. B. Saunders, 1953.

Knowles, Malcolm. *The Adult Learner: A Neglected Species.* Houston: Gulf Publishing, 1973.

Kroeker, Tirza, and Margaret Henrichs. *Reaching Adult Learners with Whole Language Strategies.* Katonah, NY: Richard C. Owen Publishers, 1993.

Martinson, Thomas H. and Juliana Fazzone. *Super Course for the ACT,* 2nd edition. New York: Prentice Hall, 1991.

Maxwell, Martha. *Improving Student Learning Skills.* Rev. ed. Clearwater, FL: H&H Publishing Company, 1997.

McLain, L. "Behavior During Examinations: A Comparison of A, C and F Students." In *Teaching of Psychology* 10(2), April 1983.

Miller, Alan. *Personality Types: A Modern Synthesis.* Calgary, Alberta, Canada: University of Calgary Press, 1991.

Neusner, Jacob. *How to Grade Your Professors.* Boston: Beacon Press, 1984.

Nist, S. L. "Teaching Students to Annotate and Underline Text Effectively: Guidelines and Procedures." *Georgia Journal of Reading,* 12(2).

Nye, P. A. "Student Variables in Relation to Notetaking during a Lecture." *Programmed Learning and Educational Technology* 15, 1978.

Pauk, Walter. *How to Study in College.* 6th ed. Boston: Houghton Mifflin, 1997.

Paul, C. and J. Rosenkoetter. "Relations Between Completion Time and Test Score." In *Southern Journal of Educational Research* 12(2).

Pierce, Charles Sanders. *The Collected Papers of Charles Sanders Pierce,* Volume 6, edited by Charles Hartshorne and Paul Weiss. Cambridge: The Belnap Press of Harvard University, 1932.

Pinnell, Gay Su and Angela M. Jagger. "Oral Language: Speaking and Listening in the Classroom." In *Handbook of Research on Teaching the English Language Arts,* edited by James Flood, Julie M. Jensen, Diane Lapp and James R. Squire. New York: Macmillan, 1991.

Postman, Neil. *The End of Education: Redefining the Value of School.* New York: Random House, 1995.

Pulvertaft, Ann. "A Collection of Letters About Books, Children and the Joys of Sharing." Excerpted in *The Whole Language Catalog,* edited by Ken Goodman, Lois Bird and Yetta Goodman. Santa Rosa, CA: American School Publishers, 1991.

Robinson, Francis P., *Effective Study.* 4th ed. New York: Harper & Row, 1970.

Rokeach, Milton. *The Open and Closed Mind,* reprinted in S. I. Hayakawa, *Language in Thought and Action,* 4th ed. New York: Harcourt Brace Jovanovich, 1978.

Rosenblatt, Louise. "What Facts Does This Poem Teach You?" *Language Arts* 57, no. 4 (April 1980).

Rubin, Donald L. and Kenneth Kantor. "Talking and Writing: Building Communication Competence." In *Speaking and Writing K–12,* edited by Christopher Thaiss and Charles Suhor. Urbana, IL: National Council of Teachers of English, 1984.

Schroeder, Charles. "The Student Learning Imperative." In *American College Personnel Association Publications* From the Student Learning Project, 1995.

Senge, Peter M. *The Fifth Discipline: The Art & Practice of The Learning Organization.* New York: Doubleday, 1994.

Smith, Frank. *Essays Into Literacy.* London: Heinemann Educational Books, 1983.

____. *Reading Without Nonsense.* New York: Teachers College Press, 1979.

____. *Understanding Reading.* New York: Holt, Rinehart and Winston, 1978.

____. *Writing and the Writer.* New York: Holt, Rinehart and Winston, 1982.

Smith, Thomas M., Beth Aronstamm Young, Yupin Bae, Susan P. Choy and Nabeel Alsalam. *The Condition of Education 1997,* NCES-97-338. Washington D. C.: U. S. Government Printing Office, 1997.

Stein, Wayne J. "Tribal Colleges: A Success Story." In *New Directions for Community Colleges* 80, Winter 1992. From *First-Generation Students: Confronting the Cultural Issues,* edited by L. Steven Zwerling and Howard B. London. San Francisco: Jossey-Bass, 1992.

Strike, Kenneth and Pamela A Moss. *Ethics and College Student Life.* Needham Heights, MA: Allyn and Bacon, 1997.

Suhor, Charles. "A Study in Media in Relation to English." Doctoral dissertation, Florida State University, 1981.

_____ "Semiotics." *Fact Sheet.* Urbana, IL: ERIC Clearinghouse on Reading and Communication Skills, 1982.

Vasquez, James. "Teaching to the Distinctive Traits of Minority Students." In *The Clearing House,* Volume 63, March 1990, 299–304.

Vygotsky, L. S. *Thought and Language.* Cambridge: The M.I.T. Press, 1962.

____. *Mind and Society.* Cambridge: Harvard University Press, 1978.

Wark, David M. and Michael J. Bennett. "The Measurement of Test Anxiety in a Reading Class." In *Reading World,* March 1981.

Weingartner, Rudolph H. *Undergraduate Education: Goals and Means.* New York: Macmillan, 1992.

Wood, Barbara. "Oral Communication in the Elementary Classroom." In *Speaking and Writing K–12,* edited by Christopher Thaiss and Charles Suhor. Urbana, IL: National Council of Teachers of English, 1984.

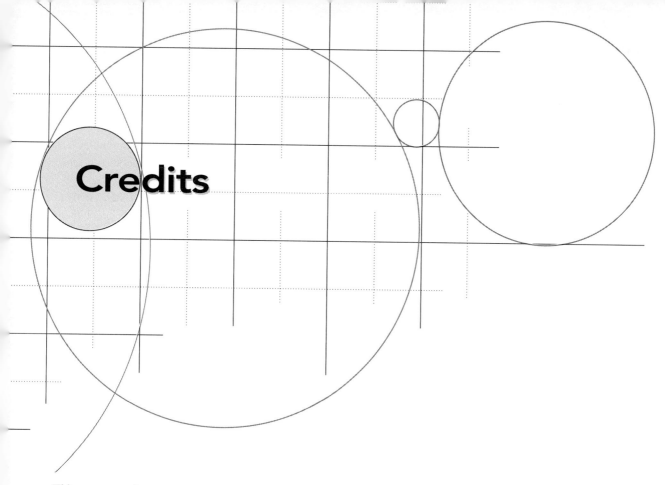

Credits

This page constitutes a continuation of the copyright page. The number at the beginning of each credit indicates the book page on which the credited material appears.

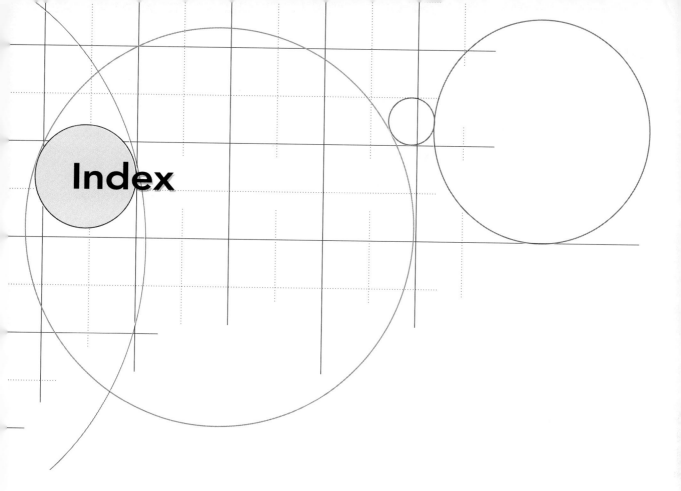

Index

Academic dishonesty, 140–141
Academic freedom and honesty, 110
ACT (American College Testing),
    85, 87
Active listening, 61
Activities, in college, 142, 144–145
Administration, in schools, 137
Advisors, 160–161, 165
Aesthetic vs. efferent reading, 35, 37
Algebra, functions of, 42
Alzheimer's disease, 48
Ambiguity, 65
Appointments, and instructors,
    111–116
Approaches to learning, 53
Arithmetic, functions of, 42
Articles, reading, 45
Articulatory loop memory, 47
Assessment of learning style,
    122–126
Associating, learning strategy, 40
Assumptions, 112–114
Attitudes, 108–109
Auditory/echoic memory, 47
Aural/auditory style, 123
Authentic learning, 36

Bacon, Francis, 36
Baddeley, A.D., 47–48
Barfield, Owen, 38
Bauer, Henry H., 44

Behavioral traits, 122
Belief/disbelief systems, 61
Belonging, 144–146
Bibliography, 207–210
Black college, defined, 136
Body language, 66
Boredom, effects on learning, 28
Boyer, Earnest, 139, 156, 187
Bronowski, Jacob, 44
Bureaucracy, school administration,
    137

Calculus/differential equations,
    functions of, 43
Campus resources, 141–142
Career exploration, 155–167
    core courses and, 156
    electronic information sources,
        161
    employment projections, 165
    interest inventories, 161
    majors and, 156–157, 158–164
    study abroad and, 157
Cause–effect, thesis statement, 80
Central executive memory, 47
Chaos system, 7–8
Charting, 21
Cheating, 141
Children, working with, 193–196
CHOICES, assessment instrument,
    163

Choosing a major, 160–164
Chronological, thesis statement, 80
Chunking, 52–53
Chunks, 72
Clark, Doug, 41
Classroom dialogue, 63–64
CLEP (College Level Exam
    Program), 88
Closet changers, 159
Cognitive styles, 123
College, purpose of, 142, 144–145
Colleges, defined, 135–136
Communication apprehension/
    anxiety, 59, 66–67
Communication systems, 57–69
Community/two-year colleges,
    defined, 137
Commuting, 175–176
Competition, 4
Comprehension, 50–53
    and reading, 18, 28
    strategy, 12
Concentration, 27
Concreteness, in message, 65
Conduct, 138–140
Confirming, and reading, 31–32
Context, in reading, 30–31
Controlling, 58
Cornell System, 9, 11–12
Cramming, 84
Credit cards, 177–178

Critical reading, 36
Critical thinking, 36, 39

Decideds, 160
Deductive reasoning, 41
Dialectical, 17
Dialects, 65
Dialogue, 58, 63–64
Difficult instructors, 117
DISCOVER, assessment instrument, 163
Dishonesty, academic, 140–141
Diversity:
    on campus, 145–150
    poll, 145
    in reading, 34
    in the workplace, 192
Drawing to learn, 7, 16, 19–21, 23, 25
Drifters, 158

Echoic/auditory memory, 47
Education IRAs, 180
Education and technology, 196
Effective vs. ineffective reading, 28–29
Efferent vs. aesthetic reading, 35, 37
Efficient note taking, 8
Efficient reading, 33
Elderly, working with, 193, 196
Electronic information sources, 161, 163–164
Embedded Figures Test, Witkin, 123
Emotional self-care, 181–182
Employment:
    and college, 174–175
    and money management, 179
    projections and trends, 164–165
Encoding, 7, 16
Endnotes, 201–206
Enforced study halls, 174
Enriched majors, 156–157
Enrollment, 146–150
Environmental function, in reading, 36–37
Episodic memory, 48
Essay:
    development/structure of, 79
    exam, 77–79 80–81, 89, *see also* Exam
    readings, 45
Estimate, in reasoning, 41
Every other line, note taking, 12, 14
Exam, 114–116, *see also* Final exams, Testing, *and* Test anxiety
Expectations of instructor, 110–111
Experts, 160
Expressive systems, 57
Extensive reading, 33

Externals, 159
EZ charge systems, 177–178

Family Educational Rights and Privacy Act, 141
Family, and college, 176–177
Faustian, 197
Field independent learners, 123–124
Field sensitive learners, 123–124
Fill-in-the-blank tests, 81, *see also* Exam
Final exams, 83–86, *see also* Exam, Testing, *and* Test anxiety
Financial aid, 178–179
First-letter mnemonics, 51–52
First-order comprehension strategy, 12
First-year orientation survey, 162–163
Foreign language texts, 39–40
Forest learners, 123
Forgetting, and memory, 49–50
Formal speaking, 65
Future, after college, 187–199

Gamesmanship, 4
GED (General Educational Development), 86
General education requirements, 156–157
Genres, in literature, 37–38
Geometry, functions of, 42–43
Gere, Ann Ruggles, 96
GMAT (Graduate Management Admissions Test), 88
Goals, and reading, 34
Goodman, Kenneth, 30, 36
GRE (Graduate Record Exam), 87
Greeks and behavioral traits, 122
Group:
    dynamic strategies, 98–102
    listening strategy, 101–102
    speaking strategy, 100–101
    writing strategy, 99–100

Heterosexism, 150
Hidden minority, 149–150
Higher math, functions of, 43
Highlighting, 32–33
Hoekema, David, 138
Homophobia, 150
Honesty, academic, 110
Hope Credit, TRA 97, 180
Humanities texts, 37–38
Humors, and personality, 122

Iconic memory, 47
Imagining, 58
Immigration, and workplace, 192
Improvement:

listening, 60–61
memory/comprehension, 50–53
speech, 64–65
In loco parentis, 138–139
Inclusion, on campus, 145–150
Independent (nonsectarian) colleges, defined, 136
Inductive reasoning, 41
Ineffective vs. effective reading, 28–29
Information management systems, 3–26, 115
Informational function, 36–37
Informing-responding, 58
Instructors, 107–120
    and assistants: 110–11
    difficult, 117
    and exam preparation, 114–116
    expectations of, 110–111
    and majors, 164
    meeting with, 118–120
    office hours strategies, 111–116
    and personality, 116–117
    shopping around for, 117
    and teaching styles, 127–129
Integrating, 31–32
Intensive reading, 33
Interactional scaffolding, 63–64
Intercommunication, 58
Interest inventories, 161
Internet, 5, 46
Internships, 163–164
Interrelationships, 49
Iconic/visual memory, 47
IRAs, education, 180

Jacobson, Debra, 194
James, William, 47
Journal:
    activities, 22, 53, 66, 88, 102, 118, 129, 151, 165, 182, 197
    articles, 45
Journal/note taking, 17

Keirsey Temperament Sorter, 124–126
Kinesthetic style learning, 123
Knowles, Malcom, 58
Kolb, David, and Learning Style Inventory, 123

Labor force, 192
Language:
    and thinking, 27–69
    intensity, 64
Learning:
    after college, 189–191
    cognitive styles, 123
    behavior, 4
    opportunities, 117

and peers, 102–105
style, 121–131
systems, 22
Learning Style Inventory (LSI),
Kolb, 123–124
Least to most, thesis statement, 80
Lectures, and note taking, 7
Left-handed students, note taking,
14–15
Lifetime Learning Credit, 180
Listening, 59–62, 101–102
Listening–reading connection,
59–60
Listening and speaking, 27–56,
58–69
Literacy, 57, 191–192
Literature texts, 37–38
Loci method, 51
Long-term memory, 48
LSAT (Law School Admissions
Test), 87

Magazines, 45–46
Majors, 158–164
and advisors, 160–161
and career exploration, 155–167
changing, 165–166
and electronic information
sources, 161, 163–164
and employment projection
trends, 164–165
and general education requirements, 156–157
and interest inventories, 161
and study abroad, 157
Managing, 169–184
employment, 174–175
family, 176–177
money, 177–180
stress, 180–182
Mapping, 20
Marking, 32–33
Master's:
degree, 188–189
thesis, 188
MAT (Miller's Analogy Test), 87
Matching tests, 75–76, see also
Exam
Mathematics texts, 41–43
Math skills, 41
Maxwell, Martha, 28
MCAT (Medical College
Admissions Test), 87
Memory:
articulatory loop, 47
and comprehension, 27, 50–53
devices, 50–53
episodic, 48
iconic, 47
improvement, 50–53

long-term, 48
sensory, 47
short-term, 47
systems, 46–53
visual, 47
Men's colleges, 136
Mentor, 108, 117–118
Message, in speech, 64
Method of Loci, 51
Millennium, impact of, 189
Mnemonic devices, , 50–53
Money management, 177–180
borrowing, 178
and credit cards, 177–178
employment, 179
financial aid, 178–179
TRA 97, 180
Most to least, thesis statement, 80
Motivation, 27
Multiple choice tests, 73–75, see
also Exam
Myers-Briggs Type Indicator
(MBTI), 123–125, 127

Narrative chaining, 52
Neussner, Jacob, 137–138
Newspapers, 45–46
Nist, S.L., 32–33
Noblitt, Brenda, 178
Note taking, 5
chaos system, 7–8
in college, 5
Cornell system, 9, 11–12
efficient, 8
every other line, 12, 14
left-handed students, 14–15
note/book consolidation systems,
12, 16
rainbow system, 8–9
traditional outline system, 9–10
Novels, 45

Objective tests, 72–77, see also
Exam
Occupational function, 36–37
Occupations, 187–188
Office hours, and instructors,
111–116
Oracy, 57
Oral communications, 58
Organization, 64
Orientation survey, 162–163
Out-of-classroom, learning opportu-
nities, 117

Page-to-page, consolidation systems,
12–13
Paperback novels, 45
Peer learning, 102–105
Pegword method, 52

Pencil-in-hand strategies, 16
People and policies, 137–141
Personal:
inquiry, 23
reading improvement log, 34–35
Personal Report of Communication
Anxiety (PRCA), 67–68
Personality:
and instructors, 116–117
types, 122–127
Physical self-care, 181
Piaget, Jean, 96
Pierce, Charles Sanders, 21
Plagiarism, 140–141
Plot, 37
Policies, 137–141
Predicting, 31–32
Prereading, 33
Preview, 170
Primary sources, in reading, 39
Private colleges/universities,
defined, 136
Probability, functions of, 43
Problem/solution, thesis statement,
80
Process study, 174
Product-based study, 174
Propositions, in testing, 75
Protestant colleges, defined, 136
Prove it, writing technique, 99–100
Proximal development, zone of, 96
Public colleges/universities, defined,
136
Public four-year colleges/universi-
ties, defined, 136
Purpose, in reading, 35–36

Qualifiers, in testing, 74
Question–answer, thesis statement,
80
Questions, in note taking, 12

Rainbow note taking system, 8–9
Reading:
ability, 30
aesthetic vs. efferent, 35, 37
and comprehension, 18, 28
context, 30–31
critical, 36
effective vs. ineffective, 28–29
efficiently, 33
environmental function in, 36–37
functions, 36–37
group strategy, 98–99
improvement, 33–34
process, 32
scanning vs. skimming, 29–30,
33
and thinking, 27
and writing, 57–69

Reasoning/thinking logically, 41–43
Recall, 7–12, 49
Receptive systems, 57
Recording information, 7
Recreational function, in reading, 36–37
Rehearsal, 8, 49
Relationships:
    and college, 95–96
    with information, 12
    with instructors, 107–120
Reorganizing text, 40
Rereading, 16
Research assistants, 111
Resource base, 144
Responsibilities, unique to college, 174–177
Retrieval, 8, 49
Review, 12, 170
Reward system, 66
Ritualizing, 58
Robinson, Francis, 28
Rokeach, Milton, 60
Roman Catholic colleges, defined, 136
Rosenblatt, Louise, 35

SAT (Scholastic Aptitude Test), 87
Scanning vs. skimming, reading, 29–30, 33
Scholarships, 179
Schools, by type, 136–137
Science texts, 44–45
Scientific writing, 44
Secondary sources, in reading, 39
Self assessment, 3
Self-care, 180–182
Self-confidence, 4–5
Self-Directed Search, assessment instrument, 163
Semantic memory, 48
Semantics, 31
Semiotics, 21
Sensory memory, 47
Sensory styles, 122–123, 129
Share the load, 101–102
Sharing feelings, 58
Short-answer tests, 81, *see also* Exam
Short-term memory, 47–48
Shotgunning, 98–99
SIGI-PLUS, 163
Sketching, 40
Skimming vs. scanning, reading, 29–30, 33
Smell, 47
Smith, Frank, 36
    communication, 57
    and language arts, 53
    and literacy, 27–28

    memory systems, 48–49
    thought and language, 56
Social:
    behavior, 4
    self-care, 182
Social/behavioral science texts, 38–39
Spatial, thesis statement, 80
Speaking, 62, 100–101
Speaking–writing connection, 62–63
Spending habits, 177
SQ3R, 28
Standardized tests, 85–88
Statistics, functions of, 43
Storytelling, 51, 57
Stress:
    management, 180–182
    speed, 34
Student:
    rights, 141
    services, 141–142
Study:
    abroad, 157
    effective, 170
    enforced, 174
    and learning, 3, 96–102
    preparation, 114–116
    strategies, 72, 115
Styles, speech/writing, 63
Subjective tests, 76–81, *see also* Exam
Success, 4–5, 12
Suhor, Charles, 22
Summary:
    in learning, 16–18
    in note taking, 12
    and reading, 34
Support services/facilities, 142–143
Survey, Question, Read, Recite, Review, 28
Syllabus, 5–7, 23–24, 78
Symbol switching, *see* Transmediation
Syntax, 31
System, the, 135–153

Tactile style, 123
Tag-team teaching, 100–101
Tape recording, 61–62
Taxpayers Relief Act of 1997 (TRA 97), 180
Teaching assistants (TA), 110–111
Teaching styles, 121–132
Teamwork, and workplace, 192–193
Technology, and education, 196
Teenagers, working with, 194–196
Tenure, 108
Test anxiety, 81–83, 88
    scale, 82

Testing, 71–91 114–116, *see also* Exam *and* Final exam
Thesis statement, 79–80,
Time/task management, 170–173, 175–176
TRA 97, 180
Traditional outline system, 9–10
Transmediation, 7, 16, 21–22
Tree learners, 123
Tribal colleges, defined, 136
True–False tests, 75, *see also* Exam
Tutors, 111
Type/category, thesis statement, 80

Undecided/changing majors, 158–160
Understanding:
    learning styles, 126
    the system, 135–153
    teaching styles, 128–129
Universities, defined, 136
Up-tighters, 160

Visiospatial sketch pad memory, 47
Visual style, 122
Visual/iconic memory, 47
Vocabulary development, 31
Vocal behavior, 65
Vocal style, 123
Vocation, 144
Volunteerism/service learning, 150–151
Vygotsky, Lev S., 96

Walker, Alice, 36
Web, World Wide, 5, 46, *see also* World Wide Web
Webbing, 20
Weekly planner, 172–173
Wilkinson, Andrew, 57
Witkin, Herman, 123
Women's colleges, defined, 136
Working:
    with children, 193–196
    with elderly, 193, 196
    with teenagers, 194–196
Workplace, 191–193
World Wide Web, 5, 46
    activities, 25–26, 56, 68, 89, 104, 119, 130, 153, 166, 183
Writing:
    group strategy, 99–100
    to learn, 16–18, 34
    and note taking, 7
    and thinking, 27

Year 2000, 189

Zone of Proximal Development, 96